EX LIBRIS

John Fraser Shaw
Balmacnaughton
1971–1995

A BIT OF BREADALBANE

A Bit of Breadalbane

ALASTAIR DUNCAN MILLAR

The Pentland Press
Edinburgh – Cambridge – Durham – USA

First published in 1995 by
The Pentland Press Ltd
1 Hutton Close,
South Church
Bishop Auckland
Durham

ISBN 1-85821-317-7

Typeset by Carnegie Publishing, 18 Maynard Street, Preston
Printed and bound in Great Britain by Bookcraft (Bath) Ltd.

Contents

Introduction

Love of one's land is a common feeling, emphasised if one lives in Breadalbane with its many assets including beauty, climate and convenience.

Curiosity is another human attribute: it was curiosity which prompted the research which now shows definitively that many birds, beasts and fishes seek to return to the place of their birth, which for a time at least had been their home.

Civilised man has lost many of his natural abilities, while acquiring the knowledge of how to manipulate modern gadgetry. It is my own curiosity as to how my homeland 'in famed Breadalbane' came into being, and my love of it, that has prompted the reading and exploration leading to the chapters which follow. They represent my own views after a lifetime at Remony and the reading of many books, but not necessarily accepting all that I have read. This is not surprising, since many chapters or even books have been written specifically to disprove the beliefs or theories held by other writers. I do not aspire to all the minutiae of scientific or historical accuracy, but seek to relate the chain of events as I believe they occurred which most affect the people and lands of Lochtayside.

Any errors of fact or of date must be my own responsibility. I am indeed grateful to Eileen Cox for all her help including correction of my spelling and use of English; also to Mike King, lately Assistant Keeper of Human History at Perth and Kinross District Council's Museum for advice on the archaeological content of the early pages.

My sons James and Ian have checked the post 1950 pages: it is with my children's and their children's interest in mind that the idea of this book as the story of their home was conceived. In course of writing I have considerably widened the scope of the story in the hope that it may become of interest also to a wider group of readers.

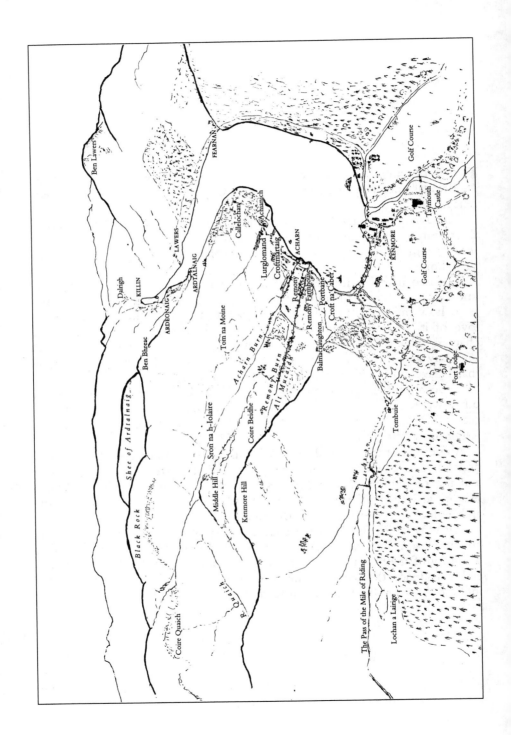

CHAPTER I

Physical Geography

A ny attempt to recount how or why the land and the people we know so well arrived at their present status must start somewhere. Since the importance of land and climate can never be over-emphasised as influencing the ways of the people living on it, at least some consideration is required as to how the land came to its present physical state.

Many books have been written and are well worth reading about the origins of planet Earth. As the surface of the planet hardened, plates of so-called land floated on its hot and liquid interior. The collision of these plates with each other produced the coruscations which we call mountains, while the gaps between them filled with water and became sea. Below the plates the interior boiled and bubbled, sometimes producing volcanoes or forcing the liquid magma up into cracks in the plates above, while heaving actions over millions of years often raised rocks or sediments which had lain below the sea high up above it, even to become mountain tops.

The land of Scotland is a microcosm of all this activity, its complexity demonstrated by study of the Geological Survey of the country. This shows how slips in the land plates produced great fault lines lying mainly from north-east to south-west, with dramatic changes in rock formations on either side of the faults.

Here in the valley of the Tay we lie on a band of schistose rock well to the north of the Highland fault which stretches from near Glasgow through Callander and Blairgowrie in an almost straight line to Stonehaven. Bands of limestone lie to the north of Loch Tay, apparent near Ben Lawers where lime loving plants flourish and further west near Blair Atholl. Through cracks in the schists bands of harder rock occur. Quarries were worked into the hard red porphyry intrusions near Remony Farm and at Callelochan to surface the public roads in these parts, red until the advent of tarmac with the use of stone of totally different colour to the common rock of the area. It is such bands of hard rock through the more general sandstone rocks around Perth which constrict the River Tay to produce white water near Stanley, at Taymount Linn and Aikenhead, which fishermen know well.

Important as is the basic rock, what lies on top of it can be even more so to dwellers on the surface. Early vegetation only became apparent on the planet's surface some 400 million years ago, no doubt helped on by cosmic

dust and fall-out which accumulated in places. A recent example of growth
on emerging magma was found in the volcanic eruption of Surtsey Island
through the sea off Iceland in 1960, where droppings from sea birds were
thought to be the origin of the first life found later on the cooling rock—a
tomato plant!

There were of course no birds or vegetation to cover the newly formed
rock these hundreds of millions of years ago, but because of the heavy molten
mass at its centre the planet was bombarded by other objects in the cosmos.
There is some evidence that a layer of black dust found world-wide in early
clays was due to the effect of a massive body, comet or asteroid, striking the
Earth 67 million years ago and splashing so great a volume of dust into the
atmosphere as to obscure the sun and exterminate the dinosaurs, the dust
ultimately falling to create this unique black band, dated by modern technology.

It is difficult to conceive of the meaning of time measured in millions of
years, or of the slow rate of growth of cover to the bare rock ultimately
leading to the emergence of life from the primeval soup and finally to the
human race. Once planet Earth existed, its climate became the major factor
governing all life on it; it is only the very particular proportions of essential
atoms producing water and oxygenated air that have allowed life on earth
as we know it, unique in all that part of the unlimited cosmos which we
are now able to explore.

Very many factors go to produce climate, not least the effect of the sun
and the rotation of the planet. We take it for granted that the poles are ice
covered while the equator is hot, but it is not so well known how the ice
cover has fluctuated over the millennia. We do know today that ice cover
in Britain at one time reached well down into England, and even the
approximate dates of the most recent ice fluctuations. Further back in time
the amount of ice and its change is less certain, but the factual evidence of
its presence is there plainly to be seen. Rock, worn smooth and polished
by ice action, can be seen in many places, for example at Remony near
the Reyvine falls on the Alt Mucaidh (the Swine Burn) and south-east of
Balmacnaughton. Valleys were gouged out by ice action to give them a
U-shaped cross section, while water, often from melting ice, eroded V-shaped
clefts and valleys.

The valley in which lies Loch Tay was once full of ice. At one period
when the ice level was near the present 290 metre contour above sea level
there may have been a partial melting and strong winds which piled up
melting ice and the debris on it to produce the well defined ridge lying
above Acharn and Achianich at this level. More water sweeping down the
slopes to the shore at that level produced banks of sand on either side of
the Acharn burn, one of which on the east side was to prove of great use

in providing hundreds of tons of fine sand to pack around the relatively fragile pipe carrying water to the Acharn Hydro plant built in 1992.

Further down the valley, its floor was subject to immense water scouring. Some 200 metres downstream of the bridge at Kenmore a shallow lair of rock forms the dam which now holds the water of the loch. Around and mainly downstream of it in the area of Taymouth and the junction with the River Lyon great banks of gravel, sand and stones were deposited on either side of the present river where excavation into the banks shows clearly well defined layers of sand or small stones from successive flood deposits of many thousands of years.

Curling is a great sport, at one time mainly Scottish because there was plenty of ice in Scotland, but now enjoyed world-wide on artificial rinks. Anyone who has curled on outdoor ice or in the Grand Match between clubs of the North and of the South, which used to be held on Carsebreck, Loch Leven or the Lake of Menteith, always had in the back of their mind the hope that the ice was thick enough to bear the weight of all the curlers and their stones. Thickness could be measured by boring a hole with an auger through the ice; 4½ inches or about 11 centimetres was deemed sufficient but it was not unknown on artificial ponds when chances were taken or ice was thawing for the ice to give way and leave the players standing waist deep in water on the bottom of the pond. Which makes it all the more difficult to conceive of ice hundreds or even thousands of metres thick which undoubtedly covered parts of Scotland in the past and still covers parts of Antarctica today.

Ice is heavy and when melted produces great volumes of water which of course flows downhill to find its own level, ultimately the sea. So sea level is dependent on the water from the enormous reservoirs of ice in the polar caps and in our time scale sea level has varied within a range of some hundred metres depending on ice melt, within the last relatively few thousands of years. But not only does ice melt cause sea level to rise (and vice versa) but the earth's plates, when relieved of the enormous weight of ice pressing down on them, tend to rise, so that sea levels at different times and at different places have varied considerably and not always in an apparently consistent manner.

Curlers on the ice, perhaps more often skaters, when they fall know to their cost how hard is the ice. It is difficult then to accept that ice is also fluid and can flow, not unlike water but at an infinitely slower rate. So from the ancient domes of ice piled high over land, parts of the ice flowed downhill, sometimes pushed by other such movements and often for con-siderable distances. Rock and debris could be and was scraped from the land surface and carried with the ice. When mountain ridges protruded above the ice it flowed between them in the valleys as glaciers. Since the middle

of the twentieth century air-line passengers flying the great circle routes from
Europe to Western Canada over Greenland could see far below them great
glaciers with dark bands of rock spoil flowing down the valleys and merg-
ing—rivers of ice. So through the millennia ice-flows covered Scotland,
carrying rocks and debris considerable distances, sometimes depositing their
burden just where the melting occurred. Isolated rocks so left are often
referred to as 'perched boulders'. High on the rounded shoulder of Creagan
na Beinne (more usually called the Black Rock) there are several of such
boulders, two well known as 'the Mare and Foal', while a number of large
rocks on the south shore of Loch Tay lie just where a later ice-melt left
them.

We know relatively little about the behaviour of thick ice-caps these
many millions of years ago, but it seems possible that one line of flow
may have been from the high ground of the Ben Lawers area in a south-
easterly direction carrying some of the Ben Lawers limestone with it. Lime
encourages good growth of vegetation: sheep, deer and hares all benefit
from good grazing. Every autumn in Perth and Stirling there are auction
sales of hill ewes and great is the competition in the market for good prices.
Is it more than just coincidence that each year ewes from Dall, Claggan,
Remony, Auchnafree, Connachan and from near Crieff are at the top end
of the market, all geographically contiguous and in an area swept south-east-
erly from the Ben Lawers limestone? And that westward, near Blair Atholl,
ewes from Monzie in the heart of the lime outcrop there are greatly sought
after?

A summit on the south side of Loch Tay lying between the Remony and
Acharn burns is known as Sron na h-Iolaire, the Eagle's Nose or Peak, and
to this day a golden eagle can be seen on many occasions circling above it.
Why? Golden eagles are partial to the mountain or blue hares, and many
hares are found on Sron na h-Iolaire. Why? Because the grazing is good.
Why? Can it be that the ancient ice-flow deposited a good sprinkling of
lime from the Ben just there, as it passed?

Temperature change, the sun's influence, can cause great changes in
climate. Climate governs vegetation's presence and growth; so it is that the
covering of Earth's plates varies geographically and according to altitude.
Here in Scotland we have a range from bare rock summits, slopes covered
by peat or clays, down to the valley floor of earth and gravel. Continuing
after the ice-melt, water has scoured deep clefts in the valley sides and floor.
The shore promontories into Loch Tay at Lawers, Ardtalnaig and Acharn
are obvious examples of gravel swept down the hillside and deposited on
the loch shore. The larger the deposit, the more probable the incidence of
soft rock or soft ground up above, for example in the heights where the
Acharn burn starts. Here sizeable landslips down the steep banks still occur

quite frequently, muddying the water and later producing an extension of the gravel fan of the burn's emergence into the loch.

Temperature variations which affect the land cannot be ignored. In the 1990s there is concern about the so-called greenhouse effect as our climate appears to grow warmer. But records make plain that temperature has fluctuated in the past, often more quickly and through a greater range than is worried about today. There is every likelihood that it will continue to show changes. The peat which we find on our hills was formed during a spell of wet and warm weather from decaying vegetation comparatively recently, probably between 5,000 and 2,000 years ago, the coal much deeper below the surface similarly, but in the far more distant past.

CHAPTER 2

Early Man

The origin of man, although much more recent than the rocks and their cover, is far more difficult to describe accurately simply because there are so very few known traces of our early ancestors. There were very few of them anyway, and until discovery of their early artifacts there was only the chance discovery of parts of skeletons, fortuitously preserved in ash or mud, to go on.

A skeleton, or rather fossilised small parts of a skeleton, later to become known as 'Lucy', was discovered in 1974 in the Awash river basin north-east of Addis Ababa and identified as an early link in the chain of human evolution. Since then in scattered places more remains have been found and even hominid footprints preserved in mud turned to sandstone, each finder proudly emphasising the importance of his or her own find and often writing a book about it. Continuing argument has taken place about the stages of human evolution, all founded on small pieces of bone or skull found in isolated places throughout the world and now dated with the increasing accuracy of modern technology.

These dating methods were only developed in the middle of the twentieth century and vary but have in common the rate of decay of radioactivity of certain atoms. This requires extremely complicated calculations; it is presupposed that a good working specimen is available of whatever is to be dated—not always easy. Further, whether the specimen is of animal, vegetable or mineral matter poses differences in technique; these allied to the minute calculations involved give rise to different degrees of accuracy of the estimated dates and hence argument about them. However, the mathematical precision about an exact date is less important than its placing in the time-scale of evolution, which is now becoming much clearer than in the past. In spite of this, the steps forward in evolution are confusing, with many different possible links between such finds as Lucy (dated about 3.5 million years ago) and the appearance of *Homo sapiens* (*c.* 0.5 million years ago). Today the arguments about which steps are correct in the evolutionary chain are interspersed with interest as to where and when they took place; it is widely accepted that there are several branches to man's family tree.

Let us accept, then, having noted the importance of climate from the preceding chapter, that mankind probably first developed where the climate was most suitable, warm and moist so that animal and plant foods were abundant. With such criteria, anywhere near the equatorial belt around the world would seem equally advantageous, but anthropologists from their study of known finds point firmly at Africa as the birthplace of mankind. Few in number, men existed alongside every other creature, many of them carnivores. In some particularly favourable place where the essential food and water occurred, some Eden-like place close to a convenient shelter, probably a cave, a couple might be able to rear a family against all the odds. Learning always from experience, others might follow; if the cave was too small or the father too brutal, some brave youngsters would look elsewhere for a place for themselves. Pursuing a favourite or easy source of food would gradually widen known territory.

Anyone who has come in contact with the tangled growth of equatorial or other primitive forest quickly finds the difficulty in forcing a passage through it. Animals of various sizes wear paths for themselves, particularly to gain access to water or around impassable obstacles such as lakes or cliffs. Many creatures lived in the trees and seldom ever put foot to land. Under those circumstances, the water surfaces of rivers or lakes, where not blocked by falls or marsh growth, provided the most easy passage; use of a floating log propelled by a stick or paddle could also give some protection from the horrid variety of water creatures all seeking food. Along the shores of lakes, or down rivers with the current to help, therefore seem the most likely routes for expansion; there was plenty of time to make progress.

Rivers from central Africa flow eastward into the Indian Ocean and westward into the Atlantic, both formidable obstacles for primitive man. A chain of lakes form the headwaters of the River Nile, flowing northwards and eventually ending in the many-channelled delta into the Mediterranean, and this seems a most likely route towards lands of different but acceptable climate in which evolving man could learn to live. His presence in Eurasia is detected since about 1.5 million years ago.

However they got there it was only in very small numbers in scattered groups over a wide area. It is thought that the use of fire was common about 0.5 million years ago or even sooner, but the next great landmark in evolution was the use of suitable stone to make arrowheads and axes, finds of which are dated from 40,000 years ago onwards.

What was their language? Did they have a language? All other animals whether in vast herds or smaller groups exist to this day without speech but not without means of communication, by facial expression, noise, gesture or action. But *Homo*, becoming more sapient, clearly evolved the use of language. Perhaps it was prompted by the need to explain just where good stone for arrowheads could be found, or to warn of the dangers to be found in some particular place, not easily explained just by gesture. Although we do not know where or when man first learned to speak and no common language could develop except where larger groups lived close together and found a need for it, language must have evolved in different groups, gradually spreading outwards from each core centre and becoming accepted over a wider area.

It goes without saying that in this period all speech and language was entirely dependent on sound and memory. Writing did not appear until man was able to find and make use of suitable material of dried hide, stone, or much later, parchment. As populations grew and spread, so the speech of the many thousands of families or tribes consolidated into, among others, what is today called the Indo-European group of tongues. That each group had contact with their neighbours is most strongly suggested by the commonality of modern words in neighbouring languages, for example:

modern word	Celtic	Latin	German	Old Irish	Sanskrit	Slavonic
mother	matres	mater	mutter	mathir	mâtár	mati
sea	mor	mare	meer	muir		morje

The river Labar, a tributary of the Rhine, is 'the talking river', with similarity to the Irish *Labrur*, Welsh *Llafar*, Breton *Lauar* and here at home our own Lawers burn.

There is a long period of little knowledge of stone age man, save of his wide distribution in small groups. Once more it would be climate and environment which allowed a few groups in favourable localities to enlarge, of necessity becoming more settled and therefore requiring to till the ground to provide adequate food supply.

The control of fire and the increased use of tools furthered the next steps of progess and an acceleration of the ability to do things. There is nothing new in 'looking over the fence' to see how other people do it. Our ancestors were equally smart to pick up the advantages of the latest tricks and in spite of language and travel difficulties, knowledge passed relatively quickly from group to group. With such knowledge, early trading or bartering developed. Near Killin at the west end of Loch Tay on the height now known as 'Craig na Cailleach', stone age man as early as 5,000 BC came across a narrow band of hard stone in the rock face, particularly suitable for making axe heads. An axe head from this unusual and easily identified stone was found in Buckinghamshire in modern times as well as in other places in Scotland, indicating the then extent of travel and of bartering. Small stone tools were easily carried; perhaps salt for food was also traded but there is no record of this save the fact that ancient salt mines have been found at or near European centres of early man. Little is known about clothing, the use of skins or

other coverings and the thongs or cords which could bind them, simply
because few traces of these remain.

Consider now the area we today call Europe some 40,000 years ago,
bounded by the seas and in the north by the polar ice cap, where small
groups of people lived in the favourable localities, making more and more
use of the land and so gaining in numbers and diversifying in skills.

Wherever the first use of copper was discovered, it soon became common
knowledge, to be followed relatively quickly by the stronger and longer
lasting iron. Vessels of clay could be substituted by those of copper or iron;
the use of pottery was widespread and still is, its style and markings giving
good indication of origin.

Each individual tribe or group, as it gained in strength and knowledge,
would become jealous of any richer neighbours, with better arms more able
to become belligerent to gain any tribal advantage, so building up a tradition
based on the necessity of strength and skill at arms plus good leadership for
survival. Successful leaders gained prestige and fame, ultimately becoming
minor kings.

Leaders, heroes, kings rose and in due course fell, often killed in battle.
To become a great leader, more than just physical prowess was required.
Somewhere in this period that characteristic which is unique in mankind,
the value and strength of moral and spiritual beliefs, must have become
apparent. Whereas a mammoth, a deer or an ape on death was either devoured
by carnivores, wasted by insects or just lost in a bog, man at this stage
developed the habit of burying his dead, or some of them, in small cysts or
sometimes in burial mounds or tombs or near places of tribal importance.
Custom clearly varied from place to place and tribe to tribe but, judging by
the relics found in many such graves, there seems to have been a common
belief in life after death, important people being provided with food, drink,
arms or ornaments for their next life. So, when a king died, he was buried
in some style. Someone must have been responsible for this; call them what
you will, shaman, priest or druid, there seems little doubt that alongside the
kings there also came into being a priestly body probably drawn from among
the population of those most given to thought and consideration of things
other than just strength at arms, those with brains as well as brawn. No
doubt the kings welcomed such support as a form of good public relations;
no doubt too that there would be rivalry between kings and priests, the
latter learning how to increase their power and position without coming
into direct conflict with the kings.

They had no god to worship but very much to fear, including the natural
phenomena of storm and tempest, thunder and lightning, with much to
observe of sun, moon and stars, climate and seasons. Sticks in the ground
cast shadows in the sunlight. Measuring these gave good indication of time

Portraits scratched onto stone in the cave of La Marche, France, about 10,000 BC
(from tracings made by L. Pales, J. Airvaux and L. Pradel, 1984).

and, if done often enough, also of the seasons. As the growing of crops increased, so also did the importance of sowing seed to the best advantage, requiring a good understanding and knowledge of sun and moon.

As time passed, such knowledge grew, no doubt fostered in the priestly groups, and of course all passed down verbally to successive generations. There is direct factual evidence of the degree of understanding of the heavenly bodies to be found at Newgrange, some thirty miles north-west of Dublin, where the tomb at the centre of the immense mound there had its inmost recess illuminated for a few minutes only each year when the rays of the sun rising above the sea at the time of the winter solstice penetrated the long narrow passage formed by huge stone slabs, contrived among others for this very special purpose. The tomb is dated about 3,300 BC. Not so many years later in Egypt, the pyramids were built with precise orientation to north and south. While such a degree and commonality of knowledge before the days of writing or any written calculations might have arisen spontaneously and almost simultaneously in widely different places, there seems at least the likelihood not only of transference of knowledge but also of the growth of recognised bodies to study the heavens and their relationship to Earth.

The Egyptians are thought to have been the first to develop a form of writing, a hieroglyphic script of symbols, about 3,000 BC. In their relatively unhampered and very favourable situation they quickly developed great skills and art forms, used to glorify their leaders and bury them with fine clothing, ornaments, weapons and even boats in their pyramids, expressing both their respect, if not love, for them and their hopes for their future survival.

Further west in central Europe, later referred to as Gaul by the Romans, things were stirring too. It was at Hallstatt on a remote tributary of the Danube fifty miles south-west of Linz in Austria, and at La Tene on the shore of Lake Neuchatel in what is now northern Switzerland that separate, particularly well placed groups developed skills and left traces of them which modern archaeologists name as the beginning of a definable Celtic civilisation about 700 BC. There were other predecessors further west and we have a first glimpse of what they looked like scratched on the stone walls of a cave at La Marche in France about 10,000 years ago. (see illustration on p. 12) This confirms local differences presumably due to different genes inherited from local tribes. The bottom right-hand face looks highly intelligent—others less so but perhaps these pictures confirm the differences between chiefs, priests and the common people.

Thus far every deduction or likelihood comes from the study of geological or archaeological facts and finds. With the advent of writing, a new phase of knowledge is reached, but one which must be treated with the greatest caution. Early writers in any language were few, as were those able to instruct writers or to read what they had written. All had varied ability and still more varied and very patchy knowledge, but being human had the characteristic of bias or slant in what they wrote, sometimes to please their masters, sometimes just to show their own cleverness. Some very early lists of names of kings or ancestors inscribed on clay tablets in the first millenium BC and discovered more recently in the Middle East have been found to be entirely fictitious, written only to glorify a ruler above his rivals as descendant from a longer line of famous names. Many early writers of history founded on what had been written before, often unaware of errors of fact and so perpetuating beliefs with scant foundation.

Until very recent years many schoolboys being instructed in Latin started with Caesar's description *Omnis Gallia in tres partes divisa est*—'All Gaul is divided into three parts'; right enough in the military sense, but there were probably far more than three groups of inhabitants each evolving in their own way within boundaries of which Caesar and his scribes were quite unaware. To the Greeks they were known as '*Keltoi*' and between the sixth and the third centuries BC some of those with the abilities found at Hallsatt and La Tene multiplied in numbers to produce pressure on living space. Some moved westward towards Britain, others south and eastward, capturing Rome in 387 BC, reaching Delphi and crossing the Dardanelles to become early Galatians.

At the height of their powers the Celts loved battle, fame and music perhaps in that order. They glorified their heroes, clad them with ornate helmets and shields and mounted them in chariots. For many centuries because of their fighting ability they were employed as mercenary soldiers by nations rich and powerful enough to do so. One wonders whether the mounted charioteer was stylised as the complete hero, and indeed, whether chariots were ever very effective in war in countries where woods, marshes and rough ground were common, but Caesar reports their presence in Britain and they were at one time raced around Roman amphitheatres.

Early Roman writers report the Celtic preference for single combat before any general engagement in battle. Their chosen heroes were supported by their followers drawn up nearby, shouting encouragement and blowing on their horns and carynxes, some of which survive today in our museums, still able to be blown. The tradition of single combat continued down the ages and was perhaps not unique among the Celts—David and Goliath; Robert the Bruce and Henry de Bohun before Bannockburn; and jousting throughout the Middle Ages. Shouts of defiance and music of a kind can still be heard at Murrayfield, especially if New Zealand are playing there.

CHAPTER 3

Early Man in Scotland

Scotland is geographically a part of Northern Britain; after the introduction telling what was happening in Europe, it is time to consider what was going on in Scotland.

Because of the changes in sea level, Britain only became an island about 7,000 BC; before then men and beasts could and no doubt did just walk across what is now the English Channel, perhaps also across the Irish Channel and across some (but not all) of the seas between the Scottish Western Islands. As already stated, walking through impenetrable undergrowth is not easy, with the only tracks made by animals, many of them carnivores. To meet a sabre toothed tiger head-on in a narrow pathway could be fatal. Far easier, then, to proceed by water or even by just walking along the shore between the tide lines, with a good source of food beside one by way of fish, limpets and mussels in the shallow sea pools. Wherever early homesteads have been found near the sea, great piles of sea shells have also been found in the accompanying middens, but as it takes 140 good-sized limpets to provide the equivalent food value of one pound of meat, comparatively few people could soon produce a good pile of shells.

Travel by boat is far more probable, but because of their perishable nature very few remains of early boats have been found. The earliest could only have been of coracle type with skins laced over pliant branches, hollowed-out logs or even crude rafts possibly with some kind of sail. One such hollowed-out log was found in 1994 in Loch Tay, only a few metres from the shore at Croftnacaber. Provided suitable materials were available there seems no reason why Western man should have lagged behind the people of the South Pacific who were reputed to have surged over the Pacific Ocean 6,000 years ago. They made cunning use of outriggers and sails, of which little trace has been found in Scotland, but one should not underestimate the abilities of our early predecessors to improvise, as Thor Heyerdahl demonstrated in crossing the Atlantic on a rush-built raft in 1978.

A starting date for human presence in Scotland is easy, as before the last great ice melt about 10,000 years ago the land was alternately covered with massive ice sheets and glaciers or swept by great rivers from the melting ice in the intermittent warmer periods, leaving no trace of life, if any in fact had penetrated so far north. Why travel or explore northwards? Hunting man pursued food where he could find it. *He* got skins from his prey; maybe *She* helped to sew them together as protection from the cold. Herds of reindeer, for example, moved seasonally up and down the fringe of the polar ice and were a valuable resource worth following.

The first firm evidence of mankind's existence in Scotland comes from traces of dwellings, amongst the earliest found dating from about 8,000 to 6,000 BC in the Isle of Rhum. Circles and tombs followed from 4,000 BC, so it must be presumed that human life had existed and indeed flourished for a considerable time before then to have achieved that degree of settlement and of population to provide a workforce to carry out such heavy works. There can be little doubt that a favourable climatic blink, coupled with a fertile and newly exposed soil with plentiful unafraid animal and fish life nearby, favoured stone age mankind and that he was widely spread out not only on the mainland but also on the outer islands, where the stone circle and avenue at Callanish in Lewis ranks second in archaeological importance to that at Stonehenge.

Consider then the requirement behind the erection of stones such as at Callanish. Firstly, a considerable number of people dwelling nearby with sufficient comfort and security to have enough able bodied people with the necessary technical knowledge to shift and erect the poles and stones. There must also have been within the group or tribe the thought or promptings to desire a formal temple or meeting place and to make it bigger and better than they had seen elsewhere.

There is widespread belief that stone age man, then copper and iron age men in central Europe, venerated oak trees, perhaps because they grew in places and on soils they found convenient for their homesteads. Mistletoe was also associated with worship and certainly formed a notable adornment to an oak tree. The origin of the word 'druid' is unknown. It first appears in early Roman writings about 200 BC and there is an association between the words '*dru*' and 'oak' in the early Celtic languages. The early members of priestly groups are most unlikely to have called themselves 'druids' but they must have been called something, so the name Druid is used here to describe the priests or shamans, even in the period some three to four thousand years before the name gained any significant acceptance.

The earliest traces found of man-made possible meeting places, henges, consisted of a bank and ditch enclosing a piece of ground usually circular, sometimes oval or rectangular. It seems clear from archaeological work that the next development, possibly many decades later, was the erection of a number of upright poles within the henge, usually in a circle and sometimes with an especially large or tall pole in the centre. It was later still that stones were used to form a further circle or alignment. The existence of holes dug within circles for poles has been found in many places and it has been suggested that the poles were used to support a roof structure conforming to the thatched roof type of meeting house used by North American Indians in a very much later age. Sometimes the centre pole was selected for its height and size. Perhaps more probable than the idea of a roof is the association with a 'grove' having a formal centre-piece.

The earliest pointer to a collegiate nature of druidical groups is the repetitive style of their henges, later circles, over such a wide area of Britain, with links to European monuments. There is no knowledge of what went on within the circles, or why. It is again only from early Roman writers that we learn of cruel druidical practices and of human sacrifices which by that time the Romans deplored. In very much earlier times human life was even cheaper; the killing of animals was an everyday occurrence so that early forms of sacrifice would seem more than probable. Further, by stepping up the importance or value of the victim, the officiating priestly body stepped up its own importance and power. The striving for power and prestige provides the most likely clue to the growth in size and extent apparently demanded for an acceptable place for meetings, prayer, sacrifice or burial. If the poles or stones associated with such places could also be used to foretell the seasons, so much more power for the druidical group.

The people of Callanish must have been under the influence of their druids for a long period. There are several other circles visible from the main one of very similar style, indicating a considerable intensity of religious belief within the community. We know nothing of these beliefs save what we can deduce from the stones themselves and the marking on them and very often on convenient outcrops of natural rock. A cup mark cut in the rock is the most common, often with one or more rings round it in circular or spiral form, occasionally with other markings. The sun and the moon were obviously to be greatly respected, the circles perhaps indicating their outward radiating power while spirals might have indicated their continuance. Although the cup marks and rings are found on bedrock they also occur on stones used for monuments and occasionally are cut in places where in the final position of the stone they were hidden from view, which carries the suggestion that their cutting was in itself a gainworthy act, while the degree and style of decoration may have represented the standing or importance of the inscriber, but all this is of course pure speculation.

Several generations of Druids must have practised at Callanish before 3,500–2,500 BC, but the climate changed, later becoming wetter, so that the whole tribe were forced to abandon their homes and circles to live elsewhere. We know this, because the Callanish stones became covered with several feet of peat and were only rediscovered in the eighteenth century and excavated down to their original ground level. What happened to the people and where they went we do not know, but they must have faced many years of growing discomfort and hardship before finally abandoning all they had created, perhaps even to find happier circumstances in this 'bit of Breadalbane'?

It has already been implied that there was a wider transference of knowledge between tribal groups than might have been expected resulting just from trade and bartering. Certainly early writers from Rome about 300–200 BC referred to traditions of learning among the Celtic peoples and also to schools of druidical teaching where aspirants had to undergo considerable periods of training before they were deemed able to join the elite schools. It would be strange if, within such centres of learning, attention was not also given to picking up knowledge from elsewhere as a means of increasing power and prestige, and thus a system of contacting fellow thinkers. Perhaps young men were specially trained and equipped for the dangers and hardships of long journeys and despatched to prestigious places in search of knowledge. Despite the difficulties and risk entailed in such journeys, some at least would return to report back to their foundations; one can imagine the joy and celebration on the return of one of these travellers in the rough home of the head Druid.

It is a common modern trait to consider early man to have been crude and almost bestial in his habits, but in the period now under consideration, the last two or three millenia BC, this was far from the case. Hardy they certainly must have been, able to withstand long periods without regular food, but from traces found at Strathallan and Sketewan there is evidence that the 'beaker people' of about 2,000 BC sometimes used their beakers to good purpose in holding special 'refreshments', brewed for example from meadowsweet and no doubt with a good kick in it. Was there then a joyful evening spent to celebrate the return of their emissary? Perhaps, and this makes one wonder just in what else the Druids were interested.

The alignment and movements of the sun, moon and stars were studied and made use of in their ceremonies with a degree of accuracy which seems incredible in an age without any form of writing or numerals. The stars (but not what today we call the Pole Star, because it wasn't then in the right place) could indicate the north by night, the sun at midday the south by day. No doubt many other alignments were studied by certain schools with varying degrees of success and used to good purpose to add importance to the ceremonies. Excitement would build up in a period of waiting for a certain event—then triumph and proof of their powers when the promised event took place, light or shadow cast on a precise spot, or the moon setting exactly as predicted.

There was a school of modern thought led by Gerald Hawkins and Alexander Thom in the 1960s and 70s which credited the ancients with detailed scientific knowledge of measurement and of astronomy. Comparison of the diameters of different circles led them to suggest that a megalithic yardstick of exactly 0.830 metres in length had been used to set out major circles and ellipses. As this measurement is almost precisely the distance that ancient man would be expected to cover in one stride it seems more likely to credit him with striding out most carefully in setting out circles rather than the adoption of mathematical precision. Belief too was held of knowledge of astronomical movements leading to the ability to foretell eclipses of the sun and moon, great events indeed. This is expecting a lot in an age without writing or system of numbers, involving detailed calculations over a span of many years at a time when the expectation of life was in the order of thirty years. Observations made over a long number of years with exact precision would not easily have been handed orally to succeeding generations, however intelligent they may have been. Even with ten-figure Napierian logarithmic tables the calculations required would have been extremely complex. Which is not to say that some druidical schools did not become exceedingly skilled with their observations, enabling them to make use of proven alignments to add solemnity and proof of divination to their ceremonies.

More down to earth was knowledge of the fruits of the earth, perhaps founded on the mystery of the mistletoe but by experiment the discovery of herbal properties for many different uses, healing, soothing, stimulating, anaesthetising—or just killing. These could more easily be demonstrated and handed down, no doubt with varying degrees of success. Perhaps medieval forms of hospitals such as that found at Soutra, south of Edinburgh, benefited from early druidical knowledge.

To summarise: stone, iron and then bronze age mankind had among their number people of intelligence who made use of every means at their disposal to uphold themselves as deserving respect and tribute without attempting to usurp the powers of those whose strength, bravery and popular esteem had risen to become leaders or tribal kings. In the graded society produced by peoples living close together, with kings at the top, fighting men, family men, workers, some almost and in later times actually, slaves, the priests formed a powerful, respected and no doubt feared group within the tribe.

CHAPTER 4

The Druids

A nd so to 'Famed Breadalbane' itself: a land of high mountains and sheltered valleys with Loch Tay giving birth at Kenmore to its river, 'meandering sweet in infant pride' as Burns described it. The River Tay flows eastwards to the North Sea; its headwaters come from far to the west, the lengthy valley forming a passageway between east and west for those with courage to penetrate among forbidding mountains.

From archaeological finds it is clear that early man was widespread in Scotland, that in the valley of the Tay there were henges, circles and rock markings dating far back into the second or third millenium BC. The circle at Croftmorag, south-east of Taymouth, has all the features of henge, post holes and upright stones associated with what has been described as the Druids. There is a smaller circle higher on the hill about 1,700 metres south-east of Acharn and other groups of stones not far away, while cup and ring markings are found on an ice-worn rocky knoll about 600 metres south-east of Balmacnaughton, on moss-covered smooth bedrock near the centre of the Queen's Drive wood and elsewhere.

Not far from the smaller circle above referred to and on a minor but commanding knoll there is a flat-topped stone block of most appropriate size to lay a human body on top of it, with smaller stones giving the appearance of a foundation or plinth on its northern side. If this is not a sacrificial altar it has every appearance of so being; although there are apparent 'henge' marks surrounding the general area of the stone, there are also remains nearby of medieval farm and stock boundaries of a much later date to cause some confusion.

There are two other suggestions of sacrifice on the southern slopes of the east end of Loch Tay. The first is a large stone or rock just protruding above the ground in the stack yard of Achianich Farm, on which a circle has been scribed which could compare in size to a cart wheel or a large mill stone. On early plans of that area the farm is noted as 'The Millstone Croft', so it is plain that the cartographer thought it was an attempt to cut a millstone—a useful and important article. But there are doubts about this intention of scribing the circle, chiefly because it looks most unlikely that a layer of stone could be lifted from the rock to form a mill stone and also because the tool marks delineating the circle include a natural crevice in the rock which

The author sitting on one of the fallen stones of the circle 1,700 m. south-east of Acharn.

The so-called 'Sacrificial Stone'.

would have made its use as a grinding stone most unlikely. On one side of the stone a short length of circular vertical face has been cut as if to form the outside edge of a grindstone, so that an early blacksmith might well have used this curved face to beat a bar of iron into a hoop or wheel shape convenient for a cart tyre.

This may well have been the objective in cutting the stone, as was often so supposed, until a second very similar circle was found scribed on a sloping rock about 1½ kilometres due east of Achianich, almost in line with the smaller circle and 'sacrificial' stone already described, lying just above the boundary of hill and in-bye land on the 260 metre contour.

This second circle is only slightly smaller in diameter than that at Achianich, but its scribing goes down into a crevice in the rock indicating its circumferencial cutting from the inscribed centre point irrespective of the flatness of the stone. Further, on two places within the circle there are uniform rows of small dots cut a few centimetres apart, uncommonly like a 'tally' of some uses to which the stone was put. A couple of metres away there is another smooth and sloping stone with a groove apparently cut in it sloping downwards towards its edge, most convenient to catch any liquid draining off the sloping face. Was it to catch blood? This is suggestive but totally without proof. All these traces of druidical use lie with excellent view of the northern horizon and of the heavens; their very number and proximity indicate a considerable population of people accustomed to druidical practices living in the district in these distant ages.

There seems a long time gap between the prolific traces of a numerous population in Breadalbane during the stone and iron ages and evidence of more recent peoples there about the time of Christ, a period in world history when enormous steps forward towards what we call civilisation were achieved. Pyramids were built; the Babylonian and Minoan empires rose and fell; writing became common particularly in the Middle East; Greek science and art blossomed. Pythagoras is always associated with the 3–4–5-sided right angled triangle, although there is good reason to think the use of that device was known long before Pythagoras, possibly by the Druids, if lacking his elegant proof calculations.

Things, and people, in Breadalbane moved more slowly. Very probably climate played an important part, first encouraging growth and then, becoming colder, forcing inhabitants down off the hillsides into the more sheltered valleys. Celtic growth and power spread slowly north and west from central Europe, both by armed intrusion and perhaps more effectively by intermarriage. There is conclusive evidence of homesteads occupied by the 'Beaker' people right up the valley of the Tay.

Arrows drawn on maps showing the likely routes of expansion suggest rapid movements, but in the time-scale of hundreds of years the spread of

Circle scribed on rock 1½ kilometres east of Achianich.
Note pock marks (ringed) on top left quadrant.

the relatively skilled Celtic people among the less advanced Northerners
must have been slow, following the easiest travel routes among which sea
travel must have ranked high. Good places to live in were already occupied

and had been occupied for thousands of years except following some disaster caused by climate, disease or tribal war. To gain a footing in 'new' country some strength would be required, that strength implying population growth in excess of that required for bare maintenence, while too many mouths to feed in one centre was the strongest inducement for planned tribal expansion. Some incursions into new territory, up a valley or over a mountain range, could be of quite minor extent. There was no supply train to support the invaders who had to live off the land, and an easy place to live would become the next settlement for them. Bad news for the original inhabitants. Some would flee, some be killed and some remain either as slaves or concubines, strengthening the invading force so that in a few years time they would feel inclined to repeat the process.

The Greek voyager Pytheas is reported to have reached the Orkney Islands about 300 BC using a gaelic type curragh 100 feet long made of hides stretched over a wooden frame. No doubt there were other voyagers who either by intent or by being storm wrecked occasionally landed on the Scottish coasts. The tradition of dark-haired people with longer noses having come from Spain or even further south is not beyond possibility, contrasting with the fair-haired races which penetrated up the south and east coasts of Britain.

To the north the people of Orkney living among so many small isles surrounded by the sea must have been well accustomed to seafaring; being reported to have been bold and quarrelsome there is good reason to suppose that some raided and settled on the north-east mainland. Mingling with those who had reached that far off corner of Britain from Europe, they may have been the forerunners of the Picts, whose origins are obscure but who are referred to by the Romans about 400 BC.

The Celts from central Europe had diversified into many different tribes, with those from the farther north and west speaking what today we call Gaelic and penetrating round the west of Britain into Ireland and north-west Scotland. Those from the more northerly parts of Europe with separate dialects became the progenitors of those that later were called Angles, Saxons and Picts. They were all of Celtic origin.

Once Ireland had become completely separated from the rest of Britain it could only be reached by boat. Early boats were small, the organisation of any form of fleet difficult, so that the incursions onto an unknown shore could only have been by relatively few well armed men or by travellers either exploring or with goods to barter. In either case tribes well away from the coast would be left relatively undisturbed on this green and pleasant land, allowing druidical schools of knowledge to flourish, to be followed after the birth of Christ by Christian monastic groups.

As far as Breadalbane is concerned in the first millenium BC, the land was still occupied by the descendants of stone age and later iron age man, making use of tools to cultivate the land on which the families had settled, clearing scrub and trees. There is no reason to suppose the numbers were greatly different from those indicated by the number and proximity of the stone circles and druidical markings already referred to: every reason to suppose that groups of families having lived in a place they found convenient to live in for several generations had grown possessive of their homesteads and prepared to defend them. When might was right, the easiest way to obtain cattle, other livestock or mates was just to take them, so that the remains of forts, duns, brochs and other defences are dated and were used for many hundreds of years onwards against aggressive neighbours and, later, invaders. Local leaders, heads of families, would gain kudos and power by saying, 'We have a good fort—have you?' But from the logistics of defence and attack against these forts one wonders just how often they were actually defended or whether they were more often used for gathering together people, stock and possessions in time of alarum, or just as meeting places.

There may be a link with the advent of the Celts in the period 700–400 BC from their original lakeside homes at La Tene and the appearance of the considerable number, at least seventeen, of lake dwellings or *crannogs* around the shore of Loch Tay dated from about 600 BC onwards, some being used, perhaps intermittently, for several hundred years.

The small island, often called Gull Island, below Croftmartaig, about half a kilometre west of the Acharn burn, is a typical example, originally connected with the shore by an underwater causeway. Opposite, on the north side of the loch near Fearnan, considerable exploration work has been done on the now totally submerged crannog at Oakbank, proving that there had been wooden piles driven down and stones placed above what may have been timber flooring, possibly to give extra height or protection against wave action. There would seem to be a link between the siting of the crannogs and adjacent areas of land on the shore convenient for a family's place of living and cultivation. If it was not easy to find a place on the land cleared of scrub for a homestead which could offer as good protection from raiding men and predators as an island, the risk of flooding and storm damage might be preferred to the dangers likely to be met with on shore.

CHAPTER 5

The Advent of Christianity

Before the time of written records our knowledge of people depends on archaeological finds. These can tell us what they did, even how they lived, but nothing of what they thought or spoke.

After 32 AD Christianity spread only slowly. St. Paul travelled widely in the Eastern Mediterranean, falling in with the descendents of the eastern Celts in Galatia. The gospels were written about 200 AD; Roman emperors professed Christianity but how far this affected the Roman soldiers is doubtful.

The first Roman invasion of Britain led by Julius Caesar in 55 and 54 BC explored and effectively conquered the people of south-eastern Britain, defeated local tribes and reached Colchester only to retire again across the Channel. It is doubtful whether the people of Breadalbane heard or cared much about this invasion; it was after all some five hundred miles away and the tribes there led by Cassivellaunus were as great potential enemies as the Romans. The next invasion under the Emperor Claudius in 53 AD reached much farther north to the Humber, but it was not till the time of Agricola that the Romans penetrated into Scotland. These dates make plain that the story of Pontius Pilate having been born at Fortingall is probably fable, no doubt owing to the coupling together of the traces of early camp sites there with lack of knowledge, only recently made firm, of the dates of the various Roman movements. Pontius Pilate must have been around the age of forty at the time of the crucifixion, c.32 AD, therefore born about 10 BC when there was no Roman presence at all in Britain. But McKerracher in his book *Perthshire in History and Legend* writes that an 'ancient chronicle' reports that a Roman Ambassador visited 'Metallanus, King of Scotissmen' about that time. While Rome, with its fleet, could conceivably have had access to a tribe which might have been persuaded to help them in a future invasion in the south, there were at that time no 'Scotissmen' in Breadalbane and Roman politics had plenty to do in Gaul without visiting a tribe in the remote north, distant from all their lines of communication.

It was not until Agricola led his legions northwards in 80 AD that the people of Breadalbane had good cause to worry and some no doubt met up with Roman soldiers. In succeeding years, with the command centre at Inchtuthill, camp at Bertha and outposts near the Sma' Glen at Fendoch and at Fortingall, while few local people actually met them in armed combat they were well within the Roman field of influence. The Romans were not slow to 'tax' their conquered peoples: they had to live in their camps without regular supply trains and no doubt their quartermasters gained their supplies by force or sometimes by way of 'tribute', which could be another word for tax. At close proximity to regular camps some trading must also have taken place—if armed foot patrols came near, it could either be a case for fleeing to the hills or for making some worth-while response to whatever they were in need of. Nearby families may even have gained a smattering of Roman speech.

The very strength of the Roman troops on the advance forced the local tribes to combine against them in order to provide any meaningful resistance. Agricola is reputed to have had over 20,000 men under his command at his furthest north encounter with the Picts at Mons Graupius in 84 AD, which may have been near Bennachie in Aberdeenshire. The Picts took a terrible hammering but the Romans withdrew after the battle, to behind their walls across Scotland, which the Picts later over-ran, and finally back across the Channel to Europe in 420 AD. The gathering of an army to fight the Romans undoubtedly helped to unite the Picts under their tribal leaders and, ultimately, kings and made a warlike people even more warlike. This implies that the people making their living on the shores of Loch Tay looked eastward with some fear, but since tradition suggests that raids by the Celts from the west also occurred, life for them must have been uncomfortable and dangerous.

Meanwhile, Christian missionaries established centres in Ireland superseding the Druids, their schools of learning becoming known and respected in Europe by 600 AD. The famous monastry at Kells was founded about 550 AD with Colum Cille, or Columba, as its most famous son. The Book of Kells was written in Latin; Columba spoke both Latin and Gaelic but is reputed to have required interpreters in some parts of his Scottish journeyings.

Ninian landed at Whithorn about 450 AD, but his Abbey there, the Candida Cassa, had little impact in the north. When Columba landed in Iona in 463 AD he landed among fellow Celts, Gaelic speakers whose leaders had a long tradition of kinship with Irish chiefs, of which Columba himself was one. It was possibly as an act of penance for his part in bringing about the great Irish battle at Cul Dreimne that Columba set out to convert to Christianity the people of Scotland and in pursuance of this aim travelled far and wide. He may well have passed along the shores of Loch Tay, although there is no specific record of this. In 585 AD he met Bridei, King of the Picts, supported by his Head Druid at Inverness and won a dramatic and important convert as part of his policy of trying first to convert the leaders of the people. Several years later he followed up this visit and travelled right around the Aberdeenshire coasts through Pictland, founding churches wherever he could.

Possible Celtic, Roman and other routes of arrival into Breadalbane.

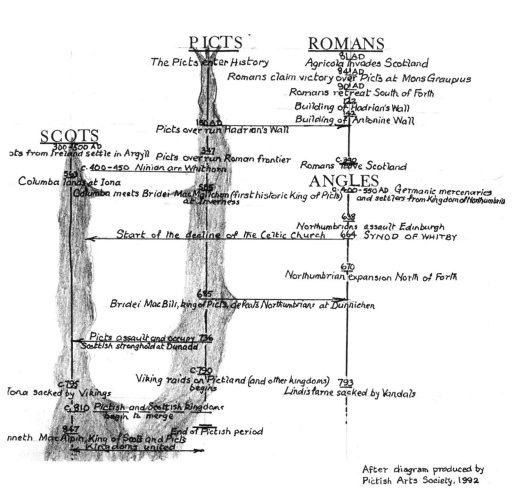

After diagram produced by
Pictish Arts Society, 1992

Timescale diagram relating influences of early races on what we now call Scotland.

Some time after Columba's death the Abbey of Iona sent out two of their number eastwards, Adamnan and Fillan. Legend has it that when the two missionaries crossed the height of land at Tyndrum and met the headwaters of the Tay they cast lots to decide how they would divide between them the lands to the east. The head of the glen fell to Fillan, who established his church at Glendochart. Adamnan, who was another descendent of an Irish chief, went on eastward and became famous in the upper Tay valley and in Glen Lyon where he set up the first water-driven meal mill at Milton Eonan, giving an indication of the state of farming at that time. More important, a monastic college was established at Dull, where the church was dedicated to Adamnan. A fair, 'Feil Eonan' was held there on his special day, 25 September, for very many years. Little trace remains today of this establishment except piles of dry stones and traces of foundations; the present local inhabitants have no knowledge or care for the site nor for the Celtic cross still standing in the centre of the village. Examination of the site, now rough and wet grazing land between the public road and the high forested land to the north, suggests there were a number of rough dwellings and one larger one with some form of lawn or more level ground perhaps used for gatherings. Careful survey and some excavation could be rewarding in gaining knowledge of one of the earliest Christian settlements in Breadalbane.

Other members of the Iona community are also known to have travelled locally, one named Ciaran setting up a church in Fearnan where his name is continued in the place name of Dalchiaran. A stone reputedly from his church is incorporated in the roadside wall just opposite the junction of the higher link road with the main Fearnan to Fortingall road. Dr Gillies in his book *In Famed Breadalbane*, gives details of many ancient place names in his carefully researched history of the area—essential reading. There are some direct relics of the ancient priests including St. Fillan's crozier and bell, both now in the National Museum of Antiquities in Edinburgh.

The written records which now begin to cover the historic times from about 300 BC onwards are themselves extremely difficult to read in whatever language they were written. Even the greatest expert is capable of mistakes owing to poor calligraphy or misunderstanding of a little known language, as successive translations of books, including for example the Bible, clearly demonstrate. Further difficulty in dating arises from the habit of early people to repeat the names of kings, leaders or priests in succeeding generations. In Ireland and in Britain at this time Latin was the only language widely understood: Gaelic with its many dialects was the universal tongue in Scotland, but all Gaelic history and tradition was handed down verbally, written Gaelic being unknown until very much later.

No doubt Druidical brains considered a written language when they perceived the uses of Latin and this may have been the origin of Ogham, a linear script with strokes across it signifying different letters. This writing is now thought to have existed in the period 200 to 600 AD and to have had an alphabet of twenty letters. It was only rarely scribed on stone, seldom using more than a few words strung together and so making translation difficult. There are only fifty-seven known examples outside Ireland, mainly of a funerary nature such as 'Here lies Niall, son of Nectan' and Latin equivalents are inferred. In Pictish areas there are a small number of similar Ogham scribings whose meanings are even more obscure, but its use seems to have died out completely by the seventh/eighth centuries AD, just at the very period when one can guess that any few remaining Druids succumbed under the growing influence of Christianity, whose representatives of course used Latin.

The Pictish sculptured stones are found mainly in east and north-east Scotland with centres of frequency in the Inverness, Aberdeen and Meigle areas, the earliest dated from the seventh century AD. The closest to Breadal-bane are stones at Logierait, Dunfallandy and Dull, all figuring horsemen. There is every indication that these sculptured stones were originally of pagan, surely druidical, origin perhaps owing to some school of expertise in design preferring symbols to the earlier cup and ring marks. Then, when the Christian presence grew, the Christians followed their policy of adapting local customs, in this case symbols, to their teaching which gives a likely reason for the growing number of Christian marks added or adapted on these stones, particularly on those of later dates.

The Picts were victorious against advancing Northumbrians in 685 AD and in 741 AD against Western Celts, but after unification of the Picts and the Scots in 843 AD under King Kenneth MacAlpin the peculiarly Pictish traits seemed to have merged or been submerged in the united kingdom. The earliest Gaelic text known in Scotland dates from the twelfth century AD and came from a long since vanished Celtic monastery at Deer in Aberdeenshire perhaps resulting from Columba's influence in going himself or sending other itinerant priests round the north-east coast.

First attempts to write Gaelic were made by speakers of 'English', perhaps with a smattering of Latin, but in either case the alphabet of letters used was very much as we know it today. This posed great difficulties, since in Gaelic there are many sounds not easily reproduced in this alphabet. The use of aspirates and the need for liquid sounds was met up to a point by the use of certain conventional combinations of letters. *Bh*, *dh*, and *mh* are all aspirates, while *gl* and *gn* for example denote liquid sounds with the *g* not sounded. Further difficulty in achieving a written language, even after acceptance of these conventions, arose from the obvious diversity of ethnic groups around both the Scottish mainland and among the islands, each speaking local dialects of a tongue long since deriving from any common ancestry.

The very real difficulty of writing, and so spreading the use of, Gaelic, continues to this day. While the ancient tradition of songs and rhymes can be learned and sung tolerably easily, to write them down is far less easy, with our modern affectation for 'correct' spelling carrying the implication of either ignorance or bad education when spelling mistakes occur. Gaelic syntax and the use of masculine and feminine forms add to the problems. Any modern critic or examiner of written Gaelic should keep in mind that early writers in both Latin and English paid little attention to spelling as long as the phonetic sounds clearly indicated the intention of the writing.

It would seem that in these early times, at an unknown starting date which is probably much earlier than might have been thought, a new class of people, other than kings, priests or common people, came to be recognised: the professional traveller who took the chance to travel unarmed and to arrive unannounced among unknown neighbouring groups or tribes. To pay his way and to become accepted he must earn some respect and interest, so had to have 'the gift of the gab' in Scotland or have 'kissed the blarney stone' in Ireland; he would also have a good knowledge of the local dialects and languages and be able to repeat happenings elsewhere, a carrier of news. Perhaps he could also sing or make some form of music, all of course at the dwelling of the tribal leader where he would seek to go if not forcibly taken there. So opens up the tradition of travelling people of many kinds and skills, some settling for longer periods where they received a special welcome. A good song or tale recounting the valour of the leader might well earn an extra 'dram', all very much in keeping with the Celtic verbal way of passing on knowledge and tradition. Those who found special favour from the chief might settle in his abode and become bard or musician, sensible that tales of mighty deeds in the past were always the most popular.

CHAPTER 6

As History Began

A s century followed century after the birth of Christ, the surviving people
of the Scottish highlands tended to combine together when they could
in ever larger groups. Fear of neighbours, greed for land, the very under-
standable herd instinct, were all influenced by the effectiveness of iron now
beginning to be forged and sharpened into weapons, sometimes 'big swords'—
the claymores. Armed strength became important and if a family group felt
vulnerable they joined with others to form a tribe with a recognised leader,
having a sphere of influence governed largely by geography and the number
of people a glen or valley could support. Might was Right. If many families
wished for nothing more than a quiet life and to get on with working their
land and tending their beasts, it was good to have links with strong leaders.
With larger families, from better survival, young men surplus to domestic
needs were only too keen to show their prowess under a good leader who
with their help might become a clan leader of even a minor king.

Here in Breadalbane, a virtual ethnic watershed between the Scots of
Dalriada and the Picts of the east, the first nearby historical grouping were
the MacDougalls and Campbells in the west and the *marmoar*, or chief, of
Atholl in the east. The considerable number of forts attributed to the Picts
in Glen Lyon suggest that this may have been an early frontier region with
strong defensive capability. Strangely, there are few such defensive works
along either shore of Loch Tay. The valley of the Tay right up to the height
of land at Tyndrum formed the direct route into Dalriada and vice versa
and so must have been often so used by raiding parties or minor armies. It
follows that those people attempting to live permanently in so attractive an
area must have been on the fringes of the protective powers of the chieftains
of both east and west and been subject to being harried by either. This may
be the reason that the history of Lochtayside lacks the feature of strong
permanent leaders until Campbell power later spread eastward from Argyll,
but instead was held by hardy families, good stockmen and farmers, willing
to take risks and ready to drive their stock up into the hills at short notice—or
even to make use of their crannogs.

Under these circumstances there can be little doubt that the objective of
the local farmers was to keep out of harm's way; where power groups existed
in Argyll or in Atholl it was wise to fall in with the wishes of the chiefs,

whatever they might be. As nationhood developed local leaders grouped together and local 'kings' elected their Ard Righ and so a presence, backed by power, at the king's seat became useful. When the 'seat' became established in some central place, Dunadd, Scone, Dunfermline or Edinburgh, it grew in size to become a court with considerable show of wealth as well as power, courtiers, guards, women folk and servants—and rivalry. To stay there for any time required not only the king's friendship but also wealth in one form or another, ultimately money. And so the functions of the leaders grew slowly over the centuries to include not only bravery in armed combat with ample supporters, a fatherly patronage over all his dependents, but also skill as taxmaster over his domaine in order to raise the funds necessary to maintain his presence at court or just to have a word with the king from time to time, useful and sometimes very essential procedures.

Coming now to the period of reasonably well documented history, it becomes a matter of choice which events and dates are deemed most important, more than tedious to attempt to record them all. The choices that follow are made with the intention of indicating the importance and sequence of events which came to affect the people living at the eastern end of Loch Tay.

Right round the coasts of Britain and far beyond, the Norsemen created terror and destruction. Abbeys, with their population of unarmed priests with relics and valuables, were obvious targets. Lindisfarne was sacked in 793 AD, Iona a few years later, the monks cruelly murdered. Columba's Celtic church had spread inland, its centre moved eastward to Dunkeld while the centre of kingship was at Scone. What was left at Iona was moved to Ireland, still regarded as the centre of the Celtic church.

The Stone of Destiny

By that time the Stone of Destiny was thought to be at Dunadd, near the Crinan isthmus of the Mull of Kintyre, where Columba had ordained Aidan as king in 574 AD. The story of the Stone rightly deserves the many books written about it. Legend, never to be scorned, tells that Pharoah's daughter, Scota, brought it with her when she married a handsome prince and that they or their descendents settled in Ireland some thousand years before the birth of Christ. Why she should have encumbered herself with what still more ancient legend held to be Jacob's Pillow is obscure, but that Stone must have been regarded as having very important mystical properties and it is just conceivable that it might have been included in a ship's ballast for a long and stormy journey. Thereafter, Irish kings were reputed to have been crowned sitting on a stone called the Lia Faill, but there is no proof, rather doubt, whether the Lia Faill was the same Jacob's Pillow. Either or both of these stones had carvings on them of a kind but their meaning is unknown at a time when there was no written language or alphabet, although no doubt they added to the mystical powers, even of speech, credited to the Stone. Then, Irish kings, Scots, settling in Dalriada might well have taken or stolen the Irish stone to add to their prestige; both Dunadd and Dunstaffnage are reputed to have held the Stone for a time.

Columba, too, is reputed to have slept with his head on a stone, but this is more probably a tribute to his hard living. He was also credited with having a portable altar which he carried with him on his travels, but portable the Stone of Destiny certainly was not, although a chip of stone as a relic could have been part of his treasured possessions. All this suggests that there may have been more than one stone deemed of symbolic importance, more certain the tradition built up that Kings should be crowned or ordained sitting on this very special Stone and that this Stone was eventually carried to Scone.

The existing seals of early Scottish kings, showing them seated above a stone, suggest that iron carrying rings were fixed to the ends or corners of the stone: it clearly had to be carried from time to time.

To get from Dunadd to Scone was quite a journey. Coming from the west, Tyndrum was a likely point on the route to the east unless the then control of the central lowlands suggested a sea route into the Clyde estuary and a shorter route by land on to Scone. Useful as any sort of cart would have been for transporting the Stone, were there any roads in these days on such a long route capable of carrying wheeled vehicles? This seems doubtful and no traces of early tracks are evident along either shore of Loch Tay other than under the existing roads, so the probability is that the Stone was literally carried from the west. It must have been quite a procession: at least eight men to shoulder the poles carrying the Stone, plus a relief team with many accompanying priests and notables and a strong guard. The folk along the route must have stared in wonder to see so large a party apparently not engaged in raiding, with its slow speed and so many in monkish habits. At Lix Toll the party might have forked southward to follow Loch Earn side and the road to Crieff, but it seems more likely that they went on down the Dochart valley and along the north shore of Loch Tay, bearing left towards Fortingall and a ford over the Lyon, then halting with known friends at Dull before going on to more at Dunkeld, all in the footsteps of Adamnan. The inhabitants of Acharn and Remony would have missed seeing the passage of the Stone if this was indeed the route taken, but word of it must surely have reached their ears very quickly and have been the subject of much speculation.

Coming now from supposition to fact, undoubtedly Balliol was crowned at Scone seated on the Stone in 1292. Nor is there any doubt that King Edward of England carried away a stone when he reached Scone in 1296, deposing Balliol, and that that Stone has been used ever since in the crowning of English and then British kings. Geologists are quite clear that the Westminster stone is of 'Old Red Sandstone', a type of rock found very commonly all round Scone. The two facts, that the powers at Scone had ample warning of Edward's coming and that the stone carried from the west was most unlikely to have been of red sandstone—legend has it of being hard and black—make it a virtual certainty that Edward was 'sold a pup' and allowed to carry off a substitute. This thinking is reinforced by Edward's action in sending back a raiding party to Scone in 1298 which tore the abbey to pieces apparently in search of something and by the lack of interest in the offer actually made after the treaty of Northampton in 1328 to return the Stone— the substitute was not required.

Back again to legend. What happened to the original Stone? There are persistant traditions that the Stone was hidden in a cave near the site of Macbeth's castle on Dunsinane Hill, even that it was found about 1800 AD by schoolboys and later carried off for examination by the then laird, a Mr Nairne, while the cave later became hidden by a rock-fall. That the Stone was taken off to be hidden in a cave seems most likely. But with the approach of Edward's army in 1296 there must have been considerable panic at Scone. Abbot Henry would receive much conflicting advice and if he were anything like more modern officials would procrastinate till the last moment. Then, with the English advance guard over the Tay, real panic, the Stone hoisted onto the most convenient cart and driven off at full speed. The Stone was undoubtedly heavy and equally certainly the track would be rough. Did an axle break or a wheel come off, tipping the Stone into the ditch? The driver and guard would be unlikely to admit to such a calamity; maybe they just threw a few branches over the Stone and fled or were killed by the English soldiers now swarming over the country. Is it still lying within a few miles of Scone? Archie McKerchar had a splendid article about the Stone in the *Scots Magazine* of December 1984, but the whereabouts of the real Stone remains unknown.

CHAPTER 7

The Coming of the Normans

I 066 AD, when William the so called Conqueror defeated King Harold of England at Hastings, is probably the best known date in the history books, not least because English history was for long considered the only British history of importance, with the whole British educational system adhering to this view. The people of Breadalbane however would take little note of this event save perhaps the passing thought that their English neighbours had taken another knock. But they little knew what was coming to them, to cause very great changes in their country within a few years.

Reference has been made to the Tay Valley being a through passage from east to west. There must have been tracks along both sides of Loch Tay, probably used in ancient times according to the knowledge held of the hostility or otherwise of the tribes of clans occupying the heights to north or south of the loch. Ewen Macdougall who was clerk at Taymouth in the early nineteenth century and whose family had lived near Ardtalnaig for many years writes:

> At Milltown of Ardtalanais opposite Lawres, stands a huge large cairn of stones called Cairn-bane, which as by tradition was gathered and piled up on the grave of one of King Duncan's nephews, who along with MacBeath and Banco, other nephews of King Duncan went at the head of an army to quell an insurrection raised by the then MacDougall, Lord of Lorn, who had rebelled against the King, and that young nobleman being mortally wounded died on his way back at Milltown, where he is buried. At this place stood a kind of Castle, where the King and his Generals rested with their army on their way to or from the west Country when a rebellion would be raised, either by MacDougall, Lord of Lorn or MacDonald, Lord of the Isles, which frequently happened, these mighty Chiefs, being very powerful and restless. The House Bell used in the said Castle was about fifty years ago found in the stance or rubbage.

Clearly the track on the south side was well known and used but from other records, the distribution of crannogs along the north shore bearing a relationship to farm lands each run by one or more families and the important access to Fortingall and Glen Lyon used by the early missionaries, it is judged that the north road was the more important. The land on the north side is also more kindly and more easily worked so that the forest and scrub persisted and still persist to a greater extent on the south shore of the loch.

In the two hundred years since Kenneth MacAlpin's day, Scotland had reeled under Norse attacks, but successive kings mainly of Pictish origin had not done a bad job in containing the damage and had even achieved some relief from it by inter-marriage with the Norse. MacBeth had had a notable reign of some seventeen years before the bastard King Malcolm, called 'Big Head' or Ceann-mohr, with Northumbrian help and the oak branches from Birnam wood defeated him at Dunsinane in 1057.

Malcolm Canmore was not only a bastard by birth, illegitimate son of King Duncan by 'the miller of Forteviot's daughter' (which is all that is known of her), but he was also a 'bastard' by nature, big, rough, callous but a good fighter. It was during one of his raids into Northumberland that quite by chance a ship, having on board the true heir to the English throne, Edward Atheling, with his Hungarian mother and his sister Margaret, all northward bound to raise trouble against King William, fell into his hands in 1070.

Margaret was a young woman of great character, born into a religious family. She is reputed to have carried with her a fragment of the 'true Cross' given to her by her grandfather Saint Stephen of Hungary, which became known in time as The Black Rood of Scotland: from it Holyrood got its name. She evidently believed she had a divine mission to spread the Christian faith, so after King Malcolm had sent her and her mother off to Dunfermline and then, overwhelmed by her beauty, asked her to marry him, it was not love at first sight, but to seize the opportunity of power as Queen of Scotland to propagate her faith, that prompted her to acquiesce.

Margaret was not only deeply religious, she was also good and kind. Coming from a background of fine stone-built abbeys with richly clad priests conforming to the practice of Rome and obedience to the Pope, she was shocked at the crudely built places of worship she found in Scotland, more horrified still at any residuary acknowledgement of stone circles, and despised the rough monkish habits used in the Celtic Church. To her belongs the credit of building the first major stone church in Scotland, the Abbey at Dunfermline near to the palace/castle there. She also restored the ruined Abbey at Iona and latterly built the tiny chapel in Edinburgh Castle; it may have been partly because of the traffic of holy men between her establishments that encouraged her to provide a free ferry across the Forth, which bears her name to this day.

On the other side of the coin, she waged an offensive war against the beliefs of the Celtic Church. Already that church had suffered a setback at the Synod of Whitby in 664 AD over the method of calculation of Easter Day, hinging on the academic question of whether or not the forty days of

Lent should include an allowance for the five or six Sundays—fast days—included in the period. Rome, with its heavier metal, won that argument, setting a precedent still extant for churchmen to argue interminably on questions themselves quite indeterminate. They had differences too about serving the wine, 'the Blood of Christ' at communion services. The Celtic practice was to dispense wine as well as bread to all communicants, while the then Roman practice allowed only the priests to sip the wine, a distinction with little apparently logical reason. Possibly there was a language difficulty in these discussions, the Celtic representatives struggling to translate their Gaelic into another tongue, while on the other side there was a mixture of Latin, Anglo-Saxon English and perhaps a smattering of French. At any rate, Margaret found the 'Kelidi', the friends of God, difficult to convince and when her fourth son Ethelred without her consent was appointed to be Abbot of Dunkeld and so nominal leader of the Columban Church, it was a major reverse which left her embittered but still resolved to eliminate the barbaric Gaelic tongue, a resolve carried down through the centuries by many good and devout persons not comprehending the importance and ancient lineage of that language. It was the start of the general decline in Gaelic to its present relatively insignificant role, of the introduction of magnificence into church buildings, their ornamentation and the adornment of their priests.

King Malcolm Canmore's reign also marks the influx into Scotland of increasing Norman and Saxon influence. As the Conqueror, King William, consolidated his hold on England, many of the Norman French who were rivals of or disappointed by King William fled north: the Princess Margaret was just one of them. Her presence as Queen was encouragement enough for many of a like mind to follow, welcomed by her and not despised by her King for their added weight and influence to his court.

Among the new customs introduced was that of holding land gifted by the King by feu charter and the accepted appointment of successors by right of birth as opposed to the ancient system of tanistry adhered to by both Celts and Picts. Tanistry had evolved from a group selection of a leader who was best suited to their needs. Naturally he came from a powerful family and must be well known, forceful and brave, but not necessarily the son of the dead chief. He could be brother, uncle, nephew, or even unrelated: women were not excluded. This was a system of strength and continuity, especially suitable for maintaining powerful groups isolated geographically and having little need or respect for an Ard Righ. From it evolved the clan system, the clan chief not only leader in time of war, but caring for his group, their customs and the land they occupied—it was not his land and he carried no documentation for it. But land held by feu charter was the land of the fortunate man named in the document. To get it he must have

been well known to the king or have carried out some signal service which
the king wished to repay, while he in turn must repay his duty to the king,
initially with fighting men on demand, ultimately by payment of money.
All depended on a written document, now, with the advent of writing and
parchment or vellum to write on, becoming more readily available.

New names also found their way north, notably those of Fraser and
Gordon. Particularly in the east the power leaders known as *marmaors* became
earls at the king's pleasure. In the west, great names were also becoming
known, names usually of Celtic origin. A chief with a crooked mouth, *caim
beul* in Gaelic, had become especially strong and founder of the clan Campbell.
Another with a face like a prize-fighter with his nose knocked crooked, *caim
srion*, became known as Cameron. Not far away, a dark stranger, *dubh gall*,
came to lead a group; his sons were of course MacDougalls. It was good to
feel kinship with famous men, such as Nechtan (Gaelic *Neachdainn*) who
probably did have many sons, one family of which came to settle in
Breadalbane, *braghaid* or braid Alban.

It is known that before 1688 Balmacnaughton and the lands below it which
later became known as Remony Farm were the property of the chief of the
clan Macnaughton, but because of the clan's support for the Jacobite cause
their lands were forfeited and later acquired by the second Earl of Breadalbane.
Another Macnaughton was tenant of Eddergol in 1480, yet another vicar of
Inchedin, Innis-cailtnigh, now Inchadney in 1510. Mac-an abba, son of the
abbot, became MacNab, while Mac an sagairt, the son of the priest, became
MacTaggart. There were no raised eyebrows in these days for the priest to
have a son, since celibacy was not a rule of the Celtic church.

Relics left by St. Fillan had been put in the care of special custodians,
who came to be known as *deoradh*, meaning literally pilgrim or wanderer,
no doubt because they carried these relics with them on their journeyings.
This word repeats as *jore*, *doire* and finally Dewar, all phonetically similar.
The name given to minor tribal chiefs or leaders was *toiseach*; he too might
have many sons all proclaiming themselves as MacIntosh, another well known
local name.

Three of Queen Margaret's sons followed Malcolm Canmore. It may give
some insight into the varied actions of these early kings to note that in the
reign of King David I (1124–53) there was time for thought to be given
about fish and fishing. Salmon were a wonderful and relatively easily obtained
source of food; 'fishing' in these days was of course catching fish for food.
Angling for sport was hardly known and the first of the very many books
on that subject was not written until well on into the fourteenth century.
Salmon could be seen running up most Scottish rivers from the sea; it was
not difficult to catch them after constructing dams or cruives across a river
at suitable places. One wonders who was the first to think that these dams

and the catches from them might come to endanger the salmon numbers, but someone at King David's court must have voiced just these fears to cause it to be enacted that such dams must have a gap left in them to allow some fish to escape upstream. This 'midstream' was to be big enough to allow a three-year-old swine, well fed, to stand in it 'so that neither the grouzie not the tail may wyn till either side'. How or whether this enactment was enforced is not known, but here is the very first official pronouncement about conserving salmon stocks.

CHAPTER 8

'Scots wha hae'

The years following the 'Margaretsons' rule saw increasing anglicisation of Scotland and subservience to England which produced widespread discontent and ultimately uprising under William Wallace, a young man, son of Wallace of Elderslie in Strathclyde. The good folk on Lochtayside no doubt shared in the indignation at what they must have perceived to be the misrule of their country, but it is more than doubtful whether any other than a few hot-heads, perhaps already in trouble at home, went out of their way to join Wallace's forces, even after his success against Edward of England at Stirling Bridge in 1298.

Here Wallace's knowledge of the long causeway over the marshes leading north from the narrow bridge over the Forth under Stirling Castle enabled him to achieve a notable success by his attack when only the head of Edward's army had crossed the bridge, in these days a narrow timber structure carried on piles, no easy passage to reinforce an endangered advance force or for them to retire over. One wonders whether the leaders on either side were aware of the ancient ford only a short distance upstream of the bridge, or whether the state of the tide at the time made its passage impossible. When United Auctions were building the market at Kildean in 1968 they uncovered the Roman road leading down to the ford, which had a good bottom and had formed the first possible place to cross the Forth on foot or horseback inland from the muddy sea estuary.

Wallace won, only later to meet a terrible death at the hands of the English. He was followed by Bruce who achieved the famous Bannockburn victory on the other side of the Forth only a few miles away when Edward, with the pride of English armed forces, marched north to relieve Stirling Castle in 1314.

By this time, Breadalbane was not yet under the control of the Campbells but Bruce would be well known to the people living there. In his early rise to power, struggling to unite the peoples of east and west, supporters of the Comyns forced him up the Tay valley into an ambush by the MacDougalls of Lorn in the narrows of Strathfillan. There, at the place now known as Dalrigh, with his Queen among his small group, while fighting hand to hand with the MacDougalls he had the brooch holding his plaid torn off his shoulder before managing to escape. The brooch, still extant, is known as the Brooch of Lorn.

Bruce was a great leader, to become recognised as the first knight of Christendom. He had a troubled and sad reign, his brothers butchered quite literally by King Edward, and his wife and daughter hung in cages outside the walls of English castles. Miraculously, they survived this cruel treatment. Because of the murder of his rival Comyn in the Greyfriars Church near Dumfries in 1306 he had been excommunicated by the Pope who gave tacit support to King Edward in spite of that king's brutality, and threatened to excommunicate the whole Scottish Church. Once established, Bruce found much support from certain leaders of the Scottish Church, especially Bishop Lamberton of St. Andrews, the Scottish Primate. It is thought to have been on his advice that a letter was sent to the Pope in 1320 putting foward the Scottish case for cessation of English raids and annulment of the excommunication. This was the famous Declaration of Arbroath, purporting to come not from the excommunicated Bruce but from the whole Scottish people, signed for by their leaders, and was a political gesture to gain the Pope's support and to weaken King Edward's position. It was of course written in Latin, which most of the signators could not read or understand, but onto which they affixed their seals on the advice of Bruce and his churchmen. They who wrote it used the most extravagant language, an indication of Christian expression at a time when Angus Ogg, Lord of the Isles, could barely understand the English used at the King's court, but the Pope was not to know that. Here is the English translation of the Declaration:

To the Most Holy Father in Christ and Lord, the Lord John, by divine providence Supreme Pontiff of the Holy Roman and Universal Church, his humble and devout sons Duncan, Earl of Fife, Thomas Randolph, Earl of Moray, Lord of Man and of Annandale, Patrick Dunbar, Earl of March, Malise, Earl of Strathearn, Malcolm, Earl of Lennox, William, Earl of Ross, Magnus, Earl of Caithness and Orkney, and William, Earl of Sutherland; Walter, Stewart of Scotland, William Soulis, Butler of Scotland, James, Lord Douglas, Roger Mowbray, David, Lord of Brechin, David Graham, Ingram Umfraville, John Menteith, guardian of the earldom of Monteith, Alexander Fraser, Gilbert Hay, Constable of Scotland, Robert Keith, Marischal of Scotland, Henry St. Clair, John Graham, David Lindsay, William Oliphant, Patrick Graham, John Fenton, William Abernethy, David Wemyss, William Mushet, Alan Murray, Donald Campbell, John Cameron, Reginald Cheyne, Alexander Seton, Andrew Leslie, and Alexander Straiton, and other barons and freeholders and the whole community of the realm of Scotland send all manner of filial reverence, with devout kisses of his blessed feet.

Most Holy Father and Lord, we know and from the chronicles and books of the ancients we find that among other famous nations our own, the Scots, has been graced with widespread renown. They journeyed from Greater

Scythia by way of the Tyrrhenian Sea and the Pillar of Hercules, and dwelt for a long course of time in Spain among the most savage tribes, but nowhere could they be subdued by any race, however barbarous. Thence they came, twelve hundred years after the people of Israel crossed the Red Sea, to their home in the west where they live today. The Britons they first drove out, the Picts they utterly destroyed, and, even though very often assailed by the Norwegians, the Danes and the English, they took possession of that home with many victories and untold efforts; and, as the historians of old time bear witness, they have held it free of all bondage ever since. In their kingdom there have reigned one hundred and thirteen kings of their own royal stock, the line unbroken by a single foreigner.

The high qualities and deserts of these people, were they not otherwise manifest, gain glory enough from this: that the King of kings and Lord of lords, our Jesus Christ, after His Passion and Resurrection, called them, even though settled in the uttermost parts of the earth, almost the first to His most holy faith. Nor would He have them confirmed in that faith by merely anyone but by the first of His Apostles by calling—though second or third in rank—the most gentle Saint Andrew, the Blessed Peter's brother, and desired him to keep them under his protection as their patron for ever.

The Most Holy Fathers your predecessors gave careful heed to these things and bestowed many favours and numerous privileges on this same kingdom and people, as being the special charge of the Blessed Peter's brother. Thus our nation under their protection did indeed live in freedom and peace up to the time when that mighty prince the King of the English, Edward, the father of the one who reigns today, when our kingdom had no head and our people harboured no malice or treachery and were then unused to wars or invasions, came in the guise of friend and ally to harass them as an enemy. The deeds of cruelty, massacre, violence, pillage, arson, imprisoning prelates, burning down monasteries, robbing and killing monks and nuns, and yet other outrages without number which he committed against our people, sparing neither age nor sex, religion nor rank, no one could describe nor fully imagine unless he had seen them with his own eyes.

But from these countless evils we have been set free, by the help of Him who though He afflicts yet heals and restores, by our most tireless Prince, King and Lord, the Lord Robert. He, that his people and his heritage might be delivered out of the hands of our enemies, met toil and fatigue, hunger and peril, like another Maccabaeus or Joshua, and bore them cheerfully. Him, too, divine providence, his right of succession according to our laws and customs which we shall maintain to the death, and the due consent and assent of us all have made our Prince and King. To him, as to the man by whom salvation has been wrought unto our people, we are bound both by law and by his merits that our freedom may still be maintained, and by him, come what may, we mean to stand.

Yet if he should give up what he has begun, and agree to make us or our kingdom subject to the King of England or the English, we should exert ourselves at once to drive him out as our enemy and a subverter of his own rights and ours, and make some other man who was well able to defend us as our King; for as long as but a hundred of us remain alive never will we on any conditions be brought under English rule. It is in truth not for glory, nor riches, nor honours that we are fighting, but for freedom—for that alone, which no honest man gives up but with life itself.

Therefore it is, Reverend Father and Lord, that we beseech your Holiness with our most earnest prayers and suppliant hearts, inasmuch as you will in your sincerity and goodness consider all this, that, since with Him whose vice-regent on earth you are there is neither weighing nor distinction of Jew and Greek, Scotsman or Englishman, you will look with the eyes of a father on the troubles and privations brought by the English upon us and upon the Church of God. May it please you to admonish and exhort the King of the English, who ought to be satisfied with what belongs to him since England used once to be enough for seven kings or more, to leave us Scots in peace, who live in this poor little Scotland, beyond which there is no dwelling-place at all, and covet nothing but our own. We are sincerely willing to do anything for him, having regard to our condition, that we can, to win peace for ourselves.

This truly concerns you, Holy Father, since you see the savagery of the heathen raging against the Christians, as the sins of Christians have indeed deserved, and the frontiers of Christendom being pressed inward every day; and how much it will tarnish your Holiness's memory if (which God forbid) the Church suffers eclipse or scandal in any branch of it during your time, you must perceive. Then rouse the Christian princes who for false reasons pretend that they cannot go to the help of the Holy Land because of wars they have on hand with their neighbours. The real reason that prevents them is that in making war on their smaller neighbours they find quicker profit and weaker resistance. But how cheerfully our Lord the King and we too would go there if the King of the English would leave us in peace, He from Whom nothing is hidden well knows; and we profess and declare it to you as the Vicar of Christ and to all Christendom.

But if your Holiness puts too much faith in the tales the English tell and will not give sincere belief to all this, nor refrain from favouring them to our prejudice, then the slaughter of bodies, the perdition of souls, and all the other misfortunes that will follow, inflicted by them on us and by us on them, will, we believe, be surely laid by the Most High to your charge.

To conclude, we are and shall ever be, as far as duty calls us, ready to do your will in all things, as obedient sons to you as His Vicar; and to Him as the Supreme King and Judge, we commit the maintenance of our cause, casting our cares upon Him and firmly trusting that He will inspire us with courage and bring our enemies to naught.

May the Most High preserve you to His Holy Church in holiness and health and grant you length of days.

Given at the monastery of Arbroath in Scotland on the sixth day of the month of April in the year of grace thirteen hundred and twenty and the fifteenth year of the reign of our King aforesaid.

One can sense the care and thought put into the document, the corrections and additions made to it. Perhaps the translation from Latin into English masks some of the tones, but it is a strange mixture of obsecration and threat, some doubtful historical facts and belittling of Scotland—'poor little Scotland, beyond where there is no dwelling place at all'—which one feels would not have been approved by Bruce. But the passage on freedom, 'for that alone, which no honest man gives up but with life itself', rings down the ages as a sentiment of which Scotland can be proud. The people of Breadalbane would be completely unaware of the letter, but may have had their own worries about the health of their well respected King, referred to in the letter ' . . . Him who though He afflicts yet heals and restores . . . our most tireless Prince . . . '—a phrase perhaps included to play down any rumour of the king being ill.

The Declaration was a success; the Pope cancelled the excommunication and Bruce died in his bed at Cardross in 1329 having been recognised as King of Scots and even offered by Edward III the return of the Stone of Destiny. He was buried at Dunfermline beside his wife, Elizabeth de Burgh who had predeceased him, his heart cut out ready to go on the Crusade he had intended but had never carried out.

After King Robert the Bruce's death, English raids and claims in Scotland continued, with retaliations which culminated at Flodden in 1513. Nearer to home, the Campbells were coming and much of what now follows comes straight from the Black Book of Taymouth, at first copied exactly as written and then paraphrased into more modern English.

CHAPTER 9

The Campbells are Coming

M uch of what follows comes straight from *The Black Book of Taymouth*, also entitled 'Papers from the Breadalbane Charter Room'.
It was privately printed by the then Marquis of Breadalbane, although undated probably near the end of the nineteenth century, with a preface by one C. Innes. The author is William Bowie who was notary and pedagogue (or tutor) to the family at Taymouth in the time of the seventh Laird of Glenurchy. He dedicated the book to his patron in 1598 and died in 1648. The book includes the Chronicles of Fortingall listing events in that parish before 1551 recounted by James M'Gregor who was Dean of Lismore and Vicar of Fortingall, and Duncan Laideus' Testament which although anonymous is thought to have been the last writing of the Duncan Macgregor who was hanged in Kenmore in 1570. There are also Bonds of Manrent, Inventories, Rentals and Court Book edicts made by the Lairds of Breadalbane.
The initial page is copied with the same spelling as written; later, the extracts are paraphased in English as we know it but using the spelling of names as written.

The Black Book of Taymouth

Ane admonitioun to the Posteritie of the Hows of Glenurquhay.

Gude redar, in this genealogie
Iff thow by blude, by lauchfull birth and name,
In richt or syde lyne is or luikis to bee
Enrold, as one by vertew and gude fame
In nobill rank to leve, think shame, think shame,
By wickit deid or sluggischnes to tyne,
Through vertew quhilk in peace, weare, field and hame
Thy predicessouris manie zeiris sine
Hes conquest, keipt and maid for to be thyne.
Thair futesteppis then if thow will imitatt,
Grerce thy witt, thy minde and whole ingyne

By thair ensample sure to lay this platt.
Will thow thy honour, howss, and rent to stand,
Conques, or keip things conquest to thy hand;
In faith feare, loue, thy God and prence
Serving with all obedience.

MB.

The first page, opposite the coloured picture of 'Dominus Duncanus Campbel de Lochlow':

The stock and immediate originall off the Hows of Glenurquhay.
Inprimis, Duncane Campbell, commonlie callit Duncane in Aa, Knicht of Lochow (lineallie descendit of ane valeant man surnamit Campbell quha cam to Scotland in King Malcom Kandmoir his tyme about the zier of God 1067, off quhom came the hows of Lochow), quhilk floorisched in King David Bruce his dayis, &c.
The foresaid Duncane in Aa, Knicht of Lochow, hade to wyffe Margaret Stewart dochtir to Duke Murdoch, on quhom he begat tua sones, the eldar callit Archibald Campbell, the other namit Colene Campbell, quha wes the first laird of Glenurquhay discendit of the hows of Lochow off the name of Campbell.

It is interesting that Master Bowie cites the origin of the house of 'Lochow' to have been apparently a Norman knight who came north, so he says, about nine years after Malcolm Canmore had been crowned. This is entirely possible and in line with the movements already mentioned, nor does it contradict the possible Gaelic origin of the name 'Campbell' since dialects of Gaelic had been spoken in Europe before the time of the Norman Conquest. Bowie presumably wrote what he had heard from the Breadalbane family—almost certainly what they would wish to read. He himself spoke English and was familiar with Latin and so possibly thought that Gaelic was a barbaric tongue. Certainly there is little use of Gaelic in the Black Book save the use of Gaelic names, so one wonders whether the Breadalbane Campbells preferred to consider themselves of Norman or French stock and considered the Gaelic/Celtic traditions to be 'Non-U', in spite of their stronghold in the west being in the heartland of Gaeldom.
The next page goes on:

Hitherto off the original: followeth the lineall and lauchfull discent.

COLENE (afterwards styled Sir Colene) received from his father on 20/10/1432 the fourscore markland of Glenurquhay, the 27 markland of Innerynan & etc. land on Lochow.

Married 1 his first wife Marriott Stewart, daughter of Waltir Stewart of

Albanie, who was the son of Isobell Duchess of Albanie and Countess of Lennox, who died shortly after.

Married 2 Jonett Stewart, eldest daughter of William Stewart, Lord of Lorne, with whom he got the dowry of the 18 markland of the Bray of Lorne, but after her father's death the Lordship of Lorne fell to William's three daughters, so the Sir Colene, through his wife the eldest of the three, came to have the superiority of the Lordship of Lorne and the first wife thereof extending to 250 marklands.

They had one son, Sir Duncan Campbel who suceeded as Laird of Glenurquhay and one daughter called Geillis Campbell who married M'Cowle in Lorne.

Married 3 a woman of Clandondoquhie; they had one son Jhone Campbell who became Bishop of the Isles and one daughter Catherine Campbell who married Waltir Stewart, baillie of Balquhidder.

Married 4 Margarett Stirling, daughter of the Laird of Keir. They had two sons, Jhone Campbell (who later succeeded as laird of Laweris) and George Campbell who died young and a daughter Helene Campbell who married firstly Makeane of Ardnamurroch and secondly a Makgregoure.

Colene was laird for 48 years in which in addition to the lands which he received from his father he acquired (conquessit) the tacks of the 10 markland of Auchmoir, the 30 markland of Ardtallonik, the heritable title of the 10 markland of the Port and Isle of Loch Tay, the 4 markland of Innerneill in Knabdale which he later exchanged with the . . . [left blank] of Balloch, the 10 markland of Drumlean and Blairboyok in Menteith which were also exchanged, to which 10 marklands the Hows of Glenurquhay sits as superior along with all the aforementioned lands. Later he acquired the 40 markland of Lawiris, the 3 markland of Correquhirk & etc. which he gave to Jhone Campbell, son of his fourth wife.

The said Sir Colene being tutor to his brother's son Colene Campbell (who was made first Earl of Ergyle) married him to the second heretrice of Lorne and thereafter (for the favour he bore him and the standing of his House) freely passed to him the superiority of the whole Lordship of Lorne.

During his time as tutor to his brother's son he built the Castle of Innerarray and later the castle of Ilankeilquhirn, the barmekyn wall of the Isle of Loch Tay and the tower of Straphillane.

Sir Colene through his valiant acts and manhood was made Knight of the Isle of Rhodos (standing in the Carpathiane Sea near Caria a country of Asia minor) and visited Rome three times.

He died in the tower of Straphillane on 24/9/1480 and was buried in the Kirk of Kilmertyne in Argyle.

From this series of facts and relationships several points emerge. Firstly, the importance of being 'in' with the right people. Colene's first wife was the daughter of the Duchess of Albanie, who was married to the Regent of Scotland during King James I's imprisonment in England—a good start.

Then, that marriage was a good springboard for power and possessions; Colene was good at it and must have been a strong and active man, always on the move. He was known as 'Black Colin of Rome' so he presumably had been there, although three visits seems a lot. As a believer in the Roman Church, no doubt a call on the Pope would have been politic, but there is no mention of this.

Not least in importance in furthering his 'hows' was Black Colin's willingness to work on his new acquisitions. The Isle of Loch Tay had long been inhabited; Queen Sybilla, the wife of King Alexander I, had been buried in the Priory there in 1122, the island being known as Eilean nam Ban, the Isle of the Women. So, today, the 'port' is Portbane, on the south shore of the loch although the island had a stone causeway connecting it to the much nearer north shore. Possibly the nuns used the port on the south shore when visiting the healing well nearby, extant and cared for until very recently. Whether the island was wholly man-made or partially natural, it had certainly been strengthened and enlarged, so the 'barmekyn wall' which Black Colin built was a continuation of this arising from his liking for the island and making it a principal residence, deeming that additional protection was required from the wind and wave action on the south and west shores. He was a great builder, with the castles at Inverary, Kilchurn and Strathfillan standing to his credit.

All this must have required money as well as power, but in the acquisitions of the variously valued marklands no mention is made of paying for them or of the people living on them. No doubt they were 'acquired' too, as tenants to pay rent, or as helpers to do the laird's will.

Finally, notice the progression eastwards, Inverary, Kilchurn, Strathfillan, Lawers, Ardtalnaig, the Isle of Loch Tay and the land at Balloch.

Thus far the first laird—followeth the secund

Sir Duncane Campbell was the eldest son of Sir Colene and succeeded as second laird of Glenurquhay.

Sir Duncane married firstly Margaret Douglas, daughter of the Earl of Angus. They had three sons, Sir Colene, Archibald and Patrick who died as a young man in the Ile Badchelich and a daughter Elizabeth who married the laird of Monivaird.

Sir Duncane married secondly . . . Moncreiff, daughter of the laird of Moncreiff and had one son called Master Johne Campbell (who was the second Bishop of the Isles of the house of Glenurquhay) and two daughters. The eldest, Katherine, married the laird of Tullibardin, the other, Annabil

Campbell married the laird of Merchistoun.

Sir Duncane lived as laird 33 years, during which he obtained tacks of the King's lands in Braidalbane and of the Charterhouse lands in the same, the tacks of the 12 markland of Cranduich. He acquired the heritable title of the Barony of Finlarig, which tacks and heritable titles together with the 'bailzerie' of Discheoir, Toyer and Glenlyoun tane of the King, he annexed to his house.

He acquired the 60 markland of the barony of Glenlyoun which he gave to his second son Archibald together with the 24 markland of the third of Lorne which he took from that house.

He acquired the 8 markland of Scheane in Glenquoich which he gave to his brother Johne Campbell of Lawiris to be held by the house.

He built the laich hall of Glenurquhay, the great hall, chapel and chambers in the Isle of Lochtay.

Sir Duncane was killed at the field of Flowdane with King James III on 9/9/1513, and was buried with his Chief, Archibald Campbell then Earl of Argyle, because they both died valiantly on that field.

Sir Duncane ably followed his father in all ways, excepting the visit to Rome. He married well and note how he looked eastward to Tullibardine and Merchiston for his two daughters.

Here is the first mention of 'Discheoir and Toyer', land respectively on the north and south side of Loch Tay but nowhere specifically defined. Discheoir possibly comes from *Deas Faire* meaning 'looking south'. 'Crown' lands, 'the King's lands in Braidalbane' were presumably lands where tenants paid rent or duty directly to the crown supervised by a baillie paid for the job, lands which had not been specifically granted to noblemen or to the Church. To become baillie of such lands, which are thought to include Eddergoll (Acharn) together with the tacks he already held, put Sir Duncane into a position of enormous power at the east end of Loch Tay. One wonders whether it was by accident or design that the buildings on the Isle of Loch Tay were burned down in 1509 as the Chronicles of Fortingall tell us: Sir Duncane rebuilt them, possibly with the stone walls still partially standing in place of the older timber construction, before setting out on his final journey. To the east lay the Earldom of Atholl; there were Menzies lands in the strath downstream of Loch Tay and there were noted lands 'acquired' at Lawers, Ardtalnaig and near Kenmore. Now Shian in Glenquaich is added and given to the laird of Lawers.

To get from Lawers to Shian would involve going over the hill from Kenmore to Glenquaich by what was called the Lairig mile Marcaidh, the 'Pass of the mile of riding', no doubt because the ground was firm and fairly level so that riders could urge their horses to greater speed. Just beyond the Lochan nan Lairig on the west side of the present road is 'Bobbie's Stone', where carving on the rock face remembers the young heir to Bolfracks Estate killed in Sicily during World War II in 1943, leading a Company of the Black Watch.

Riding had of course been the recognised means of travel for many centuries, so the breeding of horses for riding was long established. Their use in raiding or warfare was recognised; 'light' cavalry was primarily a means of getting armed men quickly from place to place, then as armour became commonplace, its weight required much heavier horses ridden by chevaliers and knights—'chivalry' was born. The principal families must have kept horses especially for getting from place to place, which they were now doing much more regularly; no doubt posting stables appeared, run either by the big families or under commercial control at some centres. So, in the armed struggle between Scotland and England, cavalry of a kind could be raised fairly quickly. In Scotland the smaller, wiry and sure-footed garron type were best suited to the terrain; in Gaeldom the clans marched on foot. In England the courtly influence, the use of armour and no doubt easier roads favoured the use of much heavier horses to carry the knights. The sheer weight of knight and horse in a charge was almost impossible to stop—given suitable ground for a charge—and this was an important aspect of kingly warfare.

And now a Campbell laird was to pay for the privileges he and his house had received from their king. Called to support King James IV, he had no option but to obey, from loyalty, pride and position, and undoubtedly called on his own supporters to provide an armed force proper for his position. There is no word in the Black Book of how many local men never returned from Flodden, but it must have been a big number with many men killed fighting on foot against English cavalry, leaving Lochtayside a glen of weeping.

The thrid laird

<u>Sir Colene Campbell</u>, eldest son of the late Sir Duncane, succeeded as third laird of Glenurquhay. He married Mariory Stewart, daughter of the Earl of Atholl and had three sons, Duncane, Jhone and Colene (which three each after the other succeeded as laird of Glenurquhay).

Sir Colene was laird for ten years and maintained all left to him. He was a great justiciar all his time. He build the chapel at Finlarg as a burial place for himself and those that followed.

He died at the Castle of Ilankeilquhirn in Glenurquhay on 12/8/1523 and was buried in the chapel at Finlarg.

Thus far the thrid laird.

The fourt laird

Duncane Campbell, eldest son of Sir Colene, succeeded him as fourth laird of Glenurquhay.

He married Mariory Colquhoun, daughter of the laird of Lus; they had one son who died in his minority.

Duncane lived as laird for 13 years, keeping all things left to him by his worthy predecessors.

He died in the Castle of Glenurquhay on 5/9/1536 and was buried in the chapel at Finlarg.

Thus schortlie of the feird.

Followeth the fyft

Jhone Campbell, brother of Duncane, succeeded as fifth laird of Glenurquhay.

He married Marion Edmestoun, daughter of the laird of Dountreith before he became laird and had two daughters, Cristiane who married the tutor of Lus and Marioun who married Alexander Home of Argadie.

John liaved as laird fifteen years and besides keeping the old living whole acquired the 12 markland of Ardbeich which he left to the house with great riches and store.

He died on the Ile of Lochtay on 5/7/1550 and was buried in the chapel of Finlarg.

This mekill of the fyft.

The Sext

Colene Campbell, brother to Duncane and Jhone succeeded as the sixth laird of Glenurquhay.

Colene married before he succeeded Margaret Stewart (daughter of Bishop Alexander Stewart) the lady conjunct fear of Inchebraky and they had two daughters. The first, Beatrx married Sir Johne Campbell of Lawiris and the second Margaret who married M'Cowle of Ragray in Lorne.

Colene, after the death of his first wife Margaret and succeeding as laird of Glenurquhay, married Katherine Ruthwen, William Lord Ruthwen's daughter by whom he had four sons . . .

Colene was laird for thirty three years during which he acquired the feu of the King's lands and Charterhouse lands in Braydalbane, the tacks of which his predecessor had obtained as stated.

He acquired the 10 markland of Auchlyne, Easter Ardchyllie and Dowinche together with the superiority of all the M'Nab's lands. Also the superiority of the 20 markland of Stronmeloquhan in Glenurquhay. Also he 'cost' an old lodging in Perth, which acqusitions and superorities remain with the house.

Colene acquired the 20 pound land of Edinambill, the 5 pound land of Edinkip under reversion and the 8 markland of Kingartt which with the 12 markland of Ardbeich and tacks of the land of Cranduich taken from the house he gave to his second son Colene.

Colene built the castle of Balloch, the castle of Edinambill in Balchquhidder, the whole lodging of Perth within the close, the four kirnellis [? corner towers] of Ilankeilquhirne in Glenurquhay, also its North chambers.

He was a great justiciar in his time, through which he sustained the deadly feud of the Clangregour for a long time. And besides that he caused to be executed to death many 'lymmaris', he beheaded the laird of M'Gregour at Kandmoir in the presence of the Erle of Atholl the justice clerk and many other noblemen.

Sir Colene died at Balloch on 11/4/1583 and was buried in the chapel of Finlarg.

Thus far the 6 laird.

The youngest son, 'Colene' once more, had lived through twenty-eight years of control by his two brothers and was fifty-one years old before he became laird, his hair beginning to go grey to earn him the name of Cailean Liath, Grey Colin.

He must have been ambitious as well as experienced; the Isle of Lochtay was not big enough for him, he wanted a castle of his own. In sight of the Isle across the loch above Acharn was a site offering easy defence. It lies on the west side of the (now called) Acharn Burn, about 160 metres above the stone bridge later built upstream of the falls, with a steep slope on three sides and a fine all-round prospect. Translated from the Gaelic of old Argyll, Campbell records can be read:

When Cailean Liath wished to build a castle at the east end of Loch Tay, Acharn was the first place he selected, and his men began to work at a hill for a foundation. A place was levelled and they began to build the wall of the castle. An old woman who had goats dwelt at the place, and she knew that when the castle should be built, she would not be allowed to remain in the place any longer, or keep goats in it. So she said to the men, 'Cold is the place where you are building the castle. It will be exposed to every wind and storm.' 'And where would you build it,' they asked her. 'Where I should hear the first thrush,' she answered. Cailean Liath told them to ascertain where the first thrush should be heard. Now there was a field where MacGregor was wont to keep his calves. It was enclosed with blackthorn and hawthorn and there was a pass through which the calves were put in and brought out. That was the first place where the men heard the thrush. The castle was built there, and it was called Caistel Balloch, the Castle of Balloch, by the common people, but Taymouth by the gentry.

The tale rings true; the squared off foundations above Acharn are there to be seen. Maybe it was just because fifty-one-year-old Grey Colin felt the cold as well as the steepness of the brae when he climbed up to inspect the work—or was there some ancient built-in, even druidical, fear of the sayings of a 'wise woman' that made him change his mind? Anyway, he got on with building at the new site and the earliest document recorded as 'signed at Balloch' is dated 12/10/1560.

The castle was only the beginning of a new era for Kenmore. Sir Colin had been a leading proponent of the Reformation and a member of the Parliament which in 1560 gave legal sanctions to Protestantism. In 1579 he received formal permission to build a church in Kenmore to supersede the ancient one at Inchadney, on the north side of the Tay about two kilometres downstream from the present main road bridge and near the old ford at Newhall. Markets used to be held there on the droving route using that ford; they too were moved to the green at Kenmore. For some time there had been a ferry and ferryman's house; now with the seasonal markets and church as well as the ferry there was need for an inn and Sir Colin granted a lease to Hew Hay and his wife to keep the inn he built on the Ferry Croft, presumably of stone, since it is described as being 'loftit' (more than one storey) with chimney, doors and windows. How many of Sir Colin's works now stand as he built them is doubtful. His castle at Balloch was pulled down and rebuilt after 1799; there is now no trace of the prison complete with iron fetters and heading axe inventoried in the original castle. The new Taymouth was built with stone from a quarry near Bolfracks and this stone was also used in the existing church. There was a huge gap in technique at this time between the wonderful masonry of many continental cathedrals and the rough stone buildings, superseding wood and turf, now being built in Scotland with or without the use of lime mortar. A gap too in the training of skilled masons and the druidical traditions of handling large stones on which the art of drystone and other walls must have been founded so that the skill of local builders must have varied enormously between these two poles. There is no doubt however that Grey Colin can be regarded as the founder of the village of Kenmore.

Perhaps the event which most stirred the people of Lochtayside was the capture and eventual execution of Gregor Roy MacGregor at Kenmore in 1570. The story of Clan Gregor is inextricably mixed with the Campbells and deserves to be told in full. It follows in the next chapter.

CHAPTER 10

The MacGregors

In the painful process of change from the clans holding their land by occupation and by force of arms to ownership of land by charter or disposition from the crown, the MacGregors fared badly while the Campbells prospered.

The MacGregor clan claimed descent from Kenneth MacAlpine; 'Royal is my race' was their motto. They occupied far flung lands in Argyllshire and western Perthshire where Glenorchy, Glendochart and Glenlyon were known as 'MacGregor's glens'. The clan followed John of Lorne and supported the English at a time when the Campbells supported Wallace and later Bruce, for which they were granted lands round the head of Loch Awe. The MacGregor chiefs lived at Stronmelochan in Glenstrae only a few kilometres from Kilchurn Castle. Traditional inter-clan rivalry and raiding developed into a love/hate relationship which lasted for hundreds of years. About 1520 a MacGregor chief of Glenstrae had carried off and married Helen, the daughter of Sir Colin Campbell of Glenorchy, while in 1561 Grey Colin, the fourth laird, was fostered with a family of MacGregors living at Stronfearnan.

In the early part of the sixteenth century, one Duncan Ladosach or Laideus (thought to have meant lordly or overbearing) had earned ill repute by robbing and terrorising the central Highlands but exerted much influence over young Gregor, now chief at Glenstrae. So when Alasdair Odhar McPhadrick V'Condoquhuy at Morenish sold his MacGregor birthright for a tack or lease of his lands from Sir Colin, pledging allegiance to him, Duncan Ladosach was only too pleased to accept his chief's injunction to obtain revenge. The unfortunate Alasdair Odhar and his supporter John McBain at Killin were duly murdered and in turn Sir Colin obtained a commission 'to pursue after Duncan Laideus, his son and their complieses', which they did successfully. Duncan Ladeus and his son were duly hanged at Balloch in 1552, but not before Duncan is reputed to have written a remarkable poem, part lament and part confession, which is quoted in full in *The Black Book*. The Clan MacGregor was harried and driven to seek safety in the remote fastnesses of Rannoch.

Young Gregor of Glenstrae had himself become a ward of the Campbells and was placed with Duncan Roy, the laird of Glenlyon, whose daughter

he eventually married, but when Grey Colin tried to persuade the Mac-
Gregors to sign bonds of friendship he failed. Among those scorning this
offer were the two sons of the MacGregor Dean of Lismore who was the
parish priest at Fortingall and it is thought that Grey Colin persuaded one
James Mac an Stalker Rioch (grizzled) who lived at Ardeonaig to murder
them. Stalker Rioch was a man of great strength, reputed to be able to shoot
an arrow from his bow from one side of Loch Tay to the other, but his
strength was of little avail when Gregor Roy and his men descended on
Ardeonaig and murdered him and his household.

Queen Mary of Scotland had shown sympathy for the landless MacGregors
but when she fled to England after her captivity on Loch Leven, Sir Colin
had little difficulty in obtaining a commission to take and execute Gregor
Roy. It was while engaged in this effort that Gregor was surprised while
visiting his wife in Glenlyon and only escaped from his pursuers by a bold
jump across the rocky gorge of the Lyon at a point known today as
MacGregor's Leap. But not for long: soon after he was indeed caught and
after a form of trial at Finlarig he was beheaded at Kenmore in 1570 in the
presence of the Earl of Argyll and the Justice Clerk to give semblance of
legality.

Gregor Roy's son Alasdair was only three years old when his father was
executed. He grew up to become known as the Arrow of Glenlyon,
handsome, athletic and much admired as a young man, but when as the heir
to Glenstrae he sought to have these lands returned to him, he was baulked
by the Campbell laird, now Sir Duncan, known as 'Black Duncan of the
Cowl'. 'Revenge,' was the cry of the MacGregors. Then came for the clan
a most unfortunate incident. Their young men had been accustomed to
poach deer from the King's forest of Glenartney but a party had been caught
and returned home with ears lopped off in punishment. Later, another party
from the Balquhidder branch of the clan, bent on the same ploy, happened
to meet Drummond Ernoch, the king's forester, unescorted. They cut off
his head and carried it homeward, stopping at Ardvorlich, where the laird's
wife was the sister of Drummond, to seek food. This they got in the tradition
of highland hospitality, but when they put the head on the table and stuffed
its mouth with bread the lady fled shrieking to the glens. When they got
back to Balquhidder a clan meeting was held in the graveyard there with
the head on a gravestone, when young Alasdair, keen to prove his leadership,
accepted full responsibility for the act. The leaders of the Scottish Government, now under young King James VI, then took every step to eliminate
the MacGregors, with a commission to Huntly, Atholl, Argyll and Glenorchy
to 'seek, tak and apprehend' Alasdair MacGregor.

With so many men of power against him, Alasdair had no one to whom
he could turn, so after a troublous period, in 1596 he sought pardon directly

from the King, then at Dunfermline. No doubt influenced by his good
appearance and manners, the 'gentle King James' did grant a conditional
pardon. Even this was not enough to cure Alasdair and his clan of their
marauding habits. At a battle in Glenfruin on Lochlomondside they killed
very many of Colquhoun's men and carried off great numbers of cattle,
sheep and horses. Alasdair was outlawed again, and finally, friendless, he
submitted to Argyll who betrayed him into the hands of the king's forces.
After a trial and confession of sorts, in 1604 he was hanged, drawn and
quartered in Edinburgh, a terrible end to a remarkable man.

Even this was not the end of the clan MacGregor, although their name
had been proscribed and all MacGregors forced to adopt other names which
they did, usually in deference to the owner of the lands in which they lived.
Many became Campbells.

About this time one Duncan Glas (pale) who lived at Glengyle at the
head of the valley of Loch Katrine, became recognised as the leader of the
remnants of the MacGregor clan in the Trossachs area. He was married to
Margaret Campbell from Meggernie in Glenlyon; their son was Robert Roy.
Duncan was a man of upright character and well educated, unlike Alasdair
who could not read English or write, as we know from a document which
he signed in 1601 'with my hand touching the notary's pen underwritten,
because I cannot write'. In his day when up until then all Gaelic tradition
and learning had been handed down orally, this was not surprising. Times
were changing and his education, added to his honesty and ability, all added
to Duncan's high reputation. Accustomed to gather cattle honestly bought
from the north, west and islands to be driven to the great annual fair, then
at Crieff, he was relied on and recognised as a leader in this trade. As a
young man, Robert Roy accompanied his father and became familiar with
the people of these remote areas, the many other drovers, their routes and
the hardships and hunger that had to be endured on these long droves in
all sorts of weather. He became an acknowledged master at this trade and
is credited later as having driven vast herds south into England as far as
Norfolk.

As he grew to be a man, Robert also grew to be skilled at arms. His
father was neither keenly Jacobite nor Royalist but supported the Highland
way of life and had been granted a colonelcy in the army of King Charles II.
Rob Roy was present with his father under Dundee at the battle of Killie-
crankie, when General Mackay after losing the battle fled across the river
and spent the next night at Castle Menzies. Both he and his father supported
law and order rather than the Stuarts, but their sympathy lay in that direction.
Rob Roy learned to distrust leaders in high places and despise bad generalship,
as at Sheriffmuir where Rob and his detachment although nominally with
the Highlanders under Mar, took little part in the battle but gained some

booty. Among his duties soon after was to garrison the castle of Balgonie in Fife which 250 years later Raymond Morris, lately forester at Remony, was to restore from its then ruinous state.

Following in his father's tradition of learning, Rob Roy sent his children to school and chose that at Acharn. Rob's wife Mary, after the destruction of their base at Craigroyston by Montrose's men in 1712, had fled to Taymouth to seek protection from Breadalbane, who treated them well. It may have been at that time that friends were made in Acharn who would care for the boys, or that the dominie there was held in special regard. Rob, for his part, in his droving days coming down from the north, would have been familiar with the track to Trinafour, Tummel Bridge and Coshieville, then by Revard (the bard's route) over Drummond Hill to the stances and inn high above Kenmore. Perhaps some stock were sold at the fair there but most would go on over 'the pass of the mile of riding' to Glenquaich and then by Amulree and the Sma' Glen to Crieff. If Kenmore had been a usual stopping place Rob would have been familiar with the area, or perhaps one of his leading drovers came from nearby Acharn. It must have been by way of further approval that he 'took' the church bell from Balquhidder and presented it to the Acharn school, where it remained until returned to Balquhidder some time after World War I, where it can now be seen. The bell, now cracked, was fixed to a stout wooden shaft about half a metre long, the ends of which would rest on bearings and the bell tolled by pulling a rope attached to a metal arm about thirty centimetres long and fixed to the shaft.

Although dubbed a rebel because of his known actions with the Jacobite forces, Rob Roy had also been in touch with Government leaders. In 1712 he had been given a very large sum by Montrose to buy cattle for him to winter in the lowlands. His leading drover, a Macdonald, absconded with the money and in spite of assurances to repay, given time, Montrose pursued his action for recovery and bankrupted Rob Roy. His bitterness at this, to him, unjust action led Rob Roy to maraud instead of buying more cattle, and naturally taken from those whom he disliked or despised. Because he generally spared the less well off and some times even returned a cow where there was great need, Rob Roy gained a Robin Hood-like reputation, hated by the powerful but well liked by the people. Many efforts were made to capture this 'rebel and thief', but by daring escapes he only added to his reputation. In 1717 he was caught and placed in the Duke of Atholl's castle at Logierait. His guards, flattered no doubt by the courtesy of their celebrated prisoner and after enjoying much of his whisky, allowed him to meet a messenger at the door. The messenger had brought a fast light-legged horse, onto which Rob Roy leaped and easily outdistanced his pursuers, heading for Loch Tay and home. It would have been quite in keeping with his character had he stopped to see his sons at Acharn and maybe have a dram with his friends there, although there is no record of this.

As the years passed, Rob Roy's fame increased; his actions, if illegal, also won many friends. Eventually, instead of being harried from his home in Glen Gyle, his stronghold of Craigroyston on Loch Lomond, his house built in Glen Shira or that at Auchinchisallen in Glen Dochart (on the south side of the public road about two kilometres east of Loch Dochart) which was burned before his eyes, Rob Roy was pardoned and allowed to live in peace at Inverlochlarig Beag where he died in 1735.

The Act of proscription of the MacGregors was repealed in 1775 and many resumed their original name.

Today little is left of the original MacGregor home in Glenstrae, while at Balloch Taymouth Castle stands empty and unused, the tenth Earl of Breadalbane living alone and unmarried in London. But both MacGregors and Campbells are to be found scattered over the lands they once used to occupy and far further afield, all proud of their name and survival through the troubled times of their ancestors.

CHAPTER II

Black Duncan of the Cowl 1552–1631

The seventh laird of Glenorchy was a very remarkable, resourceful and able man with many different interests, among which the care of the land he had 'conquesit' came only after his love of money, position and power. To achieve these objectives he used every means he could, starting with 'friendship' for the King, keeping in with his powerful friends and relations as well as extorting money from them. His overseeing of his lands was meticulous; no doubt it included seeing that all his tenants were up to date with their rents which, of course, he himself fixed.

So he had many enemies and must have been a hard man with many unlikeable characteristics. Master Bowie, author of *The Black Book*, was in his employment and so knew well on which side his bread was buttered. He refers to 'the false and forged inventiones which were never qualifiet nor prowin' which brought his laird to imprisonment in Edinburgh Castle in 1601, but these were accepted by the 'pooir and gredie courteouris for the tyme' and Black Duncan had to pay 40,000 marks to be released.

Bowie quotes separately a very great number, if not all, of the doings of his laird, occupying many pages of *The Black Book*; these are summarised below and their very extent indicates the important part the seventh laird had during the forty-eight years of his control in adding lands and power to his House of Breadalbane.

Followeth the 7

Sir Duncane Campbell, eldest and lauchfull sone to the foresaaid Colene, succeedit sevent laird off Glenurquhay.

The said Sir Duncane mariet Jeane Stewart, dochter to the Erle of Atholl to his first wyffe, on quhome he begat sevin sones, the eldest callit Colene; the second Robert . . . and 4 dochters.

After the death of his first wife Sir Duncane married secondly Elizabeth Sinclair, daughter of Henry Lord Sinclair; they had two sons and four daughters. All of his eight daughters he married off to neighbouring lairds with dowries of up to 7,000 marks apiece.

His 'conquesits' included:

The five pound land of Dunfallandy in Strathtay for 4,000 marks.

The thirteen markland of Drumnoquheill and Drumquhassil in Atholl belonging to the laird of Powrie Fotheringham, for 7,000m.

The ten pound land of Mochastyer, Duletur, Portbank, Portinellan, Tarnedown and Lochbancher for 12,000m.

The half markland of Cairndoire in Kilmahog, 500m.

The four markland of Kandnoquhane in Menteith, 4,000m.

The twenty-four markland of the barony of Glenfalloch, 24,000m.

The easter quarter of Monzie in Strathearn, 4,000m.

The ten markland of Fintolich in Strathearn and 'grass roum' of Glacorren and Beinqukuk in Glen Lednock, 7,000m.

The feus of the Chartehouse lands in Breadalbane [for the second time, perhaps because the king was hard up?] 2,000m.

The ten markland of Brayglen in Lorne, 2,000m.

The four markland of Cowle-balloch in wadsett which he then bought out in 1611 for 500m.

The eighteen markland of Tennaiffs [Duneaves] and Culdairis for 15,000m.—which he handed over to his son Patrick.

The four markland of Easter and Wester Creichanis in Strathyre, 3,000m.

The eight markland of Middell Stukis and the superiority of Garrows in Glenquoyche, 5,000m. in 1599.

The forty shilling land of Wester Stukis, 5,000m.

The glebeland of Monzie called the Ibert, 3,000m. in 1599 (handed over to his son Archibald).

The twelve markland of Crannich, the twenty pound land of Moirinche, the ten markland of Auchmoir and two markland of Kandknock extending to fifty-four marklands in all (without redemption) in Descheore and Toyer, 28,000m. in 1602.

The patronage of Insche-chaddin, 2,000m.

The long tacks of the teinds of both parsonage and vicarage of the Kirk of Glenurquhay, 3,000m.

The Isle of Inschesaill, 1,000m.

The lands of Larg, Ilemulloch, Branquhailzie, Eddraleckabeth, Strongerwald and Ardmonkmanare extending to thirteen marklands in Menteith, 13,000m. plus 400m. for the seal, in 1618.

The four markland of Leatter in Menteith, 2,000m. plus 400 for the seal in 1618.

The lands of barony of Lude extending to thirty-four marklands, also the four markland of Petnacry in the sherriffdom of Perth, for 10,460 pounds 13/4d. plus seal 1,000m. in 1619.

This considerable list of properties is scattered over a large area ever extending eastward and southward, to Lude in Atholl heartland, to Menteith and to Monzie in Strathearn. At the east end of Loch Tay, to the lands already held at Balloch, Glen Lyon and Shian in Glenquaich, were added lands at Styx and Garrows to the south-east and Duneaves and Culdares commanding the entrance to Glen Lyon, amounting to a considerable power block around Kenmore.

Black Duncan's building works included:

The Castle of Finlarig and offices and redecoration of the chapel, 10,000 pounds.
The Tower of Achallader, 1,000m.
Repair of the Castle of Ilankeilquhirn, inwardly and outwardly.
The house of Loch Dochart, 2,000m.
A large four-storied house in Benderloch 5,000m. in 1601
The house of Bachaltane in Lorne, completed in 1609, 10,000 pounds.
'The expence of the wark and travell maid by him in stopping the water of the Tay frae destroying thee place and yardis of Balloch extendit to 10,000 markis, anno 1608.'

The massive drystone floodbanks which 'stopped' the River Tay from flooding the land around Balloch must have been among the very first major flood prevention works on the Tay, cutting off an old flood channel running from these works in front of the present Castle and rejoining the present river at the Battery Pool, so formalising the meander northwards now crossed by the Chinese Bridge and protecting a large area of parkland around the Castle. No civil engineers or computers available in these days, no heavy earth-moving machinery or Planning Consent required, just common sense and using the experience of earlier floods. The work has stood the test of time and is representative of the basic right, indeed duty, of each proprietor to protect his own land.

The payment in marks for the acquisitions seems the most common but indiscriminately used alongside pounds (Scots), shillings and pence. It can be deduced that a pound was then worth 1½ marks, while a 'one markland' seems to range in value between 200 and 1,000 marks in purchase price, no doubt depending on its amenities or, more importantly, its desirability from a defence or political aspect.

Keeping in with the King and 'up with the Jones' was always a Campbell trait. Although imprisoned in Edinburgh in 1601, after buying himself out Sir Duncan did not seem to have suffered any loss of personal friendship with the king. In 1608 he gave a present of two eagles to Prince Henry and on 6 January 1609 the King's secretary replied from Whitehall:

Honorable Sir, The Prince receaved your eagles very thankfullie, and we had good sport with thame and according to his promeiss he hath sent yow a horss to be a stallon, one of the best in his stable for that purpose . . .

Some years later, in 1622, having evidently heard tales about a white deer in the Breadalbane country, the King writes:

JAMES R. Trustie and wellbeloued, wee greete you well. Hauning understood that ther is in your boundes a white hinde, we haue sente this bearer, one of our servantes, to take and transporte her hether unto us; and becaus that contrie is altogether unknowne to him, we have thought good here by to recommende him to yow most earnestlie, requiring you to assiste him and cause him to be furnished with all things necessarie, as well as for taking of the said hinde as for his oune interteynment; and nothing doubting of your best endeuour for acompishing this our pleasour, we bid you farewell. Giuen at our mannour of Theobaldes, the 13th. day of Januarie 1622.

The bearer's name was Scandoner who duly came to Taymouth, but failed to capture the hind. The postal service must have been remarkably good because on 9 March Sir Patrick Murray responds to a letter from Sir Duncan:

To my honorabill chieff the Laird of Glenvrquey theis. Noble Cheiff,—I haue reseaued from the Earll of Mar a packet of letters concerninge the takinge of this trublesum whyt hynd of yours, and hes delyuered and red them to his Maistie, he being not weill of a payne in his legs, I dar not seye the gutt. His Maiestie is weill plesed with you for the caire you hawe hed to forder his Maiestries desyr in all things concerninge this bissines of takinge thies deir; and seing his Maiestie fynds be Scandoners owine letters and all yours that it is a hard mater ather to tak hir or carey hir to the sea, by reason of the difficultie and hardnes of the place and hard tyme of the yeir; and fyndinge also be his Maiesties owine experience that iff sche cane not be takine befoir May or June, beinge so laitte in the yeir, that iff sche prowe with calf mey indenger hir owine lyff and hir calf also, his Maiesties plesour is that sche schall not be sturde this yeir, and tha his Maiestie will think of sum wther courss befoir the nixt yeir for the better effectinge of his desyrs; and his Maiestie has commanded me to wrytte wnto the Earll of Mar to send wnto all thois that borders or marcheis with Corrachaba that none presume to sture hir, under his Maiesties highest displesor. And becaus his Maiestie will trye what Scandoner can do by his arte he has wryttine his letters to the Earll of Pearthe, that he may mak tryell in Glenartnay for takinge of sum deir and rois now presently, that he mey, be his tryell their, judge what he cane do heirafter in Corrachaba. I hawe downe you the best officies that lyis in my power to his Maiestie, bothe in this and in all wther things that schall ather tuiche or concerne you, as I am bound in dewtie of blood to do. Thus, with the rememberence of my trewe loue to yourself and all yours, I rest

Your werie assured friend and kinsman to serue you,

P Murray.

Theobolls Park, the 9 of Marche 1622.

This remarkable letter shows not only the King's good sense and knowledge of country life, but also the importance of having a friend, in this case a relative, at court.

The Corrachaba mentioned in these letters, Gillies, in his book, places in Blackmount, seemingly unaware that above Remony there is the Coire Beithe, pronounced Corry Bay, the Birch Coire, although there is no birch there today except under the peat. But today in or near to Coire Beithe deer with white markings are often seen. In 1972 Herr Hatlapa from Germany who kept a deer park there enquired whether he could acquire a white-faced stag which had been reported and was given consent to try to capture it. Together with a veterinary surgeon (whose name was not Scandoner!) they made a determined attempt to 'dart' the stag but were frustrated by 'the difficulty and hardness of the place and hard time of year'—mist, in this case. However, the next June a white-faced stag calf was found not far away, brought down to Remony and ultimately despatched to Herr Hatlapa.

Surely Corrachaba was the Coire Beith, the white genes still present among the deer there: history truly repeating itself remarkably accurately.

Black Duncan took his interest in wild creatures very seriously. In 1608 he became Justice by letter patent to enforce the Acts of Parliament relating to the slaughter of red fish, smolts and fry, also of deer, roe and wildfowl between 'Grantullie . . . and within the bounds of Dischoir and Toyer . . .' In 1615 he 'causit put fellow deir and cunnyngs [rabbits] within the Ile of Inchesaile' (Innisail in Loch Awe).

He was a lover of books and is thought to have written verses. At one time he dabbled in the Black Arts.

With his fourteen legitimate children, many married and scattered throughout the area as well as several more outside wedlock, to some of which the King granted letters of legitimacy, and his immense extent of lands, Black Duncan was in a position of tremendous power, able to do what he most like doing, imposing his will.

CHAPTER 12

Campbell Characteristics

A s the people living in the more remote parts of Scotland increased in number, ultimately developing into clans, a tradition grew up of fostering sons especially of powerful leaders into other families, often distant relatives, to be brought up as part of that family, so strengthening the bonds of friendship and sometimes of blood within the clan.

The Campbells were not strictly a clan in the above sense, having 'acquired' their lands scattered over a large area and with them many tenants and followers without any blood relationship, but they were not slow to see the advantages of having supporters tied to them not merely by paying rent. Thus, in 1510, 'Grey Colin' when only eleven years old, was fostered to a family in Fearnan:

> Obligation by Johne M'Neill Vreik in Stronferna and Gregoure his brother to receive Coleyne Campbell lawful third son and heir of Sir Duncan Campbell of Glenurquhay knight in fostering and to give him a bairns part of gear; and giving to the said Sir Duncan and his heirs their bonds of manrent and calps that is the best aucht in their housis the tymes of their deceiss: the said Sir Duncan and Coleyne his son being bound to defend the saids Johne and Gregoure in the lands of Stronferna and the rest of the rowmis they possess as law will: Johne Campbell of Laweris brother to Sir Duncane Sir Robert M'Nail vicar of Killin Alexander Maknachtan Iuldonycht Talzeour Makfale and Gillechreist Clerk witnesses. Signed at the Isle of Lochtay 29 April 1510. Schir Maureis M'Naughtane vicar of Inchedin notar.

Now well into the period of written bargains, the Campbell found these bonds between apparently willing participants an excellent way of increasing their power. Fostering, as in that quoted above, formed a relatively small number of the some 145 bonds recorded between 1488 and 1681. Grey Colin executed 52, Black Duncan almost as many, spreading his net far beyond family friends nearby in Breadalbane, to Perth, Coupar Angus, Edinburgh and Stirling as well as many closer at hand.

> Marie Nikvoirest V'Causs in consideration that Duncane Campbell of Glen-urquhay is bound to defend her in her actions and quarrels, gives him and his heirs the third part of all her gear; Johne Makindewar in Portbane, Maureis M'Nauchtane in Inchadine Robertt M'Indewar and Alexander Livingstoun, witnesses. All at Illanrane 10 July 1583.

And another:

> Patrik Glas in Crief obliges him to pay to Duncane Campbell of Glenurquhay
> the sum of ten marks Scots money (yearly) during his life because the said
> Duncane Campbell promised him his protection; Johne Elder burgess of Perth,
> Laurent M'Laurent son to Laurent M'Laurent in Craigruy in Buchquhedir,
> and Walter Lindsay servant to the said Duncane Campbell witnesses. At Perth
> 20 October 1587.

It can be seen from the above bonds that the Campbells used very precise
language: they liked being precise and carried this through to listing the
quantities of food and wine used and available in their houses, the furnishing
of these houses and of course the number of men and their weapons they
could call on.

In September 1590 it is noted that in addition to the 'Laird and Ladie'
there were also in residence at Balloch the Lairds of Tullibardine and
Abercairney, the Bishop of Dunkeld, the Laird of Inchbrackie, the Prior of
Charterhouse 'with sindrie uther cumeris and gangeris'.

Between 18 and 27 September:

> Enterit and cost out of Perth be Thomas Broune off new hard fische and
> deliuerit to Elspeth Granger xxviii doz.; thairof of skait, iiii doz.; off ling iiii
> doz.; of keilling x doz.; off seythis x doz.

The good Thomas Broune must have been a very competent fishmonger
but also have had a quick delivery service. It was not until 1795 that the
Breadalbanes of Taymouth built an ice-house for themselves at the top of
Drummond Hill.

In 1626 there was an inventory of the fittings in Balloch ('called Taymouth
by the gentry') which gives a good insight on the style in which Black
Duncan lived. The list included:

> Off bousteris in Balloch, 30 . . . off coddis 31.
> Off black mantillis in the greit kist of the galarie garderob, 1.
> Off red mantillis in the household garderob, 1
> In the Ladies garderob of Balloch of quhyte Ireland caddois, 1.
> Off hewit cadddois in the Ladies garderob, 1.
> Off quhyte plaidis in the lang kist that standis on the North syde of the
> galarie, 1.
> Off courtingis ane stand of blew sey, bordourit with yallow satine conteining
> four peces with rufe and pand round about the bed, in the lang kist of the
> North syde of the galarie, 1 stand.
> Off canabies of grene plaiding, pasmentit with quhyte knittings, in the
> household garderob, 1.
> Maid by the Lady in 1598 of blew canabies pasmentit with orange, 1.
> Off lynning scheittis in the litill kist of the North syde of the galarie, 12
> pairs.

Off lynning seruiettis in the litill kist . . . 5 doz.
Off hardin seruiettis in the household garderob, 34.
Off lynning towellis in the litill kist . . . 12.
Off sewit cuscheonis with the Larde and Ladies armes, 2.
Off sewit cuscheonis in the household garderob, 5.
Off buffet stuillis red and yellow browderit with satine, 2.
Off chandillaris in the galarie garderob, 6, quhair of 2 greit chandillaris.
Off chandillaris in Balloch that Patrik M'Awyre hes, 10.

The list goes on page after page into all the separate items of linen, the pots, the pans and all the kitchen equipment, including breakages and balances of stock in hand. It would seem that Agnes Colquhoun was housekeeper at Balloch, but Magie Petir is much more frequently mentioned in that role at Finlarig; both must have been kept busy.

If the women folk kept such careful tags on their affairs, naturally the men folk did the same; the Laird would keep a particularly close eye on the list of vassals and tenants 'that ar meit to beare arms'. At the east end of Loch Tay it went like this in 1638:

PORT OF LOCHTAY—Donal M'Kerrachar, i sword, target; Callum M'Euiure, i sword; Gillechreist M'Kerrachar, i sword, target; Callum M'Lechreist Oig, bow and arrows; Johne M'Orquidill, i sword, target.

BALNASKEAG—Donald M'Houston, i sword.

KENDMOIR—Johne M'Euiure, i sword, target.

PORTBANE—Johne Campbell, i sword, target, i hakbut; Patrik Campbell, i sword, target, i hakbut.

BALLEMACNAUCHTAN—James M'Lecheir, i sword, bow and arrowes.

REMONY—Johne M'Kerlich, i sword.

TOMGARROW—Thomas Quhyte, i sword, target.

LAGGAN—John Dow Baine M'Quain, i sword, target.

AUCHARNE—Callum M'Quain, i sword, target, i hakbut.

ARDTALLONIK—Johne Robertsone, i sword, target; Gillechrist M'Achrerar, i sword, i hakbut; Duncane M'Phaderik V'Robert, i sword, target; Duncane M'Lehoneill, i sword, target; Donald M'Achrerar, i sword, i hakbut.

One wonders whether Callum M'Euiure in Port of Lochtay, Donald M'Houston in Balnaskeag and Johne M'Kerlich in Remony had lost their targets? Separate lists were made for the Parishes of Inchaddine, Weyme, Dull and Killin: from all the names listed it would seem that the Laird could call on some 115 men more or less armed, excluding his own paid servants.

Black Duncan was particularly interested that his lands in Breadalbane should be properly cared for and issued statutes from his 'court' decreeing how almost everything was to be done, under penalty of hefty cash fines for defaulters.

These start in 1621 with regulations how to carry out muirburn (heather burning), followed by listing penalties for anyone who 'schuits at deir roe blackcocks etc. nor slay blackfish in tyme coming.'

Next came rules about dykes which probably mark the start of many of the stone and turf dykes the remains of some of which can still be seen today.

> Item it is statute and ordained that all heiddykis and faulddykis within the foresaidis boundis respectine be yeirly beittit bigit and upholdin be the awneris and possessouris thairof sufficiently with divot earth and stane, under pane of ten pundis money, ilk persone failyeand thairin, toties quoties.

It is not clear who were 'the owners' thus exhorted; the Laird was the owner, but the occupiers of any land would be 'possessors'.

No one is to cut any brier or thorn save in the waxing of the moon—was this a hang-over from Black Duncan's interest in witchcraft?

All tenants are to plant young trees of oak, ash or plane (to be obtained at the not inconsiderable cost in these days of two pence each from the Laird's garden) in their kailyards on a scale of six trees per tenant and three trees per cottar for each markland 'according to samany merklands as they occupie . . . and as soon as they ar reddy to take up agane, that they be sett in the maist comodious pairtis of their said occupationes'. This was indeed an ambitious programme, but not easy to enforce. It is one of the very first records of what is today considered to be 'green' thinking and a forerunner of the immense work of tree planting and improvement carried out by forward thinking landowners.

No one may keep swine, under a penalty of ten pounds. But this statute must later have been cancelled, since piggeries were provided later in both upper and lower Acharn; the Gaelic name of the Remony Burn is the Alt Muchaid, the swine burn.

Strict rules were laid down about the grazing of the hill land and the manner of leading horses and cows to get there on the appointed dates. A common gate to be eight feet wide 'that ane horse may gang by ane uther not spilland their cornis'. In due course the areas of hill grazings became formalised and sheilings were allocated to different farms. In 1769 Remony and Balmacnaughton sheilings are shewn on M'Arthur's map as being on the north side of Glen Quaich below the steep rock outcrops there.

No one may put out a 'skabbit' horse 'unwashed', and 'aney man that findis and apprehendis the said skabbit hors to cast him over ane craig and brek his neck'. This is very drastic; the Laird must have had or heard of some terrible repercussions of having a diseased horse on the place.

Wolves must have been troublesome, because each tenant is to make 'four croscattis of irone' for slaying them. This may have been part of a general and successful war against wolves at a time of increasing numbers of stock; the last wolf in Scotland is reputed to have been killed in 1743.

No one may suffer rooks, hooded crows nor 'pyatis' (magpies?) to nest on their land; neighbours to help with this.

The rate at which oats are to be sown are laid down, under five pounds penalty.

'Browster houses', presumably public houses where ale or beer was sold, had strict regulations about the supply of ale; wives were forbidden to drink unless accompanied by their husbands!

In July 1621 for the first time it was noted that a statute was made 'with aduyse and consent of the heall tenants' and in November of 1622 'at Candmoir, it is stated and ordainit be the aduyse of the heall tennantis and millers that each tennant may have ground one firlot of barley free of multour [fee paid to the miller] each year.'

Poundfolds were to be set up in all his lands in which stray cattle or sheep could be held until claimed, each with a principal appointed by name to control it.

These strict rules were the beginning of a tradition of farming practice far ahead of its time. They must have been severely interrupted by the devastation that followed some twenty years later, but not altogether forgotten.

Among the intimate records of this time of the sixteenth and seventeenth centuries the various diarists were far more concerned in what was happening at home than in matters beyond their immediate bounds. Innes, the editor of *The Black Book* which includes 'The Chronicles of Fortingall' during the period 1550–72 says:

> There is no comment on public events . . . within the space of two leaves the deaths of Rizzio, of Darnley, of Murray . . . are noted with a remarkable avoidance of any expression of feeling. Somewhat more is elicited by the murder or death of . . . a friend or neighbour, when he deals a short eulgism,–*bonus fuit* or *non fuit avarus*.

This is the story of a small piece of the land of Breadalbane and the people on it, not a history of Scotland, but certain events ultimately affecting Breadalbane must be recorded.

Following the Reformation, the Covenant movement produced civil war between those of staunch Presbyterian outlook and those accepting religion imposed by King and Pope. Black Duncan had been succeeded by his son Colin (once again!), a lover of the arts and an extensive traveller. The luxuries listed earlier as in the Castle of Balloch would be as nothing compared to what he might have seen in Paris or elsewhere in Europe, nor would he have any concern at the contrast in the way of life in the houses, many still built of turf, of his tenants. But he was an upholder of Presbyterianism and in the last years of his life joined his kinsman the Marquis of Argyll against King Charles I with 'about ane hundred ablemen or thereby to bear weapons'.

Sir Colin was followed in 1640 by his younger brother, now Sir Robert, again living up to the Campbell tradition, having eight sons and nine daughters. He became Member of Parliament for Argyll and perhaps from this experience learned to tread very warily in choosing sides. The Earl of Atholl had earlier come to terms with Montrose, who led the King's forces, but in 1644 Montrose invaded Breadalbane from the east with among his troops wild Irishmen, also Macnabs, Macgregors and Macdonalds, all enemies of the Campbells, and swept westward along the valley of the Tay leaving a trail of desolation behind him. It was said that not a single house was left standing on the south side of Loch Tay; Kenmore was sacked, even the poor box stolen out of the church. The poor box was a large heavy ironbound chest with three clasps and padlocks; even the soldiery would have found it both cumbersome to carry and difficult to break into. Legend has it that Montrose found them at it and ordered it to be returned to the church; there must be some truth in this since the very same box now stands in its place within the Kirk of Kenmore, while in January 1645 it is recorded that the Kirk Session were able to make a distribution from it for the 'many poore people who were burned and spoyled'.

Cromwell was the next cause of concern to the people of Lochtayside. Not long after they had rejoiced at Montrose's death, when Cromwell with his army invaded Scotland in 1650 a public fast was proclaimed in Kenmore for 'the present calamities on the Kingdom be the incoming of the English'. King Charles had by this time subscribed to the Covenant and so opposed Cromwell; to avoid whose forces he withdrew from Edinburgh to Perth. The then Chancellor of Scotland, Lord Loudon, was a Campbell of Lawers and cousin of Sir Robert's. He and the Marquis of Argyll, another relative, arranged for the Honours of Scotland to be sent to Balloch for safe keeping, where they only stayed a short time before being returned to Scone for the crowning of King Charles in 1651.

These were troublous times for Breadalbane, the well-being of its people closely related to the doings of their Laird. Sir Robert was elderly, much burdened not only with supporting his large family but also in keeping his armed supporters content when they would much rather have been engaged in repairing the destruction caused by Montrose.

Sir Robert actually applied for and got an abatement in the King's taxes in 1653. He and supporters of the King were greatly helped at this time by a professional soldier, Colonel Wogan, evidently of great ability and charm, who led the Royalist forces based on Blair Atholl and Balloch in skirmishes against the Commonwealth troops based on Perth. He was unfortunately wounded and taken back to Balloch, where he died and was 'buried in great state and much lamentation with a military funeral in the Church of Kenmore.' Rev. Menzies, the then minister, did not approve, and there is a minute of the Kenmore Kirk Session which declared 'that the burial was made in the Kirk, so farre as they know without consent either of the heritors . . . or of the session . . . Their had never been such a thing befor . . . and was contrair to the law of the Kirk of Scotland.' There is no sign of Wogan's burial place today, since in 1871 when workmen were reflooring the church they came on bones, most probably Wogan's, which were then buried by the beadle 'somewhere in the churchyard'. The tradition that Wogan was buried beneath an ancient oak at Inchadney is almost certainly due to Sir Walter Scott's romancing in his novel *Waverley*.

Soon after, General Monk led the Commonwealth troops north into Scotland and established a garrison at Balloch which Sir Robert had prudently yielded to him on condition that he could still live there. Once again Lochtayside was harried. In all these reports much is said about the castles, the lairds and the military leaders, but little of the devastation of the working people already depleted in numbers by those 'ablemen' in service with the Laird, whichever side he was on.

CHAPTER 13

Now Comes Breadalbane

Sir Robert Campbell of Glenorchy died in 1657 aged eighty-two, after a troublous life, and was succeeded by his son John, born in 1635. In spite of the family lands being heavily mortgaged and the exchequer empty, Sir John served as Member of Parliament for Argyllshire from 1661 to 1663 and served for a time in the Scottish Army. He married three times and had six sons and eight daughters.

John as a boy was perhaps tutored at Balloch by William Bowie, Black Duncan's clerk and author of *The Black Book*. He certainly followed Bowie's admonitions 'to conques and keip thingis conquest'; when only twenty-two years old he set off to London and there married Lady Mary Rich, daughter of the Earl of Holland with a dowry of ten thousand pounds. One can imagine the handsome young man from the Highlands, no doubt in Highland dress, full of romantic tales of war and intrigue, sweeping a beautiful young girl (and her family) off their feet. They were married in London in 1657, then set off north with a train of garrons loaded with the lady's 'tocher' to set up house at Balloch.

Once home, John Campbell lost no time in establishing himself. First, in the Church and Presbytery of Dunkeld he succeeded in having his cousin, Patrick Campbell, appointed as minister at Kenmore. Then as an active member of the Privy Council he was rewarded by them with a commission to 'pursue, aprehend and imprison' one William Sinclair of Dunbeath in Caithness, who had moved into Sutherland with a large force, plundering and killing wherever he went. Nothing loth, John Campbell set off on this task not only with his own men but also with three hundred men of the King's Guard and a party from Lord Lothian's Regiment of Foot; when he reached Sutherland he was joined by the Earl of Caithness, whose wife was the Marquis of Argyll's daughter. Then came the first of many incidents which went to earn him the reputation of being 'as cunning as a fox, wise as a serpent and slippery as an eel'.

Lord Caithness was in trouble and very heavily in debt. Young Campbell was rich and commanding a force with which he could do what he liked in the Caithness homeland. One feels therefore that the 'agreement' reached between the two, that Campbell would redeem the debts and support the Caithness family in return for not only land but also in due course the

Caithness dignities and titles, was obtained by *force majeure* and not because of the relatively distant family relationship. At any rate, when the Earl died not long after, John Campbell took up the land and the titles and had them confirmed by the Privy Council. However, the legal heir challenged the matter and won back the land and titles. Not to be outdone, Campbell must have spun a wonderful tale to the King about his treatment after the good work he had loyally done for him; he was compensated for the loss of the land and in 1681 was created Earl of Brae D'Albane and Holland, Viscount of Tay and Paintland, Lord Glenorchy, Benderloch, Ormlie and Wick in the Peerage of Scotland, titles of which are carried down to the present day.

John, Earl of Breadalbane was now in a position of power. With land and castles, the ability to call on a large force of armed men and goodwill at court, he felt himself a leader among the Highland clans. He saw his kinsmen, the Argyll father and son, destroyed for having stood up for their political and religious views; he learned the lesson and worked hard to maintain the favour of the crown, now King William, while still showing friendship with many of the Highland leaders opposed to the King. These tactics naturally caused suspicions; Breadalbane had many enemies and had suffered cruel raids into his lands by the Macdonalds. Whether or not the Macdonald chief had signed the act of allegiance to the crown by the deadline date at the end of 1691, they were undoubtedly looked on as troublesome rebels deserving to be disciplined. Nor is there any doubt that the disciplining force came from Breadalbane country with participation by the Earl's kinsman, Robert Campbell of Glenlyon, although very few, if any, of the soldiery were Campbells. However harshly and unfairly the Government troops carried out their orders, in particular bitterly offending against ancient Highland traditions of hospitality, the government (and Breadalbane?) were not displeased at the outcome. And while 'cruel was the snow that lay in Glen Coe' in the winter of 1691–2, the Earl of Breadalbane was snugly esconced in London.

This did not prevent him from later being imprisoned in Edinburgh on charges of treason in connection with his dealing with the Highland chiefs, until King William sent a commission to Edinburgh requiring his release.

The King and the leading Scots had other things on their minds and there followed a breathing space for the people of Breadalbane when fighting and politics could at least temporarily be put aside. History does not fully relate the political manoeuvring that went on prior to the union of the Scottish and English crowns in 1707, but it does show that the Earl of Breadalbane refrained from voting on the issue, canny man. He was always thought to have had Jacobite sympathies and in 1716 joined the Earl of Mar in proclaiming the Stuart Chevalier at Moulinearn. Later, the Campbells and the Macdonalds were brigaded together on the right wing of the Jacobite forces in the inconclusive Battle of Sheriffmuir.

Breadalbane was now thrice married and eighty-two years old; he kept himself out of harm's way, pleading disability to travel, and died in 1717 having nominated his second son John, Lord Glenorchy, as his heir.

The second Earl of Breadalbane inherited the Campbell traits of longevity (he lived to the age of ninety) and of making good marriages, but he had only one son (John, again) who succeeded him—and he was a man of peace.

It is difficult to perceive accurately just what was going on along the shores of Loch Tay, since the available records are full only of lairds and their doings, now with cross-references to other historical sources. Following the 1715 attempt to re-assert the Stuart dynasty and the resulting Disarming Act of 1725 a more peaceful period ensued after local raidings by bands who had kept their arms and made the most of them against those that had surrendered theirs. The Breadalbane papers from about 1720 onwards are full of letters referring to their gardens being laid out at Taymouth, where the family were in residence when they were not travelling to Edinburgh or London, confirmed by many tradesman's accounts from these towns. The Earl was a Scottish Representative Peer and also Lord Lieutenant of Perth, while his second wife Henrietta was one of the Ladies of the Bedchamber to the daughters of King George II, all activities involving considerable expense.

It can be inferred therefore that the workers of the land were left to look after themselves for a time; that after the destruction left by the forces of Montrose and Cromwell, new homes and farmsteads could begin to take shape. One can guess that ancient dwellings largely built of turf were replaced by those built of stone, their more permanent appearance encouraging the cartographers to take note of them. Increased use of carts and carriages required rough tracks to be made suitable for the wheeled traffic, becoming more common, and this shows up in the sequence of maps made of the area.

The earliest made by Pont (c. 1590) and Bleau (c. 1654) showed no roads at all in the country areas, which is strange, since their wide travels must have made use of many principal routes, but M'Arthur in 1769 shows the beginning of tracks on the south side of the loch. Cameron's excellent map of Breadalbane in 1770 shows only a road on the north side, confirming the likelihood of the tracks on the south side just coming into increasing use. On both sides of the loch the roads shown seem to be very much on the alignment of the roads we know today.

The name Remony appears for the first time on M'Arthur's map and also on that of Stobie in 1783, referring to a farmstead on the east side of the 'Auld Vaukie' (the Alt Muchaidh or Remony Burn) about a kilometre south of the loch shore, with the Kiln Croft 200 metres downhill of it in what is now known as the Cherry Tree Park, with the remains of its lime kiln still evident and the cherry tree growing beside its east gable. Remony is clearly a Gaelic name and from its situation immediately beside the rock outcrop worn smooth by ancient ice action, the 'Re' surely comes from the Gaelic *reidh*, pronounced 'ray' and meaning smooth. The '-mony' comes from *monadh* meaning mountain or moor, but whether it relates to the small mound just beside the farmstead or to the smoothly rounded outline of the hills to the south-west is arguable. The latter concept is most appropriate to Remony, used as the name of the present Estate, the hills of which and their outline as seen from the north are indeed smooth in appearance, but the original name applied only to the small farmstead beside what were called the 'Rayvine' (smooth meadow) falls of the Remony Burn.

Just as in the present day there is a feeling of an ever accelerating rate of evolution with inventions made only a few years ago looked on as being old fashioned, perhaps the Campbell lairds at this time felt amazement at the new inventions, firearms superseding bow and arrows, journeys made to London in days instead of weeks and teams of horses with modern ploughs turning over more in a day than used to be done in a week. They were certainly forward looking; John the first Earl may have had rainbow memories of a successful London visit in his youth, which prompted him to encourage his son to send his grandson to Oxford. Sending sons away for fostering had been an ancient and provenly successful tradition—perhaps a spell at University would be even better.

Judging from the letters sent from John, Lord Glenorchy at Christs Church to John, Earl of Breadalbane at Taymouth there was a close link between the two. In a letter dated 21 July 1713 Glenorchy writes to his grandfather: 'I still take care about my Irish and some times meet with Sir Donald Macdonald's son, who is here, and another gentleman, when we talk nothing but Irish.' His University experience led to his burgeoning as a leading young Whig, a friend of Sir Robert Walpole and to his becoming Master of the Horse to the Princess Royal. He married Amabel, daughter of the Duke of Kent, then moved in high circles accepting Government posts abroad and becoming Member of Parliament for Saltash in 1727.

In 1739 the mines at Tyndrum were started, and spinning and weaving was encouraged with the produce sold at the Kenmore fairs. The second Earl's chamberlain, John Campbell of Achallader, is credited with much of the good work at this time but maybe the ideas of the young Lord Glenorchy were behind some of the innovations.

Reference has been made to 'talking in Irish', the first time that name has been noted as being used instead of Gaelic, which was undoubtedly the tongue of the common people of Breadalbane and so a basic hurdle in any conversation with their masters, while written Gaelic was unknown. Not surprisingly, there were differences in religious beliefs too, many strongly held. Already before the end of the seventeenth century very many Scots

Part of Pont's map, *c.* 1590. The 'king drowned in Loch Tay' was probably Donald IV, *c.* 647 who was reported to have been drowned 'while fishing'. 'Fishing' would have been by some form of net, and with relatively crude boats a drowning accident while handling nets could well be envisaged.

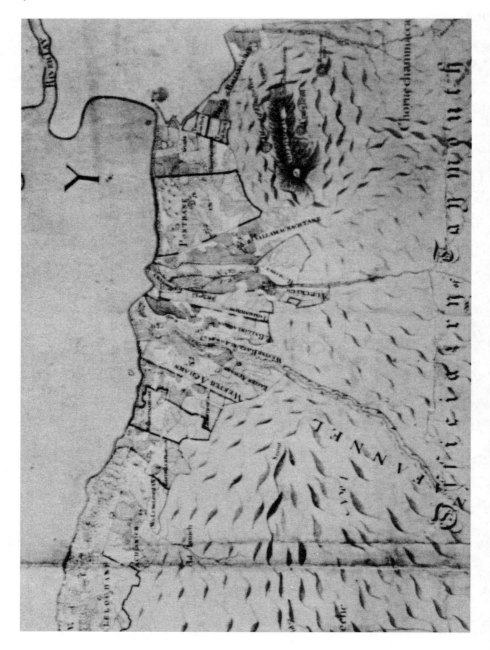

Part of McArthur's general survey of S. Lochtayside, 1769
(for detail sheets and form summaries see Appendix II).

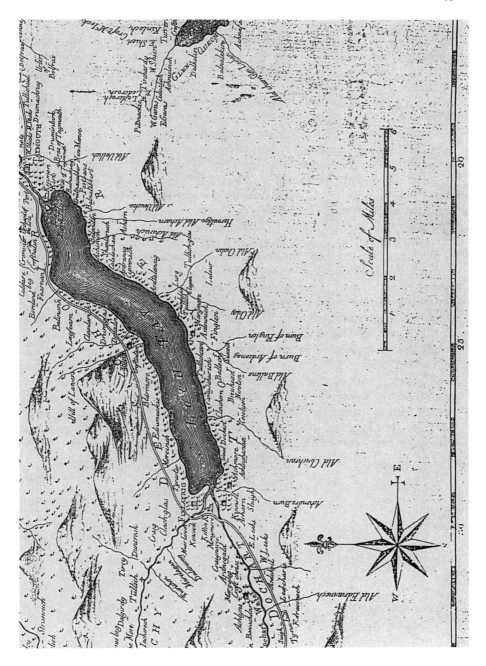

Part of Cameron's map, dated 1770.

not satisfied with things at home had left their country for the New World, some being refugee Covenanters, others mistakenly seeking their fortunes in founding a new colony of Darien on the Panama Isthmus. This migration continued in the eighteenth century, accelerating after the Jacobite defeat at Culloden.

In 1715 the ministers at both Kenmore and Killin were ardent Jacobites. In 1716 Alexander Comrie, minister at Kenmore, was deposed for refusing to conform to the new thinking, but only a few years later his successor John Hamilton had persuaded many of his charge to support the Government. Meanwhile, it is not surprising that Lord Glenorchy was able to persuade his now elderly father to 'keep his head down' and to support the Government, but in spite of this the country people were very divided in their sympathy so that when the 'fiery cross' was sent round Loch Tay in 1745, reputedly within the space of three hours, it met with results that were disappointing except from among the people of Fearnan, as many members of the Campbell families and supporters held strong views on both sides.

As in the field of religion, loyalties to the rebels or to the Government cut across family and social boundaries, but in the ultimate terrible battle on Drumossie Moor the Campbells were brigaded on the right of Cumberland's army, wearing the kilt, armed with musket, broadsword and dirk and officered by the young leaders of cadet Campbell families.

Because of these divided loyalties it may be that the east end of Loch Tay did not suffer so great a loss in men as further west, where clan hatred against neighbouring and oft raiding clans may have induced a greater proportion to take up arms, not so much in support of the Government and their now ageing laird as from hatred of their opponents. It was clan against clan at Culloden, but largely because of young Glenorchy, many of his own tenants were prevented from rising in support of Prince Charles, and so Breadalbane escaped the worst of the repercussions after 1745.

CHAPTER 14

Farms and People put on Paper

When his father died in 1752, Glenorchy became the third Earl of Breadalbane and succeeded as a Representative Peer of Scotland in the House of Lords. He would have been aware of the political rumblings which led to the passage of an Act in 1770 for the Improvement of Lands, which emphasised the importance of correct description of the land and its ownership, in which plans on parchment or other form of paper became significant, among other things greatly facilitating resolution of boundary disputes. As a result of the pressures leading to this legislation and no doubt with the Campbell love of listing every possession which has already been shown, the third Earl in 1769 appointed John McArthur to survey the south side of the loch and another surveyor, Farquharson, to do the same on the north.

Not only was McArthur to produce farm plans but he was also required to assess soil qualities and to list the tenants of each farm together with its acreage and all the stock on it. This task was accomplished in the extraordinarily short time of ten months at the cost shown on his account which was paid and receipted on 25 May 1770:

To surveying the south side of Loch Tay 146 days @ 10/-	£73
To making a plan more than bargon 90 days @ 10/-	£45
To paying of chainmen their wages @ 6d. per day	£7 – 6
To expenses of paper, books and upholstery work	£1 – 16
	£127 – 2
Received at sundry times	£55
Balance due	£72 – 2

The extent, neatness and detail of these plans must have gone a long way towards the appointment of McArthur eight years later to make a plan of the city of Glasgow and his becoming a 'burgess and guild brother' of that city.

It is not known exactly by what means the survey was carried out; the account shows that only one chainman was employed at a time to hold the end of the chain and to place the poles used in alignments, the principal equipment used. The degree of accuracy achieved was remarkable particularly in showing the burns, hills and boundaries along the high tops, depicted with such realism that a hill walker or a shooting party today would find no difficulty in using the plan. McArthur must have been a great walker and not afraid of rough country.

With the plans for the individual farms, the table of acreages in such beautiful copperplate shown in Appendix IIIA might cause eyebrows to be raised at areas being shown apparently correct to one-hundred-and-sixtieth part of an acre, surely arrived at by dividing known areas into desired proportions and then expressing the fractions in square measure. The units used were yards, feet and inches, 4840 square yards to the acre which was divided into four farthingdeals each having 40 square perches. The scale was approximately 12 inches to the mile for the farm plans and 3½ inches to the mile for the 'more than bargon' plan. McArthur was not however concerned with levels and took no account of the contouring of the land, although some rocky or steep faces are artistically indicated. Anyone viewing only the flat plan and then seeing the actual ground might have had quite a shock.

Accompanying the detail sheets there are lists (summarised in Appendix IIIA) showing a remarkably even distribution both of stock and of the areas of different types of land for each farm, which seem more orderly than would have been expected for any uncontrolled occupation of the land, as must originally have been the case. No doubt the strict rules set out by Black Duncan had been modified by time and usage under the control of successive lairds and chamberlains, ultimately aimed at optimum stocking and use of the land, and, of course, maximum rental.

One would love to know how the areas and stock lists were accepted by the occupiers. They must have been consulted to get all the names but there is the likelihood that the stock numbers were the numbers or 'soumings' allocated to each farm rather than the actual count of the cattle, horses and sheep on them. There seems a clear relationship between the acreage of moorland going with each farm and the total of stock to give a 'soum' of five acres, as McArthur mentions in his preamble to the figures for the officiary of Taymouth, stating that this is a 'low' figure 'since the quality of the grass is not to be compared with that of other officiaries'. One might doubt this, or was it just to reconcile the figures for stocking he had settled on?

Young Glenorchy had probably met General Wade when he was in the area and been impressed by his arterial road from Stirling to Fort Augustus. Road building was high on the list of priorities and the road from Balloch to Glendochart had been built with thirty-two bridges along the north side of Loch Tay. The bridge at Kenmore was completed in 1774. The commemoration stone reads: 'This building erected AD 1774; His Majesty gave in aid of it out of the annexed estates 1000 str.'

On the south side McArthur clearly shows the bridges over the Remony and the Acharn burns on their present sites, also the higher bridge across the Acharn Burn above the falls with a road up to it. A footpath is shown leading off this road between the latter bridge and the Hermitage, zig-zagging down to the foot of the falls, some traces of which still remain and down which the writer scrambled as a boy. This path could only have been of casual use for close observation of the falls, by which the Earl was obviously interested having built the Hermitage as a platform from which to view them; presumably McArthur was aware of this interest and played up to it. Beside the Remony Burn he had also written 'Pretty falls and cascades here' with the same thing in mind.

At Acharn the mill, mill-pond and lade to it are shown, also the mill and lade at its present site at Remony. The burn above that lade is shown split into two channels, the easterly one of which has been dry for so long it is scarcely recognisable today as a water channel, but it must have come into and later gone out of use on the occasion of a very major flood far bigger than has been experienced in the last century (but which might occur again?)

The big lime kiln and the pier below Croftmartaig are not shown, nor does the name 'Piercoul', which both Pont and Bleau show sited just above the present pond in Croftmartaig, appear on his plans. Had its occupiers or those accustomed to using that name become early settlers in the New World?

Passage-ways are shown leading from the farmsteads to the various areas marked as pastures, but there is no sign of the ancient fail dyke remains, mentioned earlier in the area of the Sacrificial Stone high above Remony, on what at that time must have been moorland. Is this suggestive of an earlier somewhat warmer climate to allow stock to graze at a higher altitude? Nor is there any indication of tracks leading up the hills to the sheilings which are shown, in Glen Quaich for instance, or of what we now call 'peat tracks' which can still be seen leading up towards the peat banks. Everything for the sheilings must have been carried on the backs of ponies if not of humans; was the absence of any track leading to a sheiling a safety measure in case of raids?

It would seem that by 1770 farming practice had reached a phase of small farms often shared by several tenants who were expected to cultivate as much land as possible and to adhere to the land and souming allocated to them. The better ground of the infield was ploughed regularly and given what dung and ashes that the farm could produce while the outfield was left fallow when required and not dunged. There is no mention of manure, but the Kiln Croft had its kiln presumably used to burn lime, perhaps to be spread on the field before ploughing it for oats. Where the lime came from before the ferrying of it across the loch from Lawers is not clear, but judging by the piled jetty into the loch and the size of the kiln near the house now known as Burnbank, a very considerable effort must have been made by

Breadalbane to have lime spread on the fields of his Officiary of Taymouth. The actual process used to convert the stone for use on the land appears to have required a large quantity of water, since a channel was constructed to lead water along the hillside from the Achianich burn, picking up from the small burn at Lurglomand and into a pond constructed in Croftmartaig where it could be stored before release into the burn flowing down past Tighnaldon to Burnbank as required. Small brown trout, common in the Achianich burn high up on the moor, found their way by this channel into the Lurglomand burn below the crossing place and into the Tighnaldon burn below the outfall from the storage dam, but sadly, probably owing to increased numbers of herons and successive dry seasons, they no longer exist there, where I remember catching them as a boy. The total flow thus made available must have been far in excess of that available at Balmacnaughton, where efforts were made to use water power to drive a mill. Was a mill at one time contemplated at Burnbank, or some other use of water power?

The principal crops listed by McArthur are oats and bere, a primitive form of early ripening barley. Flax was being introduced by the mid century, also potatoes. Hay was cut from the pasture if possible, but there seems to have been a great shortage of winter keep for both man and beast, the former not hesitating to bleed his cattle and to use their blood as a food supplement if necessary.

Full marks then for McArthur for giving so clear an insight of what the land looked like just after the middle of the eighteenth century. Like so many bureaucrats and, dare one say, some factors, was he more interested in paperwork than in beasts and perhaps prepared to pull the wool over his employer's eyes from time to time?

CHAPTER 15

From Strength to Strength

As far as Breadalbane was concerned, the period following Culloden was
a time of relative quiet, of progressing into the practice and enjoyment
of many aspects of culture previously missing in the harsh climate of continuing wars and clan feuds.

When his father died in 1752 the third Earl was aged fifty-eight, at the
height of his powers, politically experienced, with many friends in high
places. Feeling free from any restraint he was able to gratify many of his
wishes for improvement, not least in his home at Taymouth and the nearby
area, so that Taymouth became well known and visited by many people.

It must have been about at this time that the Hermitage, or Hermit's
Cave, was constructed as a viewing point for the Acharn Falls. McArthur's
detail plans of 1769 have the Hermitage clearly marked, while Thomas
Pennant who stayed at Taymouth in 1769 comments on the Hermitage and
the adjacent 'cataracts'. In 1776 the Rev. William Gilpin, during his tour of
the Highlands, visited the falls and wrote: 'the rock it falls from is lofty and
well broken: and it graces the centre of a little wooded theatre; which nature
seems to have made on purpose for it, and where it is shown with much
advantage. Lord Breadalbane, to whom it belongs, introduces the stranger
to it through a sort of subterranean passage, the necessity for which did not
appear'—a snub to the designer who had taken so much trouble to lead the
eye of the observer from the dark entry to the beauty of the falls framed in
the window of the chamber immediately opposite the passage.

A little later, Robert Burns visited the Hermitage while he toured the
Highlands in 1787, evidently coming over the hill from Garrows and much
struck by the beauty of the Tay Valley. He didn't stay at Taymouth; maybe
an Ayrshire poet did not rank for an invitation, but more likely no one was
aware of his intended visit. He did stay long enough at the Inn at Kenmore
to write on the wall of its parlour:

> Poetic ardour in my bosom swells,
> Lone wandering by the hermit's mossy cell,
> The sweeping theatre of hanging woods,
> Th'incessant roar of headlong tumbling floods.
> Here Poesie might wake her heav'n-taught lyre
> And look through Nature with creative fire.

and other lines including the reference to 'The Tay meandering sweet in infant Pride' which are still preserved above the fireplace.

Sixteen years later, in 1803, William Wordsworth, accompanied by his sister, included a visit to the Falls of Acharn in their Highland travels and recorded in his diary:

> Our guide unlocked a small door through which we entered and found ourselves in a narrow tunnel which I at first supposed to have been cut through the solid rock. But on our return I saw it was simply arched with rough jagged large stones, covered with a layer of earth from which sprang a wood of trees and bushes. After groping our way in total darkness along this subterranean passage, our guide, leading the way in total darkness, unlocked another small door and we entered 'the hermit's mossy cell'.

Wordsworth went on to describe the furnishings of the cell, including the hermit's bed and blankets of animal skins, with the walls displaying antlers, stuffed heads and claymores. Among the 'wood of trees and bushes' which Wordsworth described there grew up one enormous silver fir tree immediately above the underground passage, so that when it came to be felled in 1986, then showing signs of old age, there was grave fear that the crash of its fall would disturb the stone of the archway. Fortunately this did not happen.

Prior to the visit to Taymouth Castle by Queen Victoria and her Consort in 1842 no doubt the Hermitage was given a good clean up. It may have been at this time that part of the wall of the chamber was made to appear book lined, by means of false backs, leather covered with gold embossed titles, arranged on shelves. Because of bad weather, Queen Victoria never got to the Hermitage, but about 1925 I remember seeing the last of the book ends and a sorry looking fox's mask still on the wall, remnants of the furnishings long since pillaged.

When Malcolm Ferguson visited the cave in 1869, Donald Anderson was the guide, having succeeded Archibald Cameron who is listed as guide in 1793. Trade in visitors must have by that time become quite brisk, since Anderson had both a 'fause face' and the dress of a hermit which he put on when accompanying visitors. Ferguson describes the cave as 'neat and ornamental'; how long a guide was maintained is not known but no doubt the 1914–18 war put an end to visits and the control of the cave with locked doors.

By 1925 the roof was still slated but the chequered window partly broken and the interior robbed, while after the 1939–45 war the roof had been wrecked and pushed down into the ravine. When the District Council, in terms of the Access Agreement with Remony Estate completed in 1990, made safe the passages and the viewing platform as it then was, they put a plaque on the wall to record the work done. Sadly, within a fortnight, it too had gone. Too many members of the public who crave access to every place have not learned to respect their heritage and the countryside they seek to enjoy.

Thomas Gray, the poet, while staying at the Inn at Kenmore wrote:

> Lord Breadalbane's plantations and woods rise with the ground on either side of the vale to the very summit of the enormous crags that overhang it. Along them, on the mountain side, runs a terrace a mile and a half long that overlooks the course of the river. From several seats and temples perched on particular rocky eminences you command the lake for many miles . . . my Lord has built a neat little town and church with a high square tower . . .

His description of the district is easily recognisable, if somewhat patronising, and is followed by some scathing comment on the Earl's taste and his castle.

Thomas Pennant twice stayed at Taymouth and observed:

> Lord Breadalbane permits the inhabitants of the village to live rent free, on condition that they exercise some trade and keep their houses clean; so that by these terms, he not only saves the expense of sending on every trifling occasion to Perth, or to Crieff, but has got some as good workmen in common trades as any in His Majesty's dominions.

In 1773 a new Inn was built at Kenmore; the new village was well established, but forty years later the third Earl's successor noted 'Kenmore should be cleaned up . . . any stock about the village to be shot.'!

Tree planting had been carried out by Black Duncan a hundred years earlier; now the third Earl planted with an eye towards beautifying his domaine. High on the summit of Kenmore Hill on its skyline as seen from Taymouth an area was enclosed by a stockproof bank and wall, the remains of which are still evident, and fir trees planted within it. McArthur saw it and noted it on his plan as 'a mound of planted trees' together with two other adjacent 'mounds'—bonus points for him when showing the plan to the laird! It was the next laird that enclosed and planted the area we know as Tom-na-moine high above Acharn and also Wester Tom-na-moine above Callelochan, both of which are on prominent skylines. A third area above Wester Tom-na-moine still carries the remains of an enclosing fail dyke but shows no sign of having been planted. Did the money run out, was the ground at too great an altitude for successful planting, or was it perhaps over-run by deer?

In the third Earl's time James Menzies of Culdares, another noted forester, is reputed to have brought the first larch trees from the Tyrol to Scotland. It is said that some were planted both at Dunkeld and at Taymouth; some of the progeny of these trees were in due course planted by Breadalbane lairds in the wood above the present Remony, where they still flourish mightily. In 1965 naturally regenerated seedlings from these larches were uplifted and planted just below the knoll on the west side of the Acharn burn where the Breadalbanes had first intended to build their eastmost castle, so there remains a small group of larch of known and interesting progeny.

The third Earl was particularly keen on 'modernising' roads and tracks, as has already been shown. There is little reference in the archives to the types of carriages which were then in use, but love of comfort would ensure that the best were kept at Taymouth and that roads, especially near the Castle, were made fit for them. These changes, such as the new bridge at Kenmore, could bring problems too. Dated 24 August 1775 there is a Memorial to Breadalbane from Donald McNicol, fisher at Kenmore 'for compensation for ferry boats at Kenmore since the service bridge was built in 1772.'

The same year an account was paid by Breadalbane 'for curing five beds of bugs " £2-12-6'. One wonders who had complained and why the 'curing' cost what was then an enormous sum.

Day to day management of his huge estates must have taken up a good deal of time. Letters and requests came to Taymouth in great numbers. Bundles of these original letters can be found among the Breadalbane Muniments in the Records Office in Edinburgh. Among them:

In 1774 a 'Petition by tenants of Remony [not named] against William Murry, crofter there, who refused to pay rent.'

Also in 1774 there was 'a Petition by William Thomson, weaver in Tomgarrow, for money due to Patrick McNaughton in Ballinlaggan.'

> With answer for Janet McGrigor in Easter Achairn, mother of deceased Christian McKerchar, said William's wife, and his answer to her petition relating to a quarrel over ownership of a wheel [a spinning wheel?] formerly belonging to said Christian; on being refused this in a great frenzy she [Janet] threw herself among the pots and continued to knock herself against the pot till she reduced herself into her present condition, and when respondent would help her she cried out murder.

In 1776 there was a 'Petition by Alexander Robertson, waulkmiller at Acharn, for timber [of oak or ash] to repair the Mill.' Originally a waulkmill, it was later converted to a meal mill before the end of the eighteenth century and in 1924 the writer can remember it in full working order and as a boy being scared lest he fall through the hole in the upper floor down which the piled oat grains were disappearing on their way to the grindstones.

Still in 1776 there is a 'Memorial of Janet M'Grigor widow of Alexander Anderson in Croftmorig, about a debt of her husband for £1 to Duncan Robertson in Robhucky.'

In the same year the wife of Alexander Fisher, late in Aleckick, complains about the straying of goats into the Tomgarrow outfield.

John Campbell, the third Earl, lived through much of the historical period known as 'the Scottish Enlightenment', a period when men such as Adam Smith (1723–80), David Hume (1711–77), Adam Ferguson (1723–1816) and others led a group of intensive and original thinking men writing largely on philosophy, history, law and science, very much centred in Edinburgh and involved in the life of the Church, the Universities and the Law. The Adams brothers in architecture and Robert Burns were also contemporary.

There was undoubtedly a burgeoning of men capable of clear thinking living contemporaneously who by their very presence and intercourse sparked off original thought which in turn produced original action. Like many highly intelligent people, they seem to have been so busy with their own thoughts as to have little time for worldly problems. In their writing there is no mention of the Jacobite wars, which, if not world-shattering, certainly caused a lot of problems in Scotland.

Breadalbane, with his feet on the ground, moving from London to Taymouth dealing with affairs of state or his own estates, probably rarely stayed long in Edinburgh. He, in turn, makes no reference to the Enlightenment, but the gleams from that torch triggered off much new thinking of which he would be aware; particularly after the '45 he would have time to ponder and perhaps whet his own ideas. He would have spurned the efforts of the intelligentsia to use only English and to scorn the use of Gaelic (although Adam Ferguson spoke Gaelic and was born at Logierait), but he would have seen the New Town being built in Edinburgh in 1767, while the lively universities of Edinburgh and Glasgow were spawning young men full of ideas and plans for the future. Plans of his own estates he entrusted to McArthur and Farquharson in 1769; transport was to be encouraged and bridges built. Mills were built, too, at Acharn and at Remony, using better knowledge of mechanics following study of Newton's experiments. Perhaps the Macnaughton family at Balmacnaughton had had a son at university who encouraged them to attempt to build an impulse turbine to drive a corn mill there. The hollow shaft from which water emerged from two arms, each ending in a jet directed in opposing directions, is still extant, and the impulse from the jets could indeed have produced power, but the idea was too far ahead of the then metallurgy and equipment to be successful. Where water power was not available, mills driven by horses or oxen were also developed, remains of which can be seen at Lower Achianich and Lurglomand. The animal(s), which must have been short, strong and wiry, tramped round in a tight circle yoked to a horizontal beam carried on a central vertical shaft, itself connected by an underground horizontal shaft to the mill inside the stone-built barn. These were still in use up to the end of the nineteenth century, but cannot have handled more than small quantities of grain. Were they built to avoid carriage to the main mill in Acharn, or by private enterprise trying to beat the miller's monopoly charges for grinding?

In the next generation, early in the nineteenth century the new Earl's ideas for planned villages followed closely on Adam Smith's thinking. There was indeed enlightened thought and action in Breadalbane as well as in Edinburgh.

As the third Earl grew older he had many worries, not least the question of succession since both sons by his first marriage had predeceased him without issue. When he died at Holyrood House in 1782, the land and titles passed to a third cousin, one John Campbell, then twenty years old, the son of Colin Campbell of Carwhin on the north side of Loch Tay.

Far from there being change in the fortunes of the House of Breadalbane, young John Campbell fully equalled his predecessors in ability and drive. Educated at Westminster and Lausanne, two years after his succession he was elected a representative peer for Scotland in the House of Lords; in 1806 he was created Baron Breadalbane of Taymouth Castle and in 1831 he was made Earl of Ormelie and Marquis of Breadalbane. He married an heiress, Mary Turner Gavin of Langton in Berwickshire, and their son eventually succeeded him.

A romantic interest attaches to John Campbell's marriage, as is recounted by Gillies in *In Famed Breadalbane*.

Some time in the early eighteenth century a Dutch ship was wrecked off Lunan Bay, near Montrose, and the crew were sheltered by Alexander Gavin, beadle of Lunan Church, whose father had held the same office before him. The skipper of the ship, David Smith, fell in love with Margery, Alexander's sister, and in 1742 they were married in Holland, and settled down there. In due time they sent for David Gavin, Alexander's son. David became a prosperous merchant in Middleburg, Zealand. In the course of a few years he amassed a large fortune, and in 1758 he was able to leave his brother, Benjamin, to look after the business while he himself returned to Scotland. He bought the estate of Langton, Berwickshire, from the Cockburns. David Gavin had married Christina Maria Hearsey, who was a member of the English congregation at Middleburg, in 1751, and she bore him one child, a daughter who died at the age of seven years in 1765. Two years later Mrs Gavin herself died at Langton House. In 1770 David Gavin married his second wife Elizabeth Maitland, daughter of the seventh Earl of Lauderdale, by whom he had three daughters. The eldest of these, Mary Turner, born on 6 March 1771 became Countess and afterwards Marchioness of Breadalbane. Lady Breadalbane was a woman of great kindness and charity, and gave freely of her wealth to the poor people on the estates. Miss Elizabeth Gavin, sister of the Countess, who frequently resided at Taymouth, was also deeply interested in the poor of the district, and she gave to the Kirk Session of Kenmore the sum of one thousand pounds, which is secured over a portion of the Breadal-bane estates, and yields fifty pounds annually. This sum is divided half-yearly among the necessitous poor of the parish of Kenmore.

Following from this interest in the poor a gift was made of ground and the building which is today known as Tighnaldon some 300m. west of Acharn, but which at one time was known as the Poor House or Gavin Cottage. This gradually fell out of use and in terms of the original charter; it reverted in 1953 to the superior, now Remony Estate, who converted it into two flats for estate use. In turn, Tighnaldon with its plot of land was sold by the Estate and by 1994 was a little used holiday house.

Very early in the fourth Earl's time there occurred a remarkable 'disturbing of the waters' of Loch Tay on 12 September 1784. As was reported to the Antiquarian Society of Perth by Rev. Thomas Fleming after talking to an eye witness very shortly after the event, between eight and nine o'clock that morning:

The water of the bay at the east end of Loch Tay ebbed about three hundred feet and left the channel or bed of the bay almost quite dry where the water is usually three feet in depth; and, being gathered in the form of a wave, rolled on about three hundred feet further to the westward, until it met a similar wave rolling in the contrary direction. When these clashed together they rose to a perpendicular height of four feet and upwards, emitting a white foam on the top of the water. Then this wave so formed took a lateral direction southward towards the shore, gaining upon the land four feet beyond the high water mark of the Loch at that time. Then it returned from the shore to the lake and continued to ebb and flow for about an hour and a half, the wave gradually diminishing in size every time it reached the shore until it wholly disappeared. It is to be observed that during this phenomenon there was an absolute calm.

Upon the two following days, at an hour a little later in the morning, there was the same appearance, but not in any respect to the same degree.

The first who observed the phenomenon was one MacIntyre, a blacksmith, living in the village of Kenmore who went to wash his face and hands in the bay, and was greatly suprised and frightened on observing the water retiring from him while at that operation. He immediately ran and alarmed his neighbours who came running, and saw the ebbing and flowing above described.

Upon ten o'clock the same day two men standing upon the bridge of Kenmore, which is upon the river nearly where it rises from the lake, observed the weeds in the bed of the river pointing towards the loch instead of downwards with the river, and that the stream of the river flowed into the lake and not out of it.

It would seem that the cause of this disturbance must have been a movement or slip in one of the geological fracture lines below the surface of the loch. A wave having been so created would move outwards from the point of disturbance but would be constrained by the shape of the loch, mainly towards its ends where, having been halted by the shore, it would return in the opposite direction and then continue to ebb and flow for a considerable time. Such a wave can be seen oscillating, once created, in any small confined sheet of water, even one's bath, and in the large length of Loch Tay the ebbing and flowing could well continue for a considerable time. Strangely, there was no report either of a land shock or of the disturbance having been observed elsewhere. It would have been very much less noticeable along the relatively steep sides of the loch than in the very shallow and extensive east end bay where its direction was reversed by the end shore.

John, fourth Earl of Breadalbane was the youngest man to have full charge at Taymouth. No doubt he felt freer to vary or improve on the ways of his distant uncle than a son would feel in following his father; more importantly, he was of a kindly disposition as well as being able and forceful, and thoughtful in dealing with the many estate matters.

In 1786 there was a Petition by John Campbell in Tomgarrow, above eighty years of age, for charity and in the same year John McNaughton in Balnaskiag asks for help with his youngest and handicapped child.

When war broke out with France in 1793, the Earl offered to raise 'a corps of Fencible men' for internal use in Scotland. This offer was promptly accepted by Government, as was the opportunity to serve in it by the local men, so enthusiastically that having recruited one battalion a second followed within a few months and a third early in 1794. With his Lordship himself in command and each man receiving three golden guineas on attestation, there was quite a rush to the colours; the officers, many of them relatives, each received two guineas for every recruit. While clan loyalty and national patriotism were no doubt both emotive, one feels that escape from the customary hardships of winter survival and the hardest of lifestyles in a crowded community were the major reasons for recruitment.

The enlistment of Highlanders into the armed forces of the crown had been taking place for some time, a hitherto untapped and useful source of hardy recruits. In May 1760 the ten companies of the 'Highland Watch' paraded in front of Sir Robert Munroe of Foulis on the banks of the River Tay near the site of the present Black Watch Memorial. Their uniform was tartan of a dark colour and because of this they were known locally as Am Freiceadan Dubh—The Black Watch. During the parade they were formally embodied as The 43rd of Foot, Highland Regiment, but were later renumbered as The 42nd of Foot. They included many men from Lochtayside; General Stewart of Garth had encouraged recruitment.

There were however difficulties. Under the ancient clan system clan followers obeyed their clan leader and took it for granted that they should fight and if necessary die for the benefit and for the honour of their clan. But having accepted the King's warrant—and his pay—the highlanders came under a form of discipline to which they were entirely unaccustomed, and found themselves officered not by family leaders but by unknown strangers, some of whom treated their commissions as means of advancement or for financial gain. The men found to their dismay that no longer could the word or promise of the new officers be accepted and honoured, but that the promises of those now in authority were often vague and sometimes broken, particularly when coming from politicians or commanders of large forces, while any breach of discipline resulted in punishment often of the most brutal kind. To be forced to witness a luckless fellow soldier, found guilty of some act which to many of the men seemed trivial or even praiseworthy, being subjected to ghastly punishment of 250 lashes or more on his bare back sickened men who had thought nothing of wielding claymore or dirk in bloody conflict. It was principally these two causes which led to the mutiny which occurred in London in 1742, when some men of the Black Watch, deceived into finding themselves about to be despatched overseas when they had never expected to leave Scotland, proceeded without orders to march home again.

Although the Fencibles which the fourth Earl raised in 1793 were explicitly for home service only, they too found themselves subject to the 'English' form of discipline. The battalion sent to Glasgow in 1794 met trouble when one of their men, Corporal Robertson, was disciplined for allowing a prisoner held in the guard house to escape. Although their officers went through 'the proper procedures', the men were unwilling to see Robertson flogged and confronted their officers in such armed strength that Robertson was released to them from the guard house. This was mutiny, and had to be dealt with. Other units of the crown forces were called in to deal with the mutineers, now ensconsed in their billets in the streets of Glasgow. The Provost and Town Council were consulted, but it took ten days or more before a decision was made on how best to proceed.

Lord Breadalbane was summoned from his Wigmore Street home in London but was tardy in arriving and backward in dealing with his men, quite unable to persuade them to submit themselves to military discipline. In the meantime, three volunteers, McMartin, Malloch and Macnaughton, all young men under twenty-four years of age from Lochtayside, submitted themselves to the officers to stand trial in order that the company of their companions might escape the discipline which was now felt to be inevitable. They were put in irons and marched off to Edinburgh. On starting off, John McMartin appealed to the commander of the guard force, Captain John Campbell of Glenfalloch, that he should be released in order to return to Glasgow to finish some business which his honour required him to complete, after which he would rejoin the prisoners. What this business was has never been disclosed, but Captain Campbell released McMartin, who after returning to Glasgow and a hectic cross country journey back to Edinburgh, rejoined the prisoners under the gates of Edinburgh Castle, no doubt to the considerable relief of Glenfalloch who had not reported the matter.

Public opinion swung in favour of the prisoners and after going through the formal process of being tried and found guilty they were marched to the place where they were to be shot by a squad of Breadalbane men, only to be reprieved at the last moment. Under the terms of the reprieve they were required to join crown forces about to go to America, rather than joining the Breadalbane battalion. At first they refused to accept these terms, but after receiving the first daily portion of 250 of the 500 lashes which their sentence now required, unable to face the further torture the next day to their already mutilated backs, they accepted the terms and were ultimately despatched from Portsmouth to disappear from history. A terrible tale, but typical of the harshness of the discipline in those days.

The Corps existed for five years and served in Aberdeen, Glasgow, Fort George and other places. By 1797, being unable to be sent overseas, they were reduced in strength and the Earl did his best either to give employment or to settle the returning men on the land; a few joined the Regular Army while others emigrated to Canada. A further appeal for National Service was made in 1798 when there was a threat of invasion and this also met with a good response. It was estimated that three out of every four of the some 646 men between the ages of fifteen and sixty in Kenmore and Lochtayside at that time came forward to offer their services.

About the year 1800 there were many local comments and complaints about the Fencibles having 'an excess of tartan, feathers, bearskins and pipes' but the Earl played these down and in 1814 was himself appointed Lieutenant General, so perhaps his efforts to obtain a good turn-out were not in vain for his personal aggrandisement.

In 1803 there is a note of the Earl's plans for improvements and of premiums being offered. His aim was for grouping of tradesmen in planned villages. Very shortly after the start of the nineteenth century the villages of Styx, Acharn and Fearnan were in existence as well as Kenmore where the church had been reconstructed in 1760 and a new Inn built in 1773. The old graveyard at Inchadney was ordered to be levelled in 1788, which explains why there are no gravestones at Kenmore before that date.

The stone-built houses were put up by their occupiers who each had a croft in addition to their trade and so were able to make a good living, impossible with a growing family from a croft alone. Farms were rearranged generally on the McArthur pattern but with improved land management and farming practice. Linton sheep had been introduced and there was competition between the breeds until gradually the Blackface breed came to be accepted as the norm for the district. No tenant was allowed to have more than one farm and the Earl served notices to quit on several of his least efficient tenants, many of whom eventually found their way to Canada. Looking down on the pond in Croftmartaig park and close to the farmstead marked 'Piercoul' on Pont's map there are traces of what looks like a clamp or pit of potatoes lying abandoned on the hillside, as though the result of a hurried or unplanned flitting.

About this time successive lairds had come to realise the value of 'sporting' shooting as opposed to just hunting for the sake of food. Sportsmen, too, were more able to move about in the country and even to find accomodation at an Inn.

In 1785, James McCuair in Claggan of Ardtalnaig, gamekeeper there, wrote to Breadalbane asking for 'a good gun for the killing of hawks'.

Two years later, James McQuarrie (the same man using a different scribe to draft his letter?) in the 10/- land of Ardtalnaig, gamekeeper, sought remuneration for preventing encroachment by sportsmen on neighbouring properties.

In 1800 the laird was advised for the need for a fox hunter to go to Drummond Hill, while in 1821 one E. D. Davenport wrote to Breadalbane saying he 'has again failed to sight the ptarmigan; so fatigued he intends to postpone his journey to the following day.'

In 1810 there is a letter from Mary Campbell, living in the rebuilt Taymouth with the new plasterwork by Bernasconi, to her mother Elizabeth Campbell in Carwhin, describing the magnificence of the Castle and her doings, stating incidentally '. . . the grouse are however scarce . . .'

In 1833 there is a letter from Joseph Hone staying at Kenmore Inn asking Breadalbane for a day or two's shooting for himself and some Dublin friends; they had taken the moor at Kynachan and were much disappointed in it.

As the importance of sporting shooting increased, Breadalbane drafted strict instructions for the sportsmen who had his permission to shoot, which was the start of the process of written documentation now required by any shooting tenant.

Work of beautifying and improving the Estate continued. In 1789 money was advanced to tenants for enclosing (their land) for which they were liable, interest on which had to be paid at 7½%. In 1796 there is an account for building dykes in the land of the Officiary of Taymouth and references to oak being cut on Drummond Hill (for building?), and in 1797 'for building dykes and planting trees on Kenmore Hill, etc.'. There are references to 'the pleasure grounds' at Taymouth and an account 'for the cost of making falls in the burn opposite Taymouth Castle'. And another account for building the ice house on top of Drummond Hill in 1795, a small circular wall and bank like a large sheep pen over which branches could be piled on top of the ice cut from the nearby pond and piled within the pen. Was the ice for the champagne or a means of preserving fresh fish or meat in summer?

Many people must have wished to see these improvements—too many, because instructions were given for 'direction tickets', sign boards, to be made to prevent trespass around Taymouth and these were to be erected two on the Glen Quaich road, others at the Chinese Bridge and the Kenmore Gate. Tourists were not yet encouraged!

There was genuine mourning for the Fourth Earl when he died at Taymouth in 1834, to be succeeded by his son John, then thirty-eight years old. It seems almost repetitive to list the achievements and honours of the second Marquis. Educated at Eton he became Member of Parliament for Okehampton in 1820 and married Eliza, sister of the tenth Earl of Haddington, the next year. In 1832 he returned north and became Member of Parliament in the Liberal interest for his home county of Perth. He was appointed a Knight of the Thistle in 1838, a Privy Councillor in 1848 and was Lord Chamberlain to the Household between 1848 and 1858.

Clearly these many duties meant that he could not live continuously at Taymouth and in fact he left much of the running of the estates to his factor, James Wyllie, who lived at Bolfracks. But he knew his countryside and his hills; believing great wealth lay in their rocks he tramped the hills with a geological hammer seeking for ores. He re-opened the mines at Tyndrum which his father had closed and built a mini industrial estate on the shore of Loch Tay to smelt the copper extracted from the mine at Tomnadason. Both proved uneconomic and only the copper mine was continued until his death in 1862. Traces of trial excavations can be seen near the summit of Beinn Bhreac and elsewhere; legend has it that enough gold was found to make a small ring. Barites was also reported near Ardtalnaig.

The second Marquis had little time for farming and allowed his factor to clear some of his farms on the north side of the loch and in Glen Quaich for sheep, the consequent evictions causing distress and protests and more emigrants to go to Canada, many of whom settled in Ontario and called their home Perth County. Those evicted considered him a tyrant. It is thought that one of those evicted from his Lochtayside home, John Kennedy, wrote the following lines in Gaelic soon after 1834. They only became known in an abbreviated form of the first verse when they were translated into English much later and published in *Punch* in 1903:

> Frae Kenmore tae Ben More
> The land is a' the Marquis's;
> The mossy howes, the heathery knowes
> An' ilka bonnie park is his;
> The bearded goats, the towsie stots,

An' a' the braxie carcases;
Ilk crofter's rent, ilk tinkler's tent,
An' ilka collie's bark is his;
The muircock's craw, the piper's blaw,
The ghillie's hard day's work is his;
Frae Kenmore tae Ben More
The warld is a' the Marquis's.

The fish that swim, the birds that skim,
The fir, the ash, the birk is his;
The castle ha' sae big an' braw,
Yon diamond crusted dirk is his;
The roofless hame, a burning shame,
The factor's dirty work is his;
The poor folk vexed, the lawyer's text,
Yon smirking legal shark is his;
Frae Kenmore tae Ben More
The warld is a' the Marquis's.

But near, mair near, God's voice we hear—
The dawn as weel's the dark is His;
The poet's dreams, the patriot's theme,
The fire that lights the mirk is His;
They clearly show God's mills are slow
but sure, the handiwork is His;
And in His grace our hope we place;
Fair Freedom's sheltering ark is His.
The men that toil should own the soil—
A note as clear's the lark is this—
Breadalbane's land—the fair, the grand—
Will no' be aye the Marquis's.

The bitterness of the writer's feelings are plain, with his knowledge of the country and of Breadalbane's doings; particuarly noticeable his poetic ability which makes one wonder whether in fact it was written as above in Scots and not translated from Gaelic.

It almost sounds from the last line as though John Kennedy may have had in mind the curses put on the Breadalbanes by the Lady of Lawers during her lifetime in the second half of the seventeenth century. The Lady is believed to have been a Stewart from Appin who came as a bride to marry the then Campbell of Lawers in the little township there on the shore of the Loch, the ferry terminal for Ardtalnaig with a church built in 1669.

It was while this church was being built that the Lady won fame with the first of her prophecies, all said to have been written down in a great book kept at Balloch which is now lost, but which have been handed down carefully in Gaelic: 'The ridging stones will never be put on the roof.' The worked sandstone blocks duly arrived by boat and were unloaded on the loch shore, but before they could be moved a storm arose and swept the blocks down into the water, so that new materials had to be used. This very true prediction ensured that those following were feared and respected. An ash tree, which she may have planted, grew beside the north side of the church. 'The tree will grow and when it reaches the gable the church will be split asunder, and this will also happen when the red cairn on Ben Lawers falls.' The tree did reach the gable in 1833 when a violent thunderstorm that year demolished the west loft of the church, causing it to be abandoned as a place of worship. The cairn on the Ben, no doubt already eroded, collapsed in 1843, the year of the disruption of the Church of Scotland.

'When the ash tree reaches the ridge, the House of Balloch will be without an heir.' This came about in 1862 with the tree just at the ridge height, near where of course it had been for some time. The last saying about the tree: 'Evil will come to him that harms it' happened most precisely. In 1895 John Campbell of Milton farm nearby felled the tree with an axe. Shortly after, he was gored by his own Highland bull, the neighbour who had assisted him went mad and the young horse used to drag away part of the tree unexpectedly fell down dead.

Other prophecies were that: 'There will be a mill on every stream and a plough in every field'; 'The jaw of the sheep will drive the plough from the ground'; and 'the feather of the goose will drive memory from man' and all can be deemed to have been fulfilled. 'The earldom will not descend beyond a grandson in one line' came true in 1782 when the title passed to John Campbell of Carwhin and again in 1862 when the second Marquis died without an heir, indeed causing 'great and perplexing doubts to arise as to an heir' just as the Lady had foretold.

'In time the estate of Balloch will yield only one rent and then none at all' has also become true; perhaps John Kennedy had this in mind when he was finishing his poem. There can be no doubt that the prophecies of the Lady of Lawers were well known all round the loch, especially by the inhabitants of Callelochan and other holdings to the west which looked right across the loch to Lawers. Not all of her sayings were fulfilled. 'A ship driven by smoke will sink in Loch Tay with great loss of life' scared away many travellers when the Loch Tay Steamers were started. Full marks must be given to the Lady for thinking of smoke driving a ship. The biggest steamer, *The Queen of the Lake*, only operated for a short time and when it was dismantled there was some unemployment.

So far, Ben Lawers has not 'become so cold that it will chill and waste the land for seven miles.'

However one looks at the prophecies, they are a remarkable product of thought and vision.

In 1850 there is correspondence regarding eel fishing, and in 1852 about otter hounds in use at Dalmally. From 1844 to 1853 there are frequent reports on salmon in Loch Tay; in 1853 there is a plan for a new net to catch them to be sited just off the west side of the mound on which the church stands and laid out towards Sybilla's Island.

It must not be thought that the people of the lochside were so busily engaged working the land that they had no time for other things. Music evidently flourished and, no doubt under Breadalbane patronage, there was a band at Kenmore from 1849 to 1854 in charge of a Mr Foghill from whom there was much correspondence regarding its membership, resignations and uniform. On 18 May 1831 John Thomson in Lurgloman wrote to Breadalbane offering a base fiddle 'better than one which cost £50'. He had sold one like it to Mr Butter of Pitlochry.

One would guess that Wyllie, the factor, had good knowledge of the countryside and worked away while his laird was engaged in the south. Breadalbane's health was not improving, especially after the death of his wife in 1861. That year he went to Lausanne where his father had spent part of his youth and died there, aged sixty-six.

Queen Victoria's Visit

The visit of Queen Victoria and Prince Albert to Taymouth Castle in 1842 marked the very peak of Breadalbane fame and fortune. John, fifth Earl and second Marquess of Breadalbane, through his own character and ability achieved not only positions of power but also the ear and favour of the Sovereign. When the Queen accepted his invitation he must have felt it necessary for him to do all in his power to make the occasion worthy of the honour done to him by the acceptance, and set about immediately to make preparations.

An outing on Loch Tay was clearly contemplated at an early stage, and plans for it put in hand. A boat was ordered from McNicolls's yard at Greenock of special construction, while the junior member of the clan ordered to take charge of the boating activity wrote saying 'he considered the every day blue serge trousers of the thirty selected rowers should be replaced; that the kilt was quite unsuitable for rowing and that white ducks might become soiled; could he order tartan trews which would be just right?' The answer is not recorded but must surely have been favourable, since the boat in which the Queen was eventually rowed up to Auchmore at the west end of the loch is described as:

32 feet long, 6'-10'' broad and 2'-9'' deep, carvel built, 8 or 10 oared, with deep gold moulding outside, with stem head and stern beautifully carved and

gilt. The lining inside was painted in imitation of Breadalbane tartan . . . the
seats of the rowers covered with Breadalbane tartan of the finest woollen
cloth . . . the royal seat or cushion in the centre was covered with Breadalbane
velvet surmounted with the Breadalbane crest, and Scotch thistle, in tapestry,
fringed with gold.

The tartan trews were the least of it! Such detail and disregard of expense
is typical of the attention given to every aspect of the preparation and plans
for the Royal entertainment which must have involved every able bodied
member of the Campbell connection as well as the whole resources of the
immediate neighbourhood.

The following extracts are from *The National Record of the Visit of Queen
Victoria to Scotland, in September 1842*, written by James Buist in 1844. Buist
appears to be been specially appointed to the royal party and given every
facility to record the events. He wrote in very fulsome terms, no doubt
having in mind his likely readers, and this must be recognised as well as the
accuracy of his reporting.

We must say, generally, that the manner in which the Sovereign was welcomed
and entertained at Taymouth Castle by Lord Breadalbane reflects unbounded
praise, not only on the noble Marquess himself, but honour to the country
among whose nobles his Lordship occupies a foremost station.

The grounds and policies around Taymouth are of great extent, and as
they recede from the lawn immediately in front of the castle they assume a
variety of undulating slopes, interspersed with elevated mounds or hillocks,
and with innumerable clumps of trees, some of them of a prodigious size and
thickness, through whose umbrageous foliage the sun, at his greatest strength,
cannot penetrate. The Tay flows past the Castle in the rear, and throughout
the whole extent of pleasure grounds, which are upwards of two miles long
and one mile broad. There is one walk along the margins of the river,
especially, of great beauty. It is about a mile in length, formed of the finest
turf, which yields and springs to the tread like richest artificial carpeting, and
is shaded and arched over by magnificent, thickly leaved trees, which render
it 'cool as a zephyr' in the very hottest day of summer.

A very good description, still true today.

Arches were erected at the entrance to Kenmore, at the bridge over the
Tay and at all approaches to the castle, while well to the west of the castle
was pitched the tented encampment of the Ninety Second Highlanders and
of the Breadalbane Highlanders, some two hundred strong, of which Lord
Breadalbane was Colonel in Chief, with its Second in Command, Adjutant
and the officers commanding its four companies, all Campbells.

Prior to the Queen's approach on 7 September, outside the castle the
'target men' and others armed with Lochaber axes and halberds, all in full
fighting gear, formed a long single line with the Ninety Second Highlanders
and the Breadalbane Highlanders with their officers in front drawn up opposite

the castle, with the band in position and a body of nearly one hundred kilted deer hunters and beaters nearby. A Clan Menzies detachment was also on parade. Members of the public, largely wearing highland dress, thronged the lawns and approaches. James Buist writes:

> A great PRINCIPLE gleamed forth from the whole, and stood out clearly and well-defined. All this imposing array and preparation, this assemblage of all ranks and classes, was a tribute exhibiting not merely attachment and affection to Queen Victoria personally, but it displayed, also, devotion and adherence to the principle in virtue of which she holds the sceptre of England, and showed how strong and deep, and widely spread, are the roots of Monarchical Government in this country . . . the clans assembled, from all parts of the country, for no hostile or warlike purpose, but in peace and amity . . . to manifest their loyalty and regard towards the scion of a House that many of their ancestors fought against unto the death. Thus do circumstances and events irresistibly mould and change men's character and opinion. *Tempora mutantur, et nos mutantur in illis.*

Sentiments with some truth behind them, but perhaps not widely held throughout all Scotland.

The Queen's approach was signalled by flags, just after five o'clock. 'Now men,' called the Marquess, 'the Queen is at hand; prepare to give her Majesty a Highland welcome; and you men on the hill [pointing to the west of the castle] see that you are ready to send back the cheer.' It duly came, 'in thundering acclamation' amid the playing of the pipes, while the band struck up the National Anthem, a salute was fired from the Fort battery and the Breadalbane flag was hauled down above the castle, to be replaced by the Royal Standard. After being received by the Marquess and Marchioness, the Queen entered the castle where she warmly greeted the Countess of Sutherland, then moved up the decorated staircase to the gorgeous drawing room, where, from the balcony, she acknowledged the greetings of the multitude.

That evening the Royal party of thirty-nine persons sat down to dinner at eight o'clock, the dinner service of either gold or silver plate—'a large proportion of the former', with the side tables groaning with the profusion of gold and silver and the wall hung with Old Masters. Those sitting at the table are marked with an asterisk on the list of people attending the Grand Ball two nights later.

The illuminations and bonfires which followed get a chapter to themselves in Buist's account, and deserve it. Fortunately, it was a lovely evening, so that the bonfires on every peak in sight could be clearly seen. Nearby, the trees were hung with lanterns, the lawns were lit by lanterns strung as close together as possible on a line 250 yards long on their margins, while towards the west the bank spelt out in more lanterns, 'Welcome Victoria and Albert'. Straight in front of the castle a crown more than fifteen feet high had been erected and was illuminated, with a huge V and A on either side. On the hill opposite, the Fort was lit up, as was the Tower higher up on the hill (by acetylene?), long before the days of electricity. Immediately following a gunshot at ten o'clock the fireworks started, and although they may not have reached the present degree of sophistication, the number of bangs, rockets and falling showers of all kinds was immense. At one moment the Fort was enveloped with first a purple and then a green flame 'which looked transparent and singularly beautiful, and at the same time startling; on its disappearance leaving the lamps burning brightly and steadily as before.'

There followed Highland dancing on a platform in front of the castle. 'A body of Highlanders was stationed thickly around the central platform, and along the line of spectators, up to the grand entrance, carrying flambeaux or torches; and a number of splendid portable lamps were brought from the castle, rendering the scene nearly as clear as at mid-day.' The Campbell in charge of the illuminations deserved very special credit; he must have had access to a prodigious quantity of oil.

The next day broke most unpromisingly, with rain falling and a thick mist down to the tops of the trees. This caused cancellation of the intended outing on the loch, but Prince Albert was out by eight o'clock to shoot on Kenmore Hill, accompanied by the Marquess and a large number of beaters and gamekeepers. He returned to the castle at two o'clock, by which time the weather had faired, with:

20 Roe bucks,
4½ brace of Blackgame,
3 brace of Grouse,
1 brace of Capercaillzie,
1 Partridge,
1 Wood pigeon,
12 Hares,
1 Owl,
several rabbits.

This was quite a typical bag for the area shot over, but remarkable if (as was stated) all were shot by the Prince. The partridge must have been on the lower slopes near home, the roe in the well wooded slopes above and the grouse in the heather right at the top of the hill. Was the owl shot by mistake?

During a bright interval in the morning the Queen visited the dairy, built as a model of its kind, where she churned some cream in a china vase, sipped some milk and asked for a Scotch oatmeal cake. Afterwards, the dairy staff all drank some milk from the same glass as had the Queen; one, when asked what she thought about the Queen, replied, 'She's as humble a woman as ever I saw.' In the afternoon the Queen drove in her carriage to Kenmore and over the bridge, returning through the policies along the back of the castle to the east gate. That evening there was entertainment and singing in the Banner Hall.

On Friday 9 September, after a bright start to the day, the rain came down again. But the Prince 'enjoyed capital sport' on what we now call Drummond Hill, then 'the braes of Balloch'. The Queen took a quiet walk through the grounds, which had been cleared of all the public, accompanied only by the Duchess of Norfolk and attended by a single footman. The dancing exhibition on the platform in front of the castle and the parade of armed forces in the afternoon was spoilt by heavy rain which later cleared, allowing the Royal party to drive in their carriages to the east gate and up to the Fort to enjoy the fine view from that point.

After another magnificent dinner in the Banqueting Hall, the lamps on the lawn were again lit with the large crown glittering, while the guests arrived for the Grand Ball held in the Banner Hall. The list of guests is given as:

* Duke and Duchess of Buccleugh,
* Duke and Duchess of Roxburgh,
* Duchess of Sutherland and Miss Elizabeth Gower,
* Duchess of Norfolk,
* Marquess and Marchioness of Abercorn,
* Marquess of Lorne,
* Earl of Aberdeen,
* Earl of Liverpool,
* Earl of Lauderdale and Sir Anthony Maitland,
* Earl and Countess of Kinnoull and Lady E. Hay,
* Earl of Morton,
  Earl of Mansfield, Dowager Countess of Mansfield and Ladies Mansfield,
* Lord and Lady Belhaven,
  Lord and Lady Glenlyon, Dowager Lady Glenlyon and Hon. Miss Murray,
* Right Hon. Fox Maule and the Hon. Mrs Maule,
  Hon. Miss Abercromby,
  Hon. John Steuart,
  Hon. Mr and Mrs Drummond of Strathallan,
* The Hon. Miss Paget,
* The Rt. Hon. Sir John Peel,
  Sir John and Lady Elizabeth Pringle and Miss Pringle,
  Sir Neil and Lady Menzies and Miss Menzies,
  Mr Menzies and Mr F. Menzies,
  The Hon. Miss Norton,
  Sir John and Lady Richardson,
  Sir John and Lady Mackenzie and Miss Mackenzie,
  Lady Campbell and Miss Campbell of Garth,
  Sir Thomas Moncrieffe, Lady Moncrieffe and Miss Moncrieffe,

★ Sir James Clark,
Sir Adam and Miss Drummond of Megginch,
General Wemyss,
★ Col. Bouverie,
Mr Home Drummond, MP,
★ Mr G.E. Anson,
Mr and Mrs William Russell,
Mr and Mrs Gordon Campbell,
Mr and Mrs Campbell of Glenfalloch,
Mr and Mrs Nairne and Miss Nairne of Aviemore,
Mr and Mrs Stewart of Ardvorlich,
Cluny McPherson,
Mr Davidson of Tulloch,
Capt. MacDougall RN,
Mrs Campbell, Edinample,
Mr Campbell younger of Glenfalloch,
Mr Campbell Renton of Lamberton and Capt. David Campbell,
Major Hay and the Officers of the Sixth Carabineers,
Major Atherley and the Officers of the Ninety Second Highlanders,
Lt. James Campbell RN,
Lt. Patrick Campbell RN,
Mr Menzies of Chesthill,
Mr and Mrs Colquhoune of Clathick,
Mr Harrington,
Mr Lambe,
Mr Crichton Stewart,
Mr and Lady Lucy Grant,
Major and Mrs Moray Stirling,
Mr and Major Bolshes,
Mr and Mrs Smythe of Methven,
Sherriff Currie,
Mr Lawrence Davidson, Edinburgh.

Those marked ★ also attended the dinner party on 7 September.

The list is an example of the most careful preparation, selection and protocol and one wonders under whose hand it was made up before ultimate approval by the Laird and his Lady. Seating arangements at the banquets must also have caused many a heartache. Those attending the ball in addition to the house party came from a wide area, from Aviemore to Edinburgh, but mainly, naturally, from within the Breadalbane stronghold. Mr Maule was the MP for Perth; he was present at the Queen's arrival on 7 September and is described by Buist as 'deep chested and strongly made, magnificently attired and accoutred in Campbell tartan'. Mr Anson was Private Secretary to Prince Albert, while General Wemyss, Colonel Bouverie, Sir John Clark and Miss Paget were all members of the Royal suite. The link between many of the family names on the list and their lands still continues.

Saturday 10 September was the day of departure. Fortunately it was dry and calm so the decision was made to go by boat to Auchmore. Before departing there was an exchange of gifts and both the Queen and Prince Albert planted an oak and a fir tree in the old flower garden to the east of the castle, aided, and no doubt doing all the work, by the Marquess and his forester, Mr Dewar.

The bridge at Kenmore was crowded. The Royal party drove to the harbour in the river and embarked on the barge, which has already been described. It was wearing the Royal Standard and commanded by Captain MacDougall RN of Lorne and Dunolly, and was followed by four other boats carrying the remainder of the retinue and guests and two smaller boats with pipers.

> As the Royal Barge, containing her precious freight, glided slowly 'like a thing of life' from underneath the bridge, and emerged fully onto the loch, and the deafening acclamation of the spectators, the Band struck up the National Anthem and the music, swelling up from the waters through the calm clear air, mingled with the cheering of the people . . . The whole scene was among the most beautiful that was witnessed during the Queen's visit.

The fine weather held till the flotilla reached Auchmore, a row of some 14½ miles, where they were greeted by more Highlanders and an artillery salute. This gave time for the Marchioness of Breadalbane accompanied by Prince Albert to drive by carriage to Auchmore. Quite a race, and what a splendid farewell.

Lord Breadalbane finally accompanied the Royal party on horseback to the limits of his domaine on Loch Earn, where he took leave of the Sovereign and her consort. Six years later he became Lord Chamberlain to the Sovereign and retained this office for ten years.

It is noticeable that throughout Buist's account of the visit there is no mention of security and it says much for his expressed sentiments of loyalty to the Queen that she was willing to visit and stay in this highland stronghold amid the clans and men of the hills without apparent trepidation. Nor is there any record of safety precautions or of life jackets when the Queen was on board a small boat, 6' 10" wide and 2' 9" deep in the middle of a wide loch where storms are common.

Missing too from the account is any report of how carriages, horses, staff of all kinds and guests were housed and fed, an enormous administrative undertaking but evidently not worthy of mention. Times do indeed change.

Twenty-four years later in 1861, after both the Marquess and Prince Albert had died, Queen Victoria paid another and unofficial visit to the district, dressed in strict mourning. She recorded in her diary:

> We passed to the right the principal lodge of Taymouth, which I so well remember going in by, but as we could not have driven through the grounds without asking permission and becoming known, we decided on not attempting it, and contented ourselves with getting out at a gate, close to a small fort, into which we were admitted by a woman from the gardiner's house, close to which we stopped, and who had no idea who we were. We got out and looked down from this height upon the house below, the mist having cleared away sufficiently to show us everything, and here, unknown, and quite in private, I gazed, not without deep inward emotion, on the scene of our reception, twenty-four years ago, by dear Lord Breadalbane in princely style, not to be equalled for grandeur and poetic effect. Albert and I were only twenty-three, young and happy. How many are gone who were with us then. I was very thankful to have seen it again. It seemed unaltered.
>
> . . . We got into the carriage again; the Duchess of Atholl sitting near to me to prevent our appearance creating suspicion as to my being there. We drove on a short way through splendid woods with little waterfalls, and then turned into the little village of Kenmore, where a tryst was being held, through the midst of which we had to drive, but the people only recognised the Duchess. There was music going on, things being sold at booths and on the small sloping green near the church, cattle and ponies were collected—a most picturesque scene. Immediately after this we came upon the bridge; and Loch Tay with its wooded banks, clear and yet misty, burst into view. This again reminded me of the past—of the row up the Loch, which is sixteen miles long, in 1842, in several boats, with pibrochs playing, and boatmen singing wild Gaelic songs.

In 1863 there is evidence of the strength of religious beliefs among the people of Lochtayside. For some years there had been dissention as to whether parish ministers should be appointed by those in authority, basically the local lairds, or chosen by the people. In that year occurred the split in the Church of Scotland, referred to as the Disruption, when at the annual General Assembly of the Church in Edinburgh a large number of ministers led by the Moderator and many commissioners walked out of the Assembly and set themselves up as a totally independent Free Church, accepting no governmental or hierarchical authority or aid whatever. It was an unbelievably courageous act, those joining in it accepting full responsibility, financial and otherwise, for all their acts.

The division in belief cut right across congregations and families, with big variations from place to place. In Kenmore, the Kirk Session was split, but Lord Breadalbane, who was an elder, supported the Free Church and did much to build a new church at Kenmore and also elsewhere. At Lawers, the whole congregation left the Church of Scotland, which very wisely however allowed them to keep and to use their church.

It may have been due to such acts that this time the division in religious belief did not develop into civil war as had happened two hundred years earlier with the Wars of the Covenant. The Free Church at Kenmore was built at the foot of the brae down to the east shore of the loch and was commodious and well equipped; its walls now house the tourist gift shop. After the passage of time and under wise guidance from Dr Gillies, rather than having two large churches sparsely filled by the now reduced congregations, it was arranged that the service would be held each Sunday in alternate churches and the writer well remembers worshipping under Rev. Atholl Gordon in the Free Church and under Dr Gillies in the Parish Church. Eventually, in 1931, the Free Church and the Parish Church united, one of the very first reunions between the two churches then coming about, from which date the old name of the Parish Church, St. Aidan's, has been largely disused in favour of 'The Kirk of Kenmore'.

Another and very different gleam into the thoughts of local people comes from a letter on 11 December 1850 from William Grassie to Breadalbane saying his Society,

> The Kenmore Abstinence Mutual Instruction Society expresses gratitude at recipients offer of patronage; its objects; a meeting once a fortnight to dish out tracts on abstinence; all meetings to be opened and closed with prayer and no sectarian peculiarities in religion will be allowed to be introduced in any way.

Is there a hint of concern at the illicit whisky distilling probably going on locally and excessive enjoyment of the product? The writer's address is given as 'Walker's Inn, Kenmore'; Walker was presumably the Inn tenant. Was he overstepping the mark, and if so, why was Grassie staying there, unless he was a visitor? Black Duncan over two hundred years previously had issued strict regulations for 'Brewster Houses', where wives were not permitted to drink unless their husbands were present. There cannot have been much 'abstinence' during the Queen's visit, so perhaps Breadalbane's offer of patronage was an attempt to cool things down. Grassie clearly does not wish to become associated with either branch of the Church, each no doubt actively seeking to consolidate its respective position.

Communications were also under discussion. In 1845 there was word of a railway to be built between Ballinluig and Aberfeldy, while on a different level in 1854 John Sinclair, shoemaker in Acharn, was recommended for the post of runner between Kenmore and Killin, but this may have been a private arrangement for communication between the Breadalbane seats at either end of the loch.

There is evidence of continued interest in sporting and country life at this time. On 6 August 1833 James Anderson wrote to Breadalbane saying that he had failed to catch any pike in the loch, perhaps owing to the very cold weather.

In 1844 an American visitor, E. Sheppard, staying at Walker's Inn, Kenmore, and about to return to America, offered to supply Breadalbane with American deer and wood ducks. The following year he repeats the offer, quoting the deer at £8 each.

CHAPTER 16

The Breaks in Succession

John Campbell, second Marquis of Breadalbane, left no son and there were several claimants for the title and the lands. It took five years and much legal wrangling before the House of Lords finally settled the claim in favour of John Alexander Gavin Campbell of Glenfalloch, a fourth cousin twice removed of the late second Marquis, born in 1824, who then became the sixth Earl of Breadalbane. The Earl married an Irish lady by whom he had a son, Gavin, who succeeded after a protracted law suit when his father died after a period of ill health in 1871.

In the period of uncertainly the people of the lochside had an opportunity to get on with their own lives, the factor and administrators bound to 'ca canny' until the successor was finally confirmed in office. The sixth Earl was highly regarded, his family having been close friends with the late Laird and frequent guests at Taymouth, but he differed from his predecessor in being a strong Conservative and staunch supporter of the Established Church. He was a keen sportsman, especially interested in salmon fishing, which he practised on Loch Tay whenever possible.

Gavin Campbell, the seventh Earl, had a most distinguished career as Lord Breadalbane. He sat in the Lords as a Liberal, was a Lord in Waiting to Queen Victoria in 1873 and later ADC to the King. He was created a Knight of the Garter in 1894 and Marquis of Breadalbane in 1895 and was Lord High Commissioner to the General Assembly of the Church of Scotland in 1893–5. He had married Alma, daughter of the Duke of Montrose, in 1872, but they had no issue.

The seventh Earl portrayed many of the Campbell characteristics, forceful, able, favoured by royalty and one of the largest landowners in Scotland with his properties now literally stretching from near Aberfeldy westward to the sea including the islands of Luing and Seil. Of necessity he was interested in good communications and in 1892 he established the Loch Tay Steam Boat Company, selling to it his boats *The Lady of the Lake*, *Sybilla*, *Carlotta* and *Magpie*, and barges, with leases of the piers at Kenmore, Acharn, Fearnan, Lawers, Ardtalnaig, Balnahanaid and Killin—a profitable transaction as he received £8,000 from the sale and in exchange held the whole of the 800 shares of £10 in the Company. The good ship *Sybilla* did yeoman work towing the barges carrying coal, goods and passengers to the piers around the loch until she sank at anchor in the 1930s. In 1923 she carried the Duncan Millar family from Killin to Acharn on their first visit as shooting tenants at Remony Lodge.

The timetable on page 112 shows the regularity of the services in 1883 and the considerable speeds achieved. From Killin to Kenmore in ninety minutes must have meant cruising at ten miles per hour; fitting in the four stops in between at the cost of only fifteen extra minutes must have meant smart sailing and quick loading and off-loading. Acharn is not listed as a regular calling point although the pier was in use; perhaps it was 'calling on demand'. In the 1920s when the captain lived in Kenmore and the mate in Acharn, no doubt this could easily be arranged. In stormy weather the *Sybilla* was moored in Remony Bay, being the most sheltered water at the east end of the loch where the predominantly west wind with the long fetch could build up a big wave. A series of posts sticking up well above the water indicated the shallows and no doubt helped in the safe approach to Acharn pier.

The horses pulling the coach between Kenmore and Aberfeldy must have gone at a spanking trot to cover the distance in one hour having regard to the big climb to be overcome in each direction.

In his local capacity, Lord Breadalbane took great interest in the Volunteer Forces and was Colonel of the 5th Battalion, The Black Watch. He was responsible for the rifle range above Balmacnaughton, with a huge iron target no doubt whitewashed with a black bullseye, and the armoured marker's cabin beside it with a slit through which the marker could indicate with a disc on the end of a pole the strike of each shot. Firing points were at 200, 400, 600 and 900 yards, distances at which the Lee-Metford rifles could show remarkable accuracy. Regular practices were held and prizes offered at certain competitions. Duncan McArthur recounted how he came off the *Sybilla* at Kenmore after being mate on her daily trip, walking up to the range just in time to compete in a principal competition—and of course winning it.

After the Great War there were big increases in costs of all kinds, especially of wages, while the accumulated expenses of law suits coupled with heavy death duties, augmented when the succession was not directly to a son, all added to the financial difficulties of the Earl. Rumour has it there were also gambling debts. By 1922 he had resolved to sell the eastmost portion of his estate, the start of the break up of the Breadalbane empire foretold by the Lady of Lawers, but he did not live to see the sale as he died in 1922 while attending a meeting of the Caledonian Railway Company in Glasgow.

The peerage then became vested in his nephew, Ivan Edward Herbert Campbell, only child of Ivan Campbell the third son of the sixth Earl, but he survived his uncle by only a few months.

It then took further legal process once more to find the heir, the lands

Gathering near Remony Farm to mark the coronation of King Edward VII in 1902. Hence the name of the adjacent field where sports competitions were held: 'The Coronation Park'. See Appendix IV for the names of many of the people.

TIME TABLE FOR SEASON 1883.

Outward

STATIONS	a.m.
Carlisle (Caledonian),.........leaves	4.18
Edinburgh, via Stirling,............ "	4.10
Do., via Fife,............ "	6.30
Glasgow (Buchanan Street),..... "	7.0
Stirling,......... "	8.0
Dundee (Caledonian),..... "	7.40
Perth (Highland),......... "	9.30
Aberdeen,......... "	6.0
Inverness,......... "	
Aberfeldy,.............arrive	10.55

	a.m.	a.m.
Coach leaves Aberfeldy,.....	7.45	11.0

STEAMER.	a.m.	Pass.grs and Goods. a.m.	Express Noon.	Mail p.m.
Kenmore Pier,.........leaves	7.0	8.45	12.0	2.30
Fearnan,......... "	7.20	9.5	—	2.48
Ardtalnaig,......... "	7.45	9.30	—	3.7
Lawers,......... "	7.55	9.45	—	3.14
Ardeonaig,......... "	8.15	10.5	—	3.30
Killin Pier,.............arrive	8.45	11.15	1.30	4.20

STATIONS.	a.m.	Noon.	p.m.	p.m.
Killin Pier,.........Coach leaves	8.50	12.0	1.50	4.35
Do. Hotel,......... Do. arrives	9.5	12.10 p.m.	2.0	5.45
Do. Do. ......leave for South	9.5	2.0	2.50	5.39
Do. Station, ... arrives	9.50	2.0	2.50	6.20
Do. Hotel, ... leave for Oban	9.5	3.0	3.50	6.0
Do. Station, ... arrives	9.50	3.50		7.15

STATIONS	a.m.	Noon.	p.m.
Oban,.........Train arrives	12.15	6.15	9.43
Callander, "	11.8	3.45	7.18
Dunblane, "	11.37	4.20	7.57
Stirling, "	11.54	4.40	8.12
Edinburgh (Waverley), "	1.50 p.m.	6.30	9.55
Glasgow (Buchanan Street), "	1.25	5.50	9.15 a.m.
Carlisle (Caledonian),	5.17	8.40	12.8

Return

STATIONS.	a.m.	a.m.	a.m.
Carlisle (Caledonian),.........leaves	4.18	5.10	9.20
Do. (N.B.), "	4.57	4.57	8.15
Glasgow (Buchanan Street), "	7.0	9.15	1.15 p.m.
Edinburgh (Waverley), "			
Stirling, "	6.10	8.30	12 25
Callander, "	8.0	10.10	2.15
Oban, "	9.10	11.20	3.10
	5.25		12.40
Killin, ...arrive	7.43	12.10	3.57

STATIONS	Mail Noon	Express p.m.	Pass.grs and Goods p.m.
Killin,.........Coach leaves	10.30	12.15	4.0
Do. .... Hotel arrives	11.10	1.10	4.30
Do. .... Do. leaves	11.45	1.40	4.35
Do. .... Pier arrive	11.55	1.50	4.45

STEAMER.	a.m.	Mail Noon.	Express p.m.	Pass.grs and Goods. p.m.
Killin Pier,.........leaves	9.10	12.0	2.0	4.50
Ardeonaig,......... "	9.40	12.30	—	5.35
Lawers,......... "	9.55	12.45	—	5.55
Ardtalnaig,......... "	10.5	12.57	—	6.10
Fearnan,......... "	10.25	1.17	—	6.40
Kenmore,.............arrive	11.0	1.50	3.30	7.20

STATIONS.	a.m.	p.m.
Kenmore,.........Coach leaves	11.15	3.45
Aberfeldy,......... " arrives	12.10 p.m.	4.45

STATIONS	a.m.	p.m.
Aberfeldy,.........Train leaves	1.55	4.55
Ballinluig, "	2.30	5.30
Inverness, "	10.20	10.20
Perth, ... arrive	3.33	7.0
Dundee, "	4.45	8.10
Glasgow, "	6.5	9.55
Edinburgh, "	6.30	9.55 a.m.
Carlisle, "	8.40	12.8

and the title eventually passing to Charles William Campbell, born in 1889, a descendent of John Campbell of Boreland in Glenlochay, through a distinguished line of soldiers, his father being Major General Campbell who had been a claimant for the Breadalbane title when it was awarded to Gavin, the sixth Earl.

The ninth Earl adopted a military career, passed through the Royal Military Academy and went to France in August 1914, later commanding an anti-aircraft battery. He was wounded at the Battle of the Aisne and awarded the Military Cross, later becoming ADC to the Commander in Chief of the Rhine Army of Occupation and then himself commanding the 8th Battalion of the Argyll and Sutherland Highlanders. After the war he had the difficult task of overseeing the break up and sale of the Breadalbane Estates, living mainly at Auchmore near Killin and taking an active part in many local affairs. He was elected a Scottish Representative Peer, elected County Councillor for the Parish of Kenmore, was a Justice of the Peace and became chairman or president of several local bodies, among them the Scottish Salmon Angling Association and the Awe District Salmon Fisheries Board. In 1922 the Loch Tay Central Salmon Fishings Company was incorporated to regularise the salmon fishing in the main central portion of the loch and to control it in the hands of the riparian owners, no doubt having in mind the impending sales of land. A short length at either end of the loch was kept in Breadalbane control for the benefit of family and friends; these two sections were later broken up and special salmon fishing rights created within them. Later, Remony Estate as a riparian owner acquired the right for two boats on the central beat and one on the east reserved water. For many years I was chairman of the Central Salmon Fishings Company and incidentally also for a short time chairman of the Awe District Salmon Fisheries Board. Lord Breadalbane had married in 1918 Armorer Williams, widow of Captain Eric Nicholson of the 12th Lancers and in 1919 they had a son, John Romer Borland, who on his father's death in 1922 inherited the titles of Earl of Breadalbane and Holland, Viscount of Tay and Paintland, Lord Glenorchy Benderloch, Ormelie and Wick 1677; Baronet of Glenorchy; Baronet of Nova Scotia (cr. 1625), but, sadly, no land at all—it had all been sold. In 1995 the present Earl was unmarried and living in London.

CHAPTER 17

Changes on the Land

S o far the story has mainly been of acquisitions of land by successive Breadalbanes and their care of the farmsteads and villages which they created. But now it has also to be told how many of the farmsteads fell into disuse.

The main and over-riding cause was the hardness of the life of the people working the land. Cows for milk and horses for transport were essentials; all had to be fed as well as the people themselves from the produce of the land, grass, bere and oats. The latter crops required cultivation, with poorer yields on higher ground and more difficult to cultivate when the ground was steep. These factors speak for themselves, but the very access to the improved communications and all the additions to basic requirements which were becoming available was made more difficult by the long walk re-quired—even to the nearest ceilidh—and the carrying up the hill of everything not produced on the holding.

There can be no doubt that after the emigrations to Canada in the seventeenth and eighteenth centuries, augmented by the later clearances for sheep which only produced a small proportion of the stream of emigrants, letters must have reached Lochtayside telling of life in Canada, naturally in the most favourable terms, persuading many that they themselves should seeks a new life. And so the higher holdings were among the first to fall into disuse.

There are no ruins left of the farmstead of Aleckich shewn in 1769 on McArthur's map together with its stocking and acreage. It must have been vacated for one reason or another by about 1840, or soon after, when word of Queen Victoria's visit got around and it was thought that the nearby 'paved' ford across the Alt Muchaid should be replaced by a bridge so that the Queen might drive along the high road in her carriage. The bridge was duly built with fine stone abutments, using many conveniently faced and squared blocks near at hand from the walls of the adjacent house and barn, of which only the foundation stones at ground level can now be seen.

Up to about 1480 Balmacnaughton had been the centre of a branch of the Clan Macnaughton, and in that year one Donald Macnaughton was the tenant. After that the clan fell upon bad times and their name largely disappeared from the area. What had been a centre of a quite numerous population declined until in 1638 James McKerchar, as the Breadalbane tenant of Balmacnaughton, only ranked '1 sword, bow and arrows' among the Highlanders.

Soon after 1760 there was a Macnaughton back as tenant in Portbane and his son, Alexander, became tenant of the new Remony Farm just on the east side of the Alt Muchaidh and close to the public road. Quite by chance, about 1830 Sir John Sinclair, then President of the Board of Agriculture, on his travels fell in with Alexander Macnaughton and after some conversation asked him if he would be willing to start a woollen mill. With the promise of financial support, Alexander agreed, constructed a mill pond and lade and built an overshot water wheel to drive his mill (the remains of which can still be seen), establishing a spinning and weaving business. He must have been a shrewd and able man; he was also the progenitor of a burgeoning family of Macnaughtons producing outstanding lawyers, bankers, doctors, merchants and particularly men of letters who served all over the civilised world.

For a time the venture at Remony prospered. A great store to hold the wool available had to be built close to the bank below the mill pond as successive Macnaughtons enlarged and developed their sheep stock and became recognised as leading livestock farmers. A Blackface ram named Arabi Pasha was bought from Lanarkshire for the then enormous sum of £30, which was reputed greatly to have improved the stock, while their Clydesdale mare Remony Bell was a winner at the local shows and dam of foals which followed her example.

After being tenants for many years, Alexander's grandson Peter bought the farm outright in 1921 during the break-up of the Breadalbane estates. It was the family of his widow's brother-in-law who eventually sold the farm to become part of Remony Estate in 1930, when a nephew, John Campbell, was the tenant.

In 1808 a young apprentice named James Haggart was employed, who, after only a few years, asked for and got the tenancy of the mill at Keltneyburn where he worked for the rest of his life improving and extending the business. His two sons, Peter and James, continued successfully and in 1880 leased the woollen mill at Aberfeldy, now the railhead. The firm of P. & J. Haggart became well known and for many years held the Royal Warrant, supplying tartan goods and rugs to Balmoral and to many other establishments. Peter's son, James Dewar Haggart, spread his wings in acquiring much of the land of Aberfeldy, becoming Provost of the Burgh in 1914 and for very many years thereafter. Known as 'Tartan Jimmie', he prospered greatly and was

1. A genealogical tree of the Macnaughton family is included as Appendix VI.

awarded the OBE, finally acquiring with others Taymouth Castle itself and the neighbouring grounds, when their sale took place.

A branch of the Macnaughton family had moved to Pitlochry and established the woollen business there. In June 1960 Blair Macnaughton, then head of the firm, advertised his intention to beat the 'Throckmorton Record' made in 1811 when sheep were clipped, the wool spun and woven, the cloth dyed and the jacket made all within the space of thirteen hours and twenty minutes. My wife and I attended the clipping in a park behind the Pitlochry cinema at eight a.m., and then, after all the processes of manufacture were completed, were guests of honour in the evening at the dinner at which Blair appeared wearing the finished jacket to the newly composed pipe tune 'Blair Macnaughton's Jacket', having beaten the record by seven hours and ten minutes. The whole world of woollen manufacturing was present and as the present owner of Remony, where it all started, I had the honour of proposing the principal toast to 'A. & J. Macnaughton Ltd.'. It was a great occasion; the jacket is still to the fore and Blair is reported in 1994 still to be able to get into it. This business, established for over 150 years in Pitlochry and now in its fifth generation, is still wholly owned by the founding family.

The dwelling house at Balmacnaughton continued in use for many years, occupied either by a farm servant or temporarily by retired people; it was eventually sold as a holiday house in 1985.

Only a short distance below, the original Remony and the adjacent Kiln Croft had ceased to be farmed by 1861, when Sir Alexander Campbell of Barcaldine had plans prepared for a house to be built and called Remony, perhaps because he had enjoyed shooting over the land or just because the site on which Remony House now stands was convenient and had a fine view. It would seem likely that there had previously been a cottage on the site and that this was incorporated into the east end of the new house. Duncan McArthur, of whom more later, told me that he remembered a young couple who had been married at Amulree walking over the hill to spend their honeymoon night with the two old ladies then living in the Kiln Croft house.

High on the brae above the present village of Acharn there was quite a community on the west side of the Acharn Burn near the site where Grey Colin had first intended to build his castle about the year 1555; they too were abandoned as were the buildings at Piercoul and Croftmartaig.

Although life on the higher farms was hard, the village of Acharn established by the Breadalbanes as a centre for craftsmen and workers, was full of life. The list of its inhabitants in 1850 (see Appendix IIIB) shows a total of some sixty-six adults and a hundred children and young people living in the then twenty houses, more than eight souls on average to each house.

Houses in Acharn (some demolished and replaced by Council houses)
and fields to the east, in use as crofts, *c.* 1925.

Some of the houses had separate living quarters on each side of a common
entrance with a second upstairs storey. Number 6 in the upper (south side)
village had no fewer than seven adults and three children on one side and
three adults on the other. Box beds let into the sides of their walls were
common, but life must have been crowded and uncomfortable.

The list shows there were:

2 millers
3 carpenters
1 blacksmith
3 masons
1 painter
1 grocer
1 dyker
1 roadman
1 guide
1 shoemaker
15 labourers

This must have been the heyday of the village, as such a team of workmen
would require considerable development work—and money—to keep them
going. The roadman was paid 11/- a week in summer and 10/- a week in

winter; this must have been at the lower end of the wage scale. Several men walked daily to Taymouth, directly employed by the estate on garden and forestry work. The band, perhaps still led by Mr Foghill, was to the fore and a man was employed as 'guide to the falls'. Was he perhaps unfit for other work, his sister listed as 'insane' but still living with the family?

Campbell resources, much drained by Queen Victoria's visit, were feeling the strain and could not long continue on this scale. The village's reputation for longevity was being forged in spite of the crowded conditions, with nine inhabitants of seventy or over and three over eighty.

With the changes in farming practice, some farms were split up and amalgamations took place. East and West Ballinlaggan were given over largely as crofts to the tradespeople of Acharn, who, with a declining population and less work from Breadalbane, were finding things difficult.

In addition to the croftland, each crofter had the right, or 'souming', to graze cattle on land set aside for that purpose, and a committee of crofters met regularly to supervise the common grazings. In 1895 special rules and bye-laws were in force, with two of the crofters chosen each year to act as managers. A herd was engaged to take the cows daily to and from the cow park after 20 April each year, from their byres in the village convenient for milking. The crofters had to arrange for a bull, with a charge of 4/- for each service, and keep the bull shed clean. The ground, too, was cared for. 'In order to prevent waste of grass and growth of rushes, drains shall be made to draw off the surface and spring water . . . ' Moles were to be dealt with by 'a proper mole catcher' and the molehills scattered over the ground.

Fencing the cow park was a serious matter, with the cost of nails included each year in the account. In 1896 a major repair of the cow park fence was required and after a meeting held in the smithy it was resolved to draw up a specification of the work required and to advertise for tenders for the erection of a new fence. The existing fence had apparently been damaged by timber extraction, and the contractor had offered to supply new fencing posts, while Mr Dunn, the estate factor, had agreed to supply wire for a five-wire fence on the assumption that it would last eight years. At the Annual General meeting held on 7 March 1896, sealed tenders for the erection of the fence were opened, two local men quoting 3¼d. per lineal yard and an Aberfeldy man 2¼d. 'After discussion it was moved and seconded that the offer of John Macgregor, Revucky, viz 3¼d. per lineal yard including tarring be accepted' and this was unanimously agreed. Whether it was the inclusion of 'tarring' or John Macgregor's reputation (or relationship?) with the Committee is not clear.

They took their duties very seriously in these days. One wonders whether the meetings, chaired by Dugald McEwen the local school teacher who also

The new hut at Glen Quaich with Johnny Reid, Duncan McArthur and Jess.

drafted the bye-laws and wrote the minutes, were used as an opportunity by him to show his expertise and perhaps earn approval from the factor. Each year an account was prepared and audited by the managers, determining the amount to be paid by each crofter which varied considerably from year to year. In 1896 twenty-eight crofters each paid 8/11d. per cow which covered much of the cost of the new fence: next year it was down to 5/10d. In successive years the number of cows dropped, nineteen @ 6/11d. in 1910, thirteen @ 1/7d. in 1920 and ten @ 2/- in 1925. The record ends in 1926 with the note 'No income, No expenditure' signed by William Barron and John Cameron, who I remember as a tall lugubrious man who lived in Holly Cottage. The names 'The Cow Park', 'The Bullshed Park' and 'The Crofts' are still in use, but after 1926 all upkeep and maintenance of the land fell to the proprietor.

Interest in sport was growing; Sir Alexander Campbell's house was used as a shooting lodge and in 1905 the road up to the lodge was improved, with a new concrete bridge over the small burn a hundred metres below it.

Shooting became so popular that the lodge was no longer large enough to hold the tenants, so a wooden annexe with a corrugated iron roof and with four rooms was built just beside the south-west corner of the house to accommodate the gentlemen who, however, had to walk past the front door of the house to their 'convenience' which was indeed conveniently (and very draftily!) built out on stilts over the cliff above the Remony Burn. One can still see the steps leading to it.

The shooting tenants were often well known: Sir John Holder for his contribution towards the Holder Hall in Kenmore, rudely known as 'the Tin Tabernacle' and for which my wife struggled for many years to raise enough money to meet the cost of heating it for use during the winter months; Sir John Jaffray who erected a cairn in the Coire Beithe to mark the place where he received intimation of his knighthood. My own father was knighted in 1932 while living at Remony. After he had bought the estate in 1925 he demolished the annexe and made use of its materials to construct a shooting hut in Glen Quaich, up to which the whole family traipsed in 1925 for its christening. It was a soaking wet day so that we were forced to shelter in the hut, but I was keen to get down to the Quaich burn to see if there were any fish in it. There were, and I brought back two small (to all eyes except mine) trout, in triumph. The hut stood well, much used and still in use in 1995 although now badly in need of replacement.

Tomgarrow was no longer a farmstead but was occupied by a shepherd until 1925, the last by the name of Baptie, after which it was used as a hay store and stock shelter.

It is not easy to tell the exact date when old stone buildings became mere rickles of stone. One such ruin, some 200 metres below the public road and to the east of the Achianich burn plantation, had been tenanted by a man called Broadley in the late 1920s, who one day walked out and was never heard of again. It was left completely furnished with all equipment and cutlery in quite reasonable condition and I well remember visiting it with my father and wondering what was to be done with it. In the event, the answer was 'nothing', since a new tenant could not be found, so it was left vacant to become as old a looking ruin today as many abandoned a hundred years earlier.

Many other changes in the land took place during the nineteenth century. Pressures on winning food and paying rent encouraged working the land as extensively as possible, while the forward thinking Breadalbanes encouraged drainage and improvements. Field drainage for cultivation was unknown until the eighteenth century except in the south where the land was better and less steep, and where the technique of ploughing to produce the 'ridge and furrow' surface was in use. The first efforts to keep water off cultivated land was by means of open ditches, often of considerable size and length, cutting across the slope of the land to lead surface water to existing water courses. Good examples of these can be seen in the high fields on either side of the Acharn burn, so wisely sited as to be have been well worth cleaning out and renewing up to the present date. A later and most extensive

Modern bridge over old Breadalbane culvert near Balmacnaughton (see page 122).

example is the 'canal' on the upper side of the Queen's Drive to the east of the Remony burn where an open channel nearly two metres wide and almost as deep was built with a pitched stone bottom and wrought stone vertical sides to lead a relatively minor burn across the slope to the Remony burn. Floods over the years had filled up this ditch with gravel so that there was a convenient ford across it to reach the land on the uphill side, but as this ford became still shallower, in times of flood, water spilled over the Queen's Drive causing flood damage below, to prevent which the canal had been built. It was not until 1993 when a modern powered excavator was brought in to clear out the gravel that the extent and depth of the beautifully built channel came to view, so wide and deep that a bridge of steel girders and sleepers was required to regain access across it. It seems probably that the initial construction was a combination of Breadalbane and Macnaughton enterprise, perhaps encouraged by the work commencing in the quarry below through which the burn prior to its diversion had flowed. This quarry, behind the knock to the east of the Remony burn and only 150 metres from the public road, was used until the 1930s, with blasting of the rock face and heavy stone-breaking equipment, to provide surfacing for the road with its red stone. A similar quarry near Callelochan, further west, was also so used.

About 1825–50 a system of below ground surface drains was developed, called 'Deanstoning' or 'Smith's system'. Drains were cut a metre or so deep, bottomed, with stone slabs from either side leant upward together, tent-like, to form a triangular water channel. These continued for a long time, many still in use, but the change from horse to tractor was their death knell as the heavy weight of the tractor wheels flattened the stones leaning against each other and blocked the water passage. Many wet patches seen in otherwise dry fields today are due just to such blocking of the old stone drains.

The Breadalbanes in the latter part of the nineteenth century also built certain main drains some seventy centimetres square with paved bottom and wrought stone sides, sunk well underground and covered with stone slabs, which today would cost a small fortune to construct, many still functioning. It was not until the latter half of the nineteenth century that tile drains came into general use, to be followed a century later by pipe drains made of polythene or similar material: light, convenient to handle and easy to lay with modern machinery, but expensive. The large machines themselves, even when tracked, tended to make a mess of soft and boggy ground. All these different forms of drains become blocked in time, especially in peaty ground, either by silt or by the roots of rushes or trees; continuous maintenance is inevitably required leading to a modern tendency to revert to open cut drains across the slope, now easily formed by machine.

The Breadalbane leases in use after the eighteenth century required all tenants to maintain their ditches and drains as well as their fences (except march fences) and roads, and it was often the burden of these quite onerous conditions that led to tenancies being ended.

The use of sheilings had also declined, as did the demand for peat and so too the use of the hill tracks leading to the peat banks originally allocated to each farm holding.

The Breadalbane papers make little reference to events outside their immediate domain; wars, whether against the Jacobites or the French, get scant mention. The 1914–18 'Great War' took its toll from the Parish of Kenmore and the Memorial at the entrance to the Parish Church lists:

from Kenmore	John Crichton	Lieut B Watch
	John Mackie	Pte B Watch
	Harold Towner	Pte B Watch
	Fred Glover	London Regt
	Arthur Pinkney	Stoker RN
	James McLaren	Pte B Watch
	Andrew Inkster	Pte B Watch
and from Acharn	Duncan McPherson	Pte Canadians
	John McLaren	Pte Cameron Highlanders
	James Campbell	Pte KOSB
	Lachlan McCowan	Pte Scots Guards
	Thomas McRae	Cpl B Watch

and a further twenty names from the remainder of the parish, a total of thirty-two young men from an already shrinking population. The Memorial for the Dead in the 1939–45 'World War' inside the Church lists only seven names:

Donald Anderson	Guardsman, Scots Guards
Donald Beaton, Private	Argyll & Sutherland Hrs
Kenneth A. M. Gillies	Capt. Black Watch RHR
Robert Hutchinson	Major, Black Watch RHR
Donald McKerchar	Corporal, Royal Air Force
Dugald McNiven	Home Guard
Hamish McRae	Sapper, Royal Engineers

The huge number of civilian casualties, mainly in the bombed cities, are generally unrecorded. The name of Dugald McNiven, a civilian, is however included above, his death resulting from an accidental grenade explosion while on parade with the Home Guard, which also killed Major Merrilees of Garth.

Finally, the effects of World War I largely put an end to the old farming systems except for a few hardy and well placed survivors. With the break up of the Breadalbane estates in 1922–4 there was much need for reconstruction, re-thinking and better financing.

Intromission

R eaders who have progressed thus far will have understood that events affecting this 'bit of Breadalbane' have been recounted from geological, archaeological and written historical sources; also how in more recent years the landowners, successive Campbells of Breadalbane, had exercised major influence on the land and the people, superimposed on the climatic and sociological happenings affecting the country as a whole.

Following the break-up of the Breadalbane Estates in 1922–4 new land owners came on the scene. Remony Estate was bought by James Duncan Millar in 1925 and became the home of his family after 1928.

It is appropriate that mention should be made of the Duncan Millar family as landowners, succeeding the Breadalbanes, to indicate the continuing effects of their ownership in recent years. Since for the first time the personal knowledge of the writer becomes of major importance, the first person singular must come into use when recounting memories, which I have endeavoured to keep factual but which inevitably may include some errors especially of names and dates which are of course my sole responsibility.

My father was born in Edinburgh in 1871, educated at Edinburgh University, practised law in Edinburgh and eventually became a King's Counsel. In 1906 he married Ella Forrester Paton, daughter of Alexander Forrester Paton, then head of Paton and Baldwins, now Coates Viyella. Their children were my sister Sheina who married Ken Scott, and myself born in 1914. I was educated at Gresham's School, Holt, and Trinity College, Cambridge, served an apprenticeship with Sir Alexander Gibb & Partners in London and worked with that firm as a civil engineer until 1951 (interrupted by four years war service), when I retired in order to give greater attention to the lands of Remony for which, by then, my wife, Lois McCosh whom I had married in 1945, and I were wholly responsible.

My father entered Parliament as Member for St. Andrew's Burghs, Asquith's old seat, which he won in 1910. A year later, under the then Parliamentary reorganisation, that constituency was abolished and replaced by East Fife. My father and mother, having represented the constituency for only one year, were presented with handsome scrolls contained in a gold casket by the Constituency Liberal Association. I have always thought that this came about not only in appreciation of the good work which I have no doubt was done, but also from the desire by the Burgh Liberal Associations not to have their funds passed on to unknown successors but rather to perpetuate the burghs by this magnificent gesture. The casket, bearing the arms of all the old Fife Burghs, was later coverted for use as a cigar and cigarette holder and stood on my desk in Tayside House during my period of office as Convener from 1974 to 1978.

My father then sat for the constituency of East Lanark from 1911 to 1918, before winning back the East Fife seat in 1922 which he held and lost more than once before his death in 1932 as the sitting Liberal National member shortly after being knighted for his work in the then Scottish Office.

The title deed for Remony estate which my father acquired in 1925 after being its sporting tenant for a couple of years, was a formidable document.

Gavin, seventh Earl of Breadalbane, had in 1911 executed a Trust Deed and Disposition and Settlement with various codicils dated up to shortly before his death in 1922, in favour of the Duke of Montrose, KT, Lt. Col. Malise Graham DSO, MC commonly called Lord Malise Graham, and Colonel Donald Cameron of Lochiel CMG, ADC, and it was these three Trustees who signed the deed. It was meticulously executed in longhand, describing the lands transferred and boundaries of the estate with a plan also showing all the neighbouring proprietors who at that time were Mr J. K. Hutchison who had very recently acquired Bolfracks estate, Lady Campbell and Mr Maitland Campbell of Garrows and Col. A. E. Whitaker of Auchnafree, while Ardtalnaig was still owned by the Breadalbane Estates.

Also acquired were right to fish with rod and line for salmon in Loch Tay (to be reasonably exercised) and the right to land on 'the Island opposite Taymouth Gardens'. Then came a list of burdens going with the land, including a proportion of the annual stipend payable to the minister of the Parish Church at Kenmore, as follows:

Edragol—Two bolls six stones and nine pounds and three tenths of a pound of meal, seven bushels three pecks and six tenths of a quart of barley and sixteen shillings three pence and four-fifths of a penny Scots in money;

Alekich (otherwise Auchleckich, Auchlekeith or Allekach)—Two stones and nine pounds and four tenths of a pound of meal, three pecks and nine tenths of a quart of barley and one shilling and ten pence Scots in money;

Acharn—Four bolls of meal, one quarter three bushels two pecks one gallon and eight tenths of a quart of barley and one pound four shillings and five pence and four-fifths of a penny Scots in money;

Callelochan—Nine pounds and twelve shillings and seven pence and four-fifths of a penny Scots in money; (or nineteen shillings and seven pence Sterling in all.)

The pound Scots had always had a varying relationship in value to the

English pound which had tended to decline in value over the years; here we see the total of £11. 15s. 3d. Scots valued only as 19s. 7d.

These minute divisions in quantity and money must have followed from previous disposals of parcels of land and been arrived at by dividing the major burden of teinds for the whole Parish both in kind and in money in proportion to the estimated value or extent of the different parcels of land down to the last small fraction, possibly in the same way that McArthur in 1769 had arrived at figures of acreage to so minute a fraction of an acre at that time impossible to have been reached by the means of survey at his disposal. The teind system continued until 1973, when the 'augmentation' of the original 19s. 7d. required the estate to pay annually to the General Trustees of the Church of Scotland the (still very precise) sum of £15 0s. 1d.

Land Tax of £3 14s. 2d. was also allocated, but much more important were the legal and contractual obligations to farm tenants regarding sheepstock and maintenance of fences.

CHAPTER 18

A New Broom

My earliest memory of Remony as an seven-year-old boy is on landing at the old wooden pier at Acharn after a seemingly endless journey from Edinburgh, by train to Killin Junction, and changing there for the downhill run to Killin Pier Station to get on board the good ship *Sybilla* for its zig-zag journey down the loch, calling at Ardeonaig, Lawers, Ardtalnaig and Fearnan. The family was met at the pier and driven up to 'The Lodge' to settle in for their season of its occupation. I remember the shiny horse-hair covered chairs in the dining-room and the musty smell of the wood lined rooms in the annexe, but above all the joy of country freedom after town life and of finding trout in the burn.

The next summer we drove up from our Edinburgh house, 18 Abercromby Place, by car, a journey via Stirling, Callander and Killin which took four hours hard going. This was to be repeated over the years with ever shortening journey times as cars and roads improved until by 1990 the eighty-odd miles to and from Edinburgh over the Forth road bridge could be done in a little over an hour and a half.

The first action of the new owner was to extend and modernise Remony Lodge, doing away with the annexe and forming a new access up from the public

Donald Steward, head keeper, with fine salmon caught in Loch Tay.

road from near what was then the old houses of Revucky, which were demolished. I remember the houses there in a semi ruinous state with a formidable old (to me) lady who kept hens still living in the eastmost house; she later married Donald Stewart the gamekeeper and moved to live with him in the keeper's cottage near the old Remony coach house.

No doubt stone from the Revucky houses was used to form the entrance and bottoming for the new avenue, rolled by a splendid old steam road roller which could only reach the top of the quite steep slope either by screwing down the steam safety valve to what appeared from the expression on driver McLean's face to be a position of extreme danger, or by a circular route up the existing old avenue, and then downhill over the steep section at an alarming rate. The ridged bank which had stretched down from the present garden to the west of the annexe was cut through, its soil dumped to form the present north lawn and the stone bridge built over the small burn to the west of the house to complete the new access.

Stone had to be found for the new building work. This was taken from the quarry in the Remony burn just above the present wooden bridge in the wood, its predecessor taking the horses, and carts across the burn, then down through the wood to the house.

Remony Lodge, about to be modernised.

The older quarry in the small burn to the west within the wood had been used previously to obtain building stone, but the quarry in the main burn was preferred. My father and mother were worried about this as the burn was then the estate boundary and the question of ownership of the quarry in it not well defined. This uncertainty was aggravated by the fact that the burn divided a hundred metres upstream of the quarry to form an island, and if the western branch was deemed the boundary then the quarry lay outwith the estate boundary. To strengthen our claim, for a short time it became a Sunday afternoon ploy for the family, by suitable placing of sizeable stones, to try to divert as much water as possible down the eastern branch and over the quarry to prove that to be the main channel, and hence our right to make use of the stone. In the event, no trouble ever arose, except that some of the stone cut from the quarry proved slightly porous and so liable to allow dampness to penetrate the new walls of the house, especially the west gable exposed to the strong wind beating rain onto it.

One of the wisest innovations made by my father was the installation of a hydro electric plant driven by water from the Acharn burn. He had first

Remony as reconstructed, 1926. Architect J. Melvin, Alloa.

visited another early hydro scheme at Inverpolly, accompanied by the whole family in our Wolseley car, which suffered a broken back axle on the pot-holed and not so great North Road at Drumochter, but repair by the local blacksmith enabled us to continue and complete our journey. I will never forget catching my first salmon in the Polly River, and weeping all the way home because the fish my sister had helped to catch, after she saw me catch mine, was – very generously – given to my mother, while my beautiful salmon was left lying on the slab! The Remony plant could originally generate about 39 kw Direct Current as was normal at that time, which kept 'The Lodge' warm and well lit as well as being used for cooking and water heating for almost seventy years. Without it, we would have been pushed to be able to live in the house.

Typical of the situation found by many new landowners, there was lots to do and much money required to do it. It was fortunate that the estate purchase had included a considerable block of mature timber, mainly spruce, situated high above the Queen's Drive, for which there now developed a good demand during the expansion and building work which followed after the end of the war. The sale of the timber greatly helped to offset the purchase price and the cost of subsequent works.

The trees had been planted by the Breadalbanes about 1850 along with

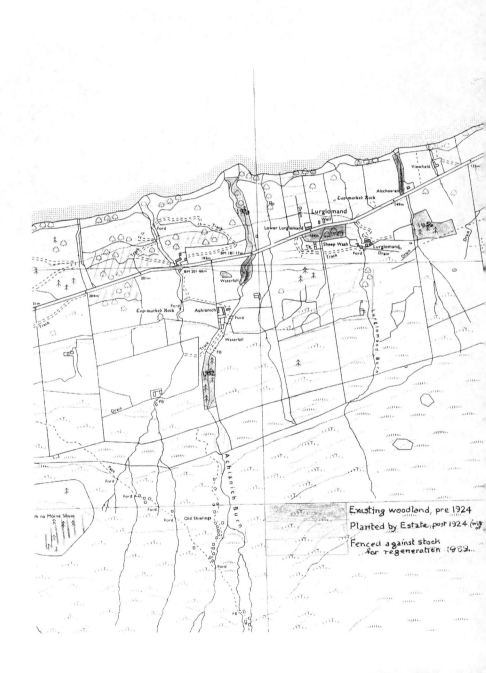

Viewfield

135m

Aitchoarant

Cup-marked Rock

149m

Lurglomand

Well

Lower Lurglomand

Sheep Wash

Track

Lurglomand
Drain

Ford

Lurglomand Burn

Track

Ford

BM 181·17m

193m

BM 201·66m

201m

Waterfall

204m

31m

Ford

Cup-marked Rock

Achianich

Ford

Track

Waterfall

FB

252

FB

Drain

Pen

Ford

Ford

Ford

Achianich Burn

m na Moine Shuas

Ford

Old Shielings

FB

Existing woodland, pre 1924

Planted by Estate, post 1924 (with

Fenced against stock
   for regeneration 1982.

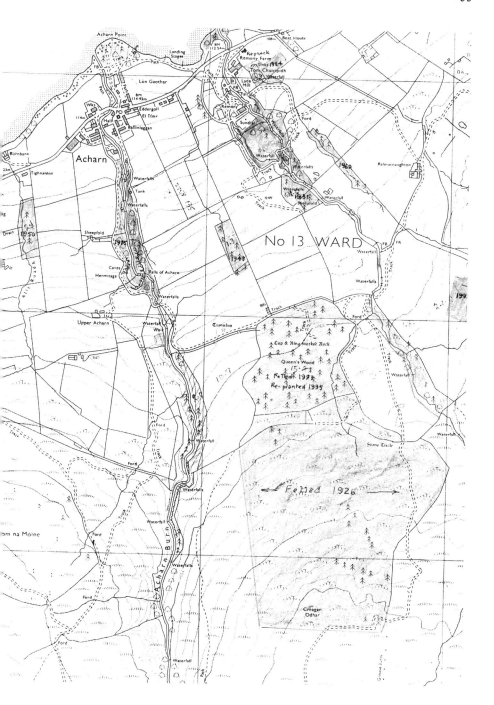

many other areas including the northern slopes of Kenmore Hill, the Target Wood and Drummond Hill. Now timber reached its pinnacle of wealth in terms of money as opposed to prestige and beauty; being mature, all these areas were felled with considerable financial benefit. Felling was carried out by men using cross-cut saws; after snedding and cross cutting to suitable lengths the trees were hauled by horses to the mills – rough and dangerous work especially on steep ground. Two mills were built for the Remony wood, with steam powered circular saws and rolling mill bench. Only the milled baulks of timber cut to optimum sizes depending on trade demand and the type and dimension of each tree had to be handled on the final journey to the public roads and merchant's yards. The engines were of course fired by the unwanted side 'slabs' of the round timbers, self generating fuel at hand without any haulage. Large mounds of sawdust accumulated with any unwanted waste. The remains of these can still be seen with the access tracks for wheeled vehicles leading to the mills.

Wild life was considerably affected, the capercailzie most of all, this being the start of the general reduction of its homeland territories. The Kenmore Hill slopes and the Target Wood were both felled before the Remony high wood, so the whole local population of caper moved into our wood where the first phase of felling had been arranged to leave standing a strip of trees at its west side for shelter, and a further group at the top of the wood where the trees were less well grown. The caper had to be culled, and in one day's shooting, magnificent sport for those taking part who included my father and myself with Jervis Molteno and Edmond Fergusson, the numbers were reduced to what the remaining area of trees could sustain. I have never seen or shot so many caper in a single day, but am glad to say they can still be seen (but not shot!) in the woods at Callelochan and on Drummond Hill.

Deer, too, lost much of their shelter, but became amazingly accustomed to the felling and to the mills. I remember seeing two or three hinds nibbling at the succulent tips of a felled larch tree within a few yards of the mill where men were working and the saw singing.

It may be appropriate here to continue with the subject of timber, when, as I write, extraction is taking place of the crop my father planted as an act of prudent estate management to replace the area he had felled, from what is known as the Queen's Drive Wood. In course of time, Drummond Hill became the first acquisition of the newly created Forestry Commission, was replanted and is now most suitably under perpetual forestry. The northern slopes of Kenmore Hill were replanted in 1992 by Bolfracks Estate with native species, in contrast to the general commercial inevitability of sitka spruce as the most economically productive species.

Which leads to the discussion on land use and the economics of forestry today, now overshadowed by fluctuating Government policies and incentives.

There is no doubt there is a place for forestry in Scotland, both because of the national shortage of timber and because in many places there is no better use to which the land can be put. In straight economic terms, trees can be made to pay well when planted in good ground at a suitable altitude, in large blocks for economy of scale in the costs of fencing and of extraction roads, and within easy reach of public roads or of sea extraction. Where these criteria less well pertain, the financial results become more doubtful and other objectives may become dominant. These include tax or other incentives, employment, shelter, tourism, wild life, amenity, sport and the acidification effect of trees on watercourses, so that forestry policy, whether local or national, has many facets.

There is also the widely held belief that, after hundreds of years of extraction from the land by the human race, whether of trees, grazing animals or grouse, with nothing returned to it, the land has become so denuded of fertility and essential elements that only a prolonged period of natural regeneration, including trees of mixed ages and kinds, can restore it to a healthy state. This may well be correct, indeed applicable throughout the world with its huge increase in population, but the snag is to make such regeneration both pay its way and also support a reasonable density of people. The aim, however, of only exercising a sustainable rate of extraction of any crop whether animal or vegetable is undoubtedly correct.

Here on Remony Estate for the last forty years there has been the decision that tree planting should be integrated with other land uses and that large blocks of trees do not fit in with the policies of this small estate, having widely different objectives centred on maximum sustainable economy and continuing population. As a result, there has been intermittent planting with mixed hardwoods and conifers in small areas, often unsuitable for cultivation or good grazing, aimed at shelter, wild life, sport and amenity but each group with a core of spruce hoping it will help with the cost of replanting when the time is ripe. The maps on pages 132 and 133 shows recent plantings, the largest being that of the Queen's Drive wood, obligatory under current legislation following the granting of a felling licence for the previous crop, but with diversification of tree species and with open spaces for wild life and sport.

Having extended and settled in to their new home, the family were soon busied with the responsibilities of managing the estate. A factor, Mr Macdonald from Aberfeldy, was employed, who gave advice, collected rents and produced annual accounts. He was familiar too with the complication of hill sheep and of farm and crofting tenancies, until then largely outwith my father's experience except for his wide general knowledge of the law. On the farming side, the hill sheep were 'bound to the land', which meant that the owner of the land was bound to acquire them at market prices where

BalMacNaughton in wintertime, W. Tunnicliffe 1995.

not already the subject of farm tenancies. In our case this meant a considerable outlay and the responsibility of around a thousand Blackface ewes which were cared for by the shepherd, James (always called Jimmie) Macgregor and ran over the Middle Hill and the eastmost portion of the Acharn hill. Further west the sheep were owned by the then tenants of Lurglomand, Achianich and Callelochan farms and other smaller holdings.

The 1920 Valuation Roll (see Appendix IIIC) showed that the subjects within the bounds of Remony Estate were valued at an annual rent of some £868 and the names of the holdings of the tenants are shown. Ten years later the estate accounts showed an annual rental of £1,260, the increase being almost entirely due to the increased value of the shootings, while almost all the rents and in most cases the tenants of the smaller possessions remained unchanged. Thus there was minimum social or population upset by the change in ownership, although farming changes were on the way. The picture above shows the fields now known as The Crofts and Lonnaguy (the windy meadow) under the system of crofting cultivation. The crofters lived in the village of Acharn in houses which they had themselves originally built, with various degrees of expertise. Windows were difficult and expensive, so there were few of them. My mother was a kindly soul and noted that one old gentleman in the upper village used to sit outside his house, which had no window at all facing west, to enjoy the summer sun, on a very decrepit camp stool. She presented him with a much more comfortable folding chair, which he gravely accepted with polite thanks. Shortly afterwards the man died and left an estate (which he had recently inherited) of such magnitude, that we thought that it was he who should have provided a gift to my mother!

Water was supplied to all the houses by a stand-pipe in both the upper and lower parts of the village, a good supply, spring fed through a series of tanks and pipes. There was of course no water or services of any kind inside the houses. Each house had a wooden privy built out over the burn, crude, draughty but most efficient and labour saving. All ashes and rubbish were likewise just dumped into the burn, to be swept down to the loch in the next spate.

The estate accounts for 1930 show a loss of £439, a sizeable sum in relation to the rental of £1,260, but which included the privilege of living in 'The Lodge' and all the estate amenities and sport.

Jimmie Macgregor looked after the sheep and their sale either in Aberfeldy or in Perth. Until the advent of lorries capable of carrying stock, becoming more common in the 1920s, he and the sheep walked to the market with little interference from the almost non-existent road traffic. The factor attended to the sale entries and the sale notes which were duly accounted for in the year's accounts. It took over a day to walk the sheep to Perth and the market there (Macdonald Fraser and Co.) provided overnight layerage in grass parks, one of which later became the St Johnston's Muirton football field until they moved to the McDiarmid Park in 1990. These fields and the adjoining Muirton Farm, famous for its Clydesdale horses, are now covered by Council housing.

A lambing shepherd was employed in the spring and another to help with the sheep grazing the Acharn common ground above the head dyke and to the west of the Acharn burn, leaving the family having little direct contact with the sheep. The crofters had grazing rights (soumings) for both horses and cattle, in theory overseen by the clerk of the common grazings. It was his duty to have a bull to serve the cows, which was wintered in a stone-built byre on the east side of the Acharn burn about 300m. above the village. It was well built, its walls still standing, and hence the names still in use of neighbouring fields, the Bullshed Park, the Cow Park and the Horse Park for example.

After 1930 there were a series of changes, not least my father's death in 1932, leaving my mother as proprietrix. She made changes in management, employing Mr Skelton from Killin in place of Mr Macdonald, and took advice regarding the farm and the sheep. I remember the kindly help given by Ian McRae of Fendoch farm near Crieff and of visiting him there with my mother. Fendoch was, and still is, a 'namely' farm where stock are known both to do and to sell well; at that time we felt quite envious of them, although Ian McRae had his problems too. We got to know and still know his family, now widely scattered.

During this period many of the crofters voluntarily gave up their crofts, the land and the grazing rights reverting to the proprietor, but the small farms to the west were able with their greater stock numbers to continue in their own rights. To the east of the Remony burn John Campbell farmed what was then called Remony farm, outwith the estate boundary.

Since my school days starting in 1928, while at university and then working as a civil engineer, I had only been at home during brief holidays, taking for granted that the estate just proceeded on smooth wheels, providing wonderful recreation and sport, but I gave so little support to my mother that I now feel guilty for my lack of understanding of all that was going on. But she and Skelton worked away, just able to make ends meet with the now lessening burden of my own and my sister's education.

When the war started in 1939 I was only at home for a very few weeks in all until 1945, so there was even greater pressure on the proprietor to keep things going with minimum change and cost. I was serving with 7th Armoured Division in the Western Desert when my mother died in 1943 and, although inheriting the estate, could do nothing except by correspondence, difficult enough in war-time, with the object just of 'keeping going', which my relations and my mother's trustees advised would be far from easy.

CHAPTER 19

Rose Coloured Spectacles 1945–60

To have survived the war was wonderful. To get married nine weeks later was bliss: only towards the end of a never-to-be-forgotten honeymoon spent in Galloway did Lois and I get down to thinking about the future.

It was at that time that the decision was made not to sell the estate, as was advised as being inevitable, but to live at Remony and to do our best to keep it going. In the few weeks before going back to Germany there were many meetings with Skelton, still the factor, and with many others while basic decisions were being made.

One of these concerned the land lying just to the east of the Remony burn. Our house, which we called Remony, was technically The Lodge going with the estate shooting and for a long time our note paper was headed 'Remony Lodge'. We lived within a few metres of our eastern boundary and shared the Remony burn, being the boundary, with our neighbours.

The lands beyond were described as 'the Farm and lands of Remony and part of the Farm and lands of Balmacnaughton' when Mr Henry James Kennoway bought them from the Breadalbane Estates soon after the death of the seventh Earl in 1922. How and why this came about is not clear, but since these lands lay so close to and overlooking Taymouth Castle there may have been some connecting factor with the estate of the widowed Lady Breadalbane, who had been appointed Commissioner by Lord Breadalbane only a few days before his death. Whatever the reason, Mr Kennoway immediately resold the lands to Peter Macnaughton, farmer at Remony, where he and his brother had lived for some time, the family there already having been referred to. These were the two wise old men of the district, who sat on every local committee, consulted and very often having the last word on every local problem.

The property included the arable fields in the narrow strip between the Remony burn and the boundary of Portbane farm, with the much larger extent of ground to the south of the Queen's Drive known as Kenmore Hill and the Target Wood, in all some 850 hectares with a few hectares of good heather ground on the summit of Kenmore Hill.

Peter Macnaughton died in 1943 and it was the trustees of his heir headed by James Macnaughton of McKerchar and Macnaughton, merchants in

Aberfeldy, who sold the property to me in 1946. Two years later I sold the
hill land to Douglas Hutchinson, a mutually convenient arrangement in view
of march boundary dykes, and kept the lower ground as good farmland just
across the Remony burn. The whole farmland was tenanted by John Campbell, a shrewd farmer and stockman.

When I was finally demobilised in May 1946, once more it was only for
a brief stay at Remony, then back to Sir Alexander Gibb in London to earn
some money, where Lois and I lived in a horrid little flat in Sussex Gardens.
Fortunately this lasted only for a few months, because in August 1946 I
contrived to get a posting to Pitlochry to work on the Hydro Board's
Tummel Garry scheme. This enabled me to live at Remony and was the
start of what so far has been a continuous period of forty-eight years of
living there.

Once more, as a new proprietor, there was lots to do and lots of money
required. Our first resolve, or rather absolute necessity, was to provide decent
houses for our estate staff.

As a start, two new houses were built, later known as Tighanlaggan and
Lonnaguy. No difficulty with planning consent in those days, nor thought
of ribbon development; an easy and convenient site was chosen between
Acharn and Holly Cottage. The choice of an architect was also easy. A
fellow Royal Engineer officer with whom I had soldiered during the war
was a qualified architect and in our talks about what we both would do
'after the war' we had often said how good it would be if I were to be in
the position of being able to give him a first professional commission when
he set up on his own. Here was the chance. Geoffrey Fairweather was known
in Sapper circles as 'Stormboat Fairweather' because of a famous incident
when in an exercise he was in command of a stormboat, a small collapsible
boat with canvas sides capable of holding about twelve men and of going
at considerable speed with its outboard engine. Crossing the river with the
boat containing not only his Sappers but also the senior officer in charge,
he had driven it at full speed into the shore so catapulting everyone headfirst
onto the land. Geoffrey later lived up to his name in doing gallant work in
charge of stormboats carrying the assault units of the Highland Division across
the Rhine just downstream of Rees in the spring of 1945.

We were both new to our jobs in 1946 and my commission was indeed
one of Geoffrey's first when he started up his own business in Sevenoaks.
We collaborated in the design details and ignored all the criticism that this
was no time to build new houses after the war when building supplies,
particularly of seasoned timber, were scarce. Drawings were made, estimates
obtained indicating a final cost of £3,000 and contracts eventually let. All
went well until the builder reached the upper storey and turned to the plans
of it, to discover that the chimneys showed a difference of two feet from

their position on the ground floor – a real draughtsman's error. Consternation, but the builder just said that all good chimneys had a kink in them, and built the bend into the upper gables of the houses. The chimneys eventually drew very well. Fifty years later both houses look well, are still occupied and are commanding good rents, while one which became surplus to estate requirements in 1980 was sold for £19,000. so the decision to go ahead with their building wasn't such a bad one after all.

A new farm grieve, John Milligan, was the first to occupy Lonnguy in 1948, the year that my son James was born, succeeding faithful Davidson who had loyally supported my mother. John was a big red-headed man and led the way with more up-to-date farming practice. I remember his tussles with the big Aberdeen Angus bull which he had helped to select, called Eerielaw but always referred to as Eerylugs, a splendid stock-getter but with the annoying habit of just putting down his head and walking through the gate of any field in which he was not inclined to linger, especially if he could see some heifers in the distance. The gates were all pretty old, but it was an expensive habit so he had to go, realising £50 in the market having originally cost £70, no doubt because his previous owner was well aware of his habits.

Our first tractor, a David Brown, was provided with little except a tow-bar, but it had a driving seat on which two people could sit abreast, the spare seat being much in demand when the tractor with it trailer was used as a hill pony to take the members of our shooting tenant parties up to the butts.

In 1949 the dam and power station at Pitlochry where I had been resident engineer was almost complete; I gave up my post with Sir Alexander Gibb and Partners in order to give more time to affairs at Remony and also to stand in the General Election as the Liberal Candidate for Kinross and West Perthshire, which was won by the Conservative McNair Snadden.

The post war Hill Farming Act was a godsend to Remony and to many hill farms. It provided a 50% grant towards the cost of improvements deemed necessary in an approved scheme covering all aspects of a farm, so we entered a scheme for Remony which was I believe No. 3 in Scotland. Without it the works of improvement would have been impossible.

A new farm steading was planned and built at Acharn with the best advice then available. It is still there, but now hopelessly outdated as our advisors had been old fashioned and out of touch with post war farming. The building included a byre for cattle tied by the neck, stalls and a loose box for horses, a threshing mill and grain storage space, but only two very small courts for cattle which had to be fed by hand and only pokey implement sheds. At the time it got a great write-up, even an article in the *News Chronicle*: 'A young laird's challenge to the hills'. Perhaps the most forward looking part of the steading was a small kitchen and eating space with convenient power and water and WC, much used particularly at times of sheep handlings.

Then further Hill Farming Act schemes were promoted, for Lurglomand Farm tenanted by Jimmie Sutherland and for Achianich farm when the tenant, McSwan, relinquished his lease in 1950. The Estate was legally bound but also willing to take over the sheepstock, valued at £2,182, and the tenant's improvements; we also bought some cattle and the pair of working horses. Norman Cree, the excellent auctioneer from Macdonald Fraser who conducted the away-going sale, was in great form. A cow which had escaped from the sale ring was sold while scampering up the hill towards the horizon: 'Look how fit she is!', and when it came to the hens: 'They must be grand layers – just look at the view they have.'

That year I took over the accounts as well as the day to day management of the farms and estate, and produced an archaic form of accounts enormously bulky and extravagant in paper but with minute accounting in every department, no fewer than twenty-five different accounts, including one for 'Pigs and Poultry' (which we then kept), all of which must have given the accountant who dealt with my accounts for Income Tax purposes quite a headache but which gave me a close insight of all estate costs.

1950 saw the first of the small property sales, when the shop at Acharn was sold to what seemed then a most suitable buyer to keep it going. The shop was in a poor state of repair and would have required considerable outlay in order to let it, while money was badly required for all the improvements and new work in hand. The option of selling was inevitable, but like other subsequent sales was always regretted; the shop was re-sold only a few years later and more than once in succeeding years and is now a dwelling house, leaving Acharn without a shop, like many other small villages. Other sales of vacant properties followed over the years, always with the knowledge that the interest on the sale price would far exceed the likely rent obtainable, itself likely to require still more outlay on repair and modernisation. The policy led to lack of control over continuing occupiers, sometimes with unfortunate results, but nevertheless it enabled improvements to be made where they were essential for the efficient running of the estate as a whole and which otherwise would have been impossible.

By 1951, when my second son Ian was born, the bulk of the Hill Farming Act improvements were complete and the lands of Remony were better cared for than they had been for very many years, their lack of attention being largely through force of circumstances. The sporting side was also going well with grouse bringing in a reasonable rent from short periods of shooting by tenants, then the Lowthers, accompanied by the Trenchards.

Rabbits were present in great numbers. Winter came early in the autumn of 1951. A field of turnips in the Pony Park intended to be lifted for winter feed for the cattle had one quarter of about two acres left in the ground when the snow came, followed by a prolonged period of hard frost. This made lifting impossible, while the hard weather made food for all animals very scarce. The rabbits found the turnips and came in their hundreds, the tracks in the snow showing that some had come from Kenmore Hill, more than a mile away. We shot and snared as hard as we could; this didn't save the turnips but it did result in some 2,000 couple being sold off this one field, probably at far greater profit than from the intended use of the turnips. In the following years the rabbit numbers gradually declined until the advent of myxomatosis which virtually wiped them out. By 1994 they were returning in small numbers, again requiring control to prevent damage, particularly to brassica crops.

Winter feed for both cattle and sheep is of vital importance on a hill farm. The advent of the pick-up baler, used after modern tedding machines, made hay-making easier and far less laborious than in the days of building ricks and then stacks. The bales were convenient to feed, too, so a large corrugated iron hay shed was added to the steading at Acharn in 1952, built by A. & J. Main, which included a garage bay to house the Austin lorry we had bought for transporting stock, principally to and from market. The use of the shed worked well for several years, but under snow and ice conditions hauling the bales up the hill to feed to the sheep was difficult and sometimes impossible. That problem was solved by building a small hay shed high up on the Queens Drive, where baled hay harvested from the neighbouring fields could be stored near to where sheep coming down from the hill could be fed.

By 1955 the farming enterprise was up and running tolerably satisfactorily. Callum McCallum succeeded Jimmie McGregor, who married Mr Lamont's widow and went to live at Altchoaran.

Lois and I had bought light-legged horses in Ireland which gave us great fun. We were helped by Hendry Smith and later by a part time girl groom who doubled as my secretary. Paper work was increasing with my own work load. I had become chairman of the Highland District Council, chairman of the Perth and Kinross Council's Planning Committee and served on the Scottish Agricultural Advisory Council of the BBC and on the Regional Advisory Council of the Eastern Conservancy of the Forestry Commission.

The mobility of being able to go anywhere on the estate in quick time on horseback was a great blessing and helped to offset the time spent on paperwork. Furthermore, this mobility, used daily in exercising the horse, enabled prompt and correct attention to be given to any trouble whether of open gates, damaged fences, blocked drains or couped ewes by the limited labour available or by myself. I was proud that at this period I could ride anywhere over the estate without dismounting, either by opening easily opened gates or by jumping fences or dykes at known or prepared places. This in turn made the horses handy and versatile, so aiding their sale later and replacement with a younger horse. Girl grooms-cum-secretaries came and went, some excellent, others not so good, but in economic terms the cost of this ability to get about on horseback must compare very favourably with the modern cost of running a 4 × 4 vehicle of any sort, taking all things into consideration. Perhaps more important, there was no tracking of soft ground which can so easily lead to scouring and erosion, no necessity to keep to roads, tracks or hard ground but the ability to get into any corner of a field or the hill with ease.

Lois, a keen and expert horsewoman, was a great source of encouragement in all our horse-borne activities, participating with me in some early One Day Events which in these days were fun even if one ended with an astronomic score, and picking me up when I came to grief in the Fife Point to Point in 1956. She also had the gift of understanding horses and being able (usually!) to make them do what she wanted.

While taking part in a Farm Forum broadcast, I had heard and participated in an excellent debate when it was argued that for proper control of grazing on open moorland one should have not only sheep and cattle, in addition to the wild creatures, but also ponies, which with their two sets of teeth could and would bite through tough stems of coarse reeds and grasses unpalatable to sheep and so reduce their extent. When it was proposed to put a small herd of Shetland ponies onto our hill, Lois was enthusiastic and from the beginning took full charge of the herd until their ultimate disposal. We took the necessary steps and in 1954 bought direct from Shetland four mares with two fillies, all of the natural brown colour, and a chestnut coloured stallion, for the princely sum of £68, hoping that their offspring, if chestnut, might sell well in addition to the benefit of improved grazing.

After acclimatisation in a hill park they were released onto the open hill on the west side of our Middle Hill, where they behaved just as Shetland ponies should. Initially the mares were very wild, particularly when they had just foaled, but with Lois's careful handling, after a few years she could catch any of them on the open hill. Hill sheep 'heft' on a fairly small area of hill and, except in unusual circumstances, can generally be found there, so that a good shepherd, if a certain ewe is found missing from a gathering, can go straight to where he knows she will be. Grouse tend to remain within a few kilometres of where they are born. Wild red deer too have their territory, a larger one of some 25,000 hectares to include their required range of grazing, shelter and altitude, from which, with the exception of a frustrated stag seeking a mate, they seldom stray. These ponies then, 'hefted' onto the Middle Hill, an area of some 1,000 hectares, but behaved differently from the sheep or the deer in that they remained in a group and moved from time to time a distance of 800 metres or so, virtually round and round the hill, presumably following Nature's guidance never to graze on the ground fouled by their droppings. The only exception to this was when a young filly, just put out to the hill after being wintered in a lower park with the other youngsters, was rejected by the stallion who chased her away down Glen Quaich towards Amulree. Feeling lost she started to make her way home and was picked up by a fellow farmer at Scotston on the road between Amulree and Aberfeldy. Knowing we were the only people in the district with Shelties, he phoned to us; I duly got a message in the market in Perth where I was selling stock, so stopped at Scotston on the way home with the Austin lorry, picked up the filly and took her home.

Whether or not the herd improved the grazing is debatable. They certainly did no harm and tended to follow and to make tracks which were also used by the sheep. The shepherds were very cagey about them at first, but the ponies took no notice of the sheep and when following a sudden snow storm after an open spell, they were seen trudging down in single file through deep snow with a score or so of ewes, which had also been well out, following the track they had made, criticism turned to mild approval.

We maintained the herd for many years, always on the open hill except for the first winter for the foals, but the commercial demand for them was disappointingly small – of any colour – and we didn't like selling colt foals for a few pounds knowing they would be exported for their meat. Keeping an eye on the herd was also a minor trouble, often involving a long walk or ride, but it was only about 1985–6 that the herd was dispersed except for an 'old faithful' used as a childrens pony.

1957 saw a big step, in the Breadalbane trait of the family, when we acquired Tirinie Farm. Every experience in hill farming showed the advantage of being able to work in conjunction with a nearby arable farm so when, quite unexpectedly, Tirinie came on the market, being the nearest sizable arable farm to Remony, I put in a bid which today seems ridiculously small but which was fortunately accepted. Lying at the head of the broad Tay valley above Aberfeldy on the north side of the confluence of the Lyon and the Tay, it consisted of 120 hectares of almost all arable ground, offering great potential for availability of hay and corn for Remony plus grazing for hoggs and wether lambs. We learned later that its reputation of not being a good wintering for hoggs was borne out in practice, but in every other respect the two farms had, and continue to have, many mutually beneficial features. Putting the farm in order was another challenge, the details of which do not feature in this book, but at the time it provided an easy and enjoyable ride from Remony and we could soon ride all over the farm.

By 1960 the new broom had made a good sweep with considerable modernisation of old buildings. These included the Manufactory block in

Lower Acharn which was gutted and rebuilt within the old front walls in 1958–9. These old front walls built in Breadalbane times probably by the then crofters were well out of plumb and the architect advised that they also should come down. But we kept them, adding the small porches, and their being out of plumb is never noticed while the old stone gives an attractive frontage.

In 1960 Tom Pringle, the tenant of Callelochan Farm, gave up his lease, but this time after a lot of thought and calculations it was resolved not to try to improve this steep and difficult farm, but to sell it. The house was sold to Professor Fergusson and and land to the Forestry Commission for so derisory a sum that it might have been accounted for as petty cash, but we escaped the responsibility of upkeep and maintainance to be added to our many other commitments.

Forestry was the obvious use for the land; it would have been wonderful and a great additional asset for the estate to have been able to plant the area ourselves, but we concluded that the cost of planting, fencing and making roads was not economic for us. With hindsight, the decision was probably correct. Certainly the Commission made a first rate job of planting the ground, especially with their admirable roads, while the trees, especially the sitka spruce, grew well. Harvesting of them commenced in 1994.

In this period between 1950 and 1960 the estate wages bill had gone up from under £4,000 to £8,000 a year, an increase of 100%, while the income from rents only rose from £343 to £509, an increase of less than 50%. The sheepstock was in good heart; cultivations had been pushed far up the hillside, where we found Breadalbane had been before us. We produced potatoes and oats as well as sheep and cattle and were well established in the farming community.

CHAPTER 20

Estate and Farm Management, 1960 into the Eighties

In 1963 John Campbell, tenant of Remony Farm, just over the Remony burn, relinquished his tenancy and I took occupation of the land bought in 1946, with some 130 Blackface ewes and gimmers and twenty-two head of cattle, starting yet another Hill Farming Improvement scheme. With all the farms 'in hand', owned and run by the family, now was the time to develop a sustainable and economic management plan.

As with many Perthshire hill farms, sheep and grouse formed the basis of the economy.

Callum McCallum proved to be a top class shepherd and stockman and with his help we began to achieve improvement of the sheepstock. As well as careful handling and feeding of the stock, selection of good sires is an obvious step on the road to improvement. We made a start in 1956 by buying a Woolfords ram for £200 and followed this with another next year for £450, then big prices. With better sires we were ourselves able to sell some shearling rams. In 1963 we sold 25 shearlings at the respectable average price of £53 each, while our ewes began to win attention at the local shows. At the 1964 Aberfeldy Show our ewe won the overall and bred championships; our gimmer was also first in her class and she later went on to be a champion more than once. That year I had the honour of accepting cups from Lady Douglas Home, wife of Sir Alec Douglas Home who had defeated me to become Prime Minister in the famous Kinross and West Perthshire 'Prime Minister's by-election' in 1963. Three years later we won the Perth championship and went on to win the Aberfeldy championship for the third time.

Callum was well supported these days at the shows. Sandy Paterson, our grieve's young son, was a keen helper and went on to become one of the best known and respected shepherds in Scotland both for producing and also for selecting top Blackface rams, frequently in the six-figure class, while working at Connachan Farm. George Reid was a junior at Balmacnaughton and not long after won the title of Best Scottish Shepherd while at Glen Quaich.

In 1961 I had the honour of being asked to join the Board of Macdonald

8 *The Courier and Advertiser, Monday, August 10, 1964.*

Sir Alec's rival gets "treble" at Aberfeldy

Lady Douglas-Home, wife of the Prime Minister, made the trip to Aberfeldy from Edinburgh on Saturday to present trophies at the Atholl and Breadalbane Show.

And three times she had to hand a cup to Mr I. A. Duncan Millar, Remony, the man who put up the stiffest fight against Sir Alec in his West Perth by-election last year.

Of special interest to Lady Douglas-Home was the triumph of a Highland pony from the Derculich stables of R. W. Honeyman.

The two-year-old filly which won the junior championship and was runner-up for the breed championship was named after her daughter Meriel.

She was shown for the first time and, like the Derculich champion Mayfly, is by Iain of Derculich.

The increased entry of Highland and trekking ponies compensated for the dwindling turn-out of Clydesdales.

Champion Clydesdale out of a field of only seven was a three-year-old filly by Dunsyre Benedictine, shown by John Robertson, Newton.

The filly, bought earlier this year, was second in her class at Perth and first at Braco.

At his 18th Aberfeldy Show in succession, 19-year-old Vic, shown by George Stewart, Duireaskin, again won the award for the best home-bred animal.

Vic owes his name to his birth on V.E. Day 1945.

In the beef cattle, A. C. Fotheringham, who has a commercial herd of 60 at Ballinloan, had a great day.

He won the over-all championship with an April stot calf by an Aberdeen-Angus bull, the McDougall Cup for the best breeding cow and calf, the special award for the best animal bred by exhibitor, and the Derculich trophy for the best calf.

Runner-up for the over-all award was Major F. H. Read Easter Dunkeld. The Ballinglash Cup for the best cow of any cross went to Grandtully Estates.

Dairy champ

The dairy champion was a seven-year-old pure Jersey from R. W. Honeyman, Derculich. Wm. Blain, Dunalastair, was runner-up.

Mr Duncan Millar had a remarkable day in the Blackface sheep section, where competition is always fierce.

He won the over-all championship, female and reserve tickets, the bred championship, the special for the best lamb, the female group, reserve male group, the fleece award and four class firsts.

His female and breed champion was a two-crop home-bred ewe out of Glencuilt and East Yarthouse strains.

Reserve for the female award was ewe, shown for the first time.

Male winner and runner-up for the breed championship was a three-shear ram from R. W. Honeyman, bred at Kilburn and bought at Perth two years ago for 420 gns.

Reserve male and runner-up for the bred award was a shearling from Atholl Estates, Rotmell, by a home-bred son of a Moorfoot sheep out of a Parkhall ewe.

The reserve lamb champion also came from Rotmell, as did the leading male group.

The attendance was well up to previous years' figures in spite of the threat of rain which developed in the early afternoon.

Though it dried up later on many people left early, missing an attractive afternoon programme of sports.

The wet grass led to a spill in the final lap of the three-mile Scottish cycling championship, involving the holder, A. D. Richardson, Hawick, who was lying about fifth place. He finished second to G. D. Fraser, Dundee Roads, the previous holder.

THE RESULTS

HORSES

CLYDESDALE.—Mare—1 J. Robertson, Newton; 2 and 3 Atholl Estates, Rotmell. Gelding—1 George Stewart, Duireaskin; 2 R. Kennedy, Borlick; 3 John McIntosh, Coilavoulin. Cart harness—1 Atholl Estates; 2 John McIntosh. Best decorated horse and harness—1 Atholl Estates; 2 George Stewart; 3 Atholl Estates; 3 John McIntosh Hagart. Trophy for best turnout—Atholl Estates.

HIGHLAND PONIES.—Mare with foal—1 and 3 Major F. H. Read Easter Dunkeld; 2 R. W. Honeyman, Derculich. Foal—1 Major Read; 2 Lieut.-Col. Sir Edward Wills, Meggernie; 3 R. W. Honeyman. One or two-year-old—1 W. Honeyman; 2 Sir Edward Wills; 3 Donald Lamont, Invervack. Mare or gelding—1 and 3 R. W. Honeyman; 2 Donald Lamont. Best shod pony—1 Donald Lamont; 2 Miss C. Adam, Lundin; 3 Sir Edward Wills

PONY TREKKING.—Mare—1 Mrs Duncan Millar, Remony; 2 Duke of Atholl, Atholl Estates; 3 Gail Masterton, Cluny House. Gelding—1 Mrs R. W. Honeyman; 2 Duke of Atholl; 3 John Blain, Dunalastair Home Farm. Duke of Atholl Cup for best pony—Mrs Honeyman. Team of three ponies (Duncan Millar Shield)—Atholl Estates.

CHILDREN'S PONIES.—Pony ridden by child between 12 and 17 years—1 Pat Moffat, Grandtully; 2 David Ferguson, Dunellan; 3 Alison Cameron, Tummelbridge. Best rider—P. Moffat. Pony ridden by child under 12—1 Barbara Duff, Dalraoich; 2 F. Duncan Millar, Remony. Best rider under 12—1 McDougall, Blackhill, Strathtay. Performance test (Mrs Campbell-Preston Trophy)—Miss P. Carmichael, West Tempar. Best novice rider in performance test—Miss Ruth Wilson. Points trophy—Atholl Estates.

CATTLE

BEEF CATTLE.—Cross cow off A.-A. bull—1 Grandtully Estates, Strathtay; 2 John McIntosh, Coilavoulin; 3 Col. C. B. Sheriff, Pitnacree. Cross cow off S.H. bull—1 and J A. C. Fotheringham, Ballinloan; 2 Major F. H. Read, Easter Dunkeld. Highland or cross Highland cow—1 A. C. Fotheringham; 2 J. H. Macaulay, Comrie Farm; 3 M. G. McDiarmid, Mains of Murthly. Breeding heifer—1 A. C. Duncan Millar, Remony; 2 J. Robertson, Newton; 3 Atholl Estates, Rotmell. Stot calf by A.-A. bull (born between

davie; 2 R. W. Honeyman; 3 Col. C. B. Sheriff. Stot calf by A.-A. bull (born after April 1)—1 A. C. Fotheringham; 2 Grandtully Estates; 3 A. J. Low, Balchroich, Keltneyburn. Heifer calf by A.-A. bull (born after April 1)—1 Major Read; 2 John McIntosh; 3 I. A. Duncan Millar. Stot calf by S.H. bull (born between November 1, 1963 and April 1, 1964)—1 D. Martin, Blairfettie; 2 A. C. Fotheringham. Heifer calf by S.H. bull (born between November 1, 1963 and April 1, 1964)—J. Robertson. Stot Calf by S.H. Bull born after April 1—1 J. & T. Borrie, Auchnague; 2 J. Robertson. Heifer calf born after April 1—1 and 2 J. & T. Borrie; 3 Atholl Estates. Stot Calf by Hereford Bull born between November 1, 1963, and April 1, 1964—1 and 2 Messrs McDiarmid, Castle Menzies. Heifer Calf by Hereford Bull born between November 1, 1963, and April 1, 1964—M. G. McDiarmid, Mains of Murthly. R. J. Cameron Cup for Home-Bred Calf (small farmers)—1 A. J. Low; 2 A. J. Low; 3 G. & J. McLaren, Litigan, by Aberfeldy. Special Prize for Yearling Stot or Heifer—1 J. McIntosh; 2 and 3 Atholl Estates. McGrouther Cup for Two-Year-Old Stot or Heifer—1 and 2 Atholl Estates. Fisher Trophy for a Pair Bred by Exhibitor—1 Atholl Estates; 2 John McIntosh; 3 J. Robertson. Highland or Cross Highland Stot Calf—M. G. McDiarmid; 2 A. C. Fotheringham; 3 R. S. R Trevor, Moulincarn. Highland or Cross Highland Heifer Calf—1 M. G. McDiarmid; 2 A. C. Fotheringham; 3 J. H. MacAulay.

DAIRY CATTLE.—Cow in Milk—R. W. Honeyman. Back Calving Cow due to Calve before October 15—1 R. W. Honeyman; 2 William Blain; 3 R. S. R. Trevor. Back Calving Cow due to Calve after October 15—1 William Blain; 2 R. W. Honeyman; 3 Duncan Menzies, Rathonnais. Heifer in Milk or Calf—1 and 3 Duncan Menzies; 2 R. W. Honeyman. Bulling Heifer—R. W. Honeyman. Cow in Milk or Calf (small farmers)—1 William Blain; 2 John McIntosh; 3 Duncan Menzies. Calf Bred by Exhibitor (small farmers)—1 A. J. Low; 2 John McIntosh; 3 William Blain.

SHEEP

BLACKFACE. — Ram — 1 R. W. Honeyman; 2 I. A. Duncan Millar; 3 Major Read. In-Wintered Shearling—1 Atholl Estates; 2 and 3 I. A. Duncan Millar. Out-Wintered Shearling—1 and 2 I. A. Duncan Millar; 3 D. Scott, Kennacoil. Ram Lamb — 1 and 3 Atholl Estates; 2 I. A. Duncan Millar. Two

Aberfeldy Show

Mr Millar makes it three in a row

For the third year running Mr I. A. Duncan Millar, Remony, dominated the Blackface sheep section at the Atholl and Breadalbane Show at Aberfeldy on Saturday.

But, although it was a successful day for Mr Millar, afternoon torrential rain made it a dismal one for spectators.

A fine, though sunless forenoon helped the attendance to reach about 2500.

The Blackface sheep section was the big event in the show, and Mr Millar won his honours in the face of stiff competition. He made an almost clean sweep of the Blackface special prizes.

His one-crop ewe took the female championship, the home bred championship and the over all championship.

The ewe, by a Chamberwells sire, was female and over all reserve champion at Perth last week. This is the second successive year it has been over all winner at Aberfeldy.

Male champion

The male champion and reserve over all champion was Mr Duncan Millar's four shear ram.

Both the male and female group championships also went to Remony. The reserve groups in each case went to Atholl Estates, Rotmell, Ballinluig.

The reserve male champion was shown by Messrs McKerchar, Orchilmore. It was a two shear ram, Tangy Express, bred at Tangy, Campbeltown, by a Shielbank sire.

The reserve female was a ewe lamb from J. & W. King, Kindrochat. By a Claggan sire it was being shown for the first time.

Honeyman Trophy

It was the turn of the cattle section this year for the Mrs Gertrude C. Honeyman Trophy.

This trophy moves round the various sections annually in the manner of the Royal Highland Society's Queen's Cup.

The winner was the champion in the beef cattle section. For the trophy it was paraded against the champion dairy animal.

The beef champion was a 14-month stot from Miss E. M. Honeyman, Ballechin. A first cross, it was reserve champion in the cross cattle section at Perth last week.

Miss Honeyman's father, Mr R. Wemyss Honeyman, Derculich, showed both the dairy cattle over-all and reserve champions.

His four-year-old Jersey cow Bonnie was champion for the second year running. Home bred, it was sired by Holliesley Kahokas Magician III. The reserve was her half sister, Daisy Bell, a five-year-old.

Mr Donald Lamont, Invervack, was the most successful exhibitor in the Highland pony section.

His four-year-old yellow dun mare, Lady Nancy of Invervack, was over-all champion and home-bred champion. Reserve was a grey mare, Quicksilver VI., from the executors of the late Major F. H. Read, Easter Dunkeld.

Clydesdale

The Clydesdale champion and reserve were both shown by Atholl Estates, Rotmell—who went on to win the Jones Cup for most points over the whole show.

The champion was a nine-year-old mare sired by Muirton Sensation, and reserve was last year's champion, Charlie, a four-year-old gelding by Tarraby Student Prince.

Best home-bred Clydesdale was a two-year-old filly from Mr William Birrell, Balnald. The filly forced Vic, the 21-year-old gelding who has won this prize on countless occasions, into second place. Vic, from Mr George Stewart, Duireaskin, has only missed one Aberfeldy show.

The society's long service awards went this year to Mr John McDiarmid, who until lately was head gamekeeper on Kinnaird Estate and had 44 years service, and Mr R. Menzies, cattle

at Gallin, Glenlyon, for 37 years' service.

There was a record entry in the athletics and cycling events. The three-mile Scottish grass cycling championship went to S. Allan, Dundee Thistle. Second was another Dundee man, L. Wylie, also of Thistle.

The 13-mile road race (running) was won by A. J. Wood, Aberdeen A.A.C., in 1 hr. 11 min. 22 sec.

A new trophy for the athletic team with the most points went to Edinburgh Southern Harriers with 18 points. Runners-up were Dundee Hawkhill Harriers with 11 points.

SHEEP

BLACKFACE.

Ram three-shear and over—1 A. and 1, Duncan Millar, Remony; 2 R. Wemyss Honeyman; 3 late Major F. H. Read. Ram two-shear—1 Messrs McKerchar, Orchilmore; 2 late Major F. H. Reid; 3 Lieut.-Colonel A. M. Lyle, Riemore. One shearling—1 and 3 R. Wemyss Honeyman; 2 Duncan Millar. Ram lamb—1 Lieut.-Colonel A. M. Lyle; 2 Atholl Estates; 3 late Major Read. Two wether lambs—1 Colonel C. B. Sherriff; 2 Colonel F. W. R. Douglas, Turrerich; 3 James Borrie. Ewe in milk without lamb—1 and 2 Duncan Millar; 3 Duncan Millar, Achiamich. Gimmer — 1 and 2 Atholl Estates; 3 Duncan Millar. Ewe lamb—1 J. and W. King, Kindrochet; 2 Duncan Millar; 3 late Major Read. Two ewe lambs—1 Atholl Estates; 2 Duncan Millar; 3 R. Wemyss Honeyman. Sheep with best fleece—1 Messrs McKerchar; 2 Lieut.-Colonel Lyle; 3 Duncan Millar. Leicester and cross section—Ram—1 J. Borrie; 2 W. A. Thomson, Tullochvile; 3 Atholl Estates. Pen of three, cross lambs—1 John Robertson, Newton; 2 James Borrie; 3 A. Campbell, Dull Farm.

PERTH

Sheep

BLACKFACE

Fraser and Company and two years later also became a director of United Auctions formed under the aegis of that doyen of auctioneers, Lovat Fraser. Sadly, he died shortly afterwards and to my considerable surprise I found myself elected chairman of that Company. At that time United Auctions were building a new market at Kildean farm to the west of Stirling to replace Livestock Mart's old and rather squalid market near Stirling railway station and I was able to persuade Lord Clydesmuir to perform the opening ceremony in 1967. That autumn at the annual sale of Blackface rams I bought the champion ram from Glenuig for £1,000, which not surprisingly became known as 'Kildean'. He proved extremely profitable and even before his offspring came to be sold, in 1968 we sold 45 rams at an average price of £75 with a top price of £850 and, next year, had the champion ram at Oban. These were among the highlights of the sheep sales, but there were many disappointments as well with big fluctuations in prices, particularly of rams.

In 1966 I became a member of the governing body of the Hill Farming Research Organisation, always known just as 'the HFRO', where I learned about and was much impressed by the work being done on in-wintering of hill ewes. So much so that when two years later Lois and I went on a salmon fishing trip to Iceland, where virtually all stock have to be housed in winter, I took the time to visit some of their large sheep sheds and to learn their techniques. Armed with all this information, I designed and built at Acharn a large and airy shed, approximately 60 metres long and 29 in width, intended to be able to house, and if necessary lamb, 1,000 ewes, which cost some £8,000 including the pens and fittings.

From experience, we had found that the Acharn hirsel (flock) had the highest death rate and lowest lambing percentage, largely owing to the geographical situation whereby they hefted onto the highest ground but had only a very limited area of low ground for wintering; the in wintering of the hirsel was intended to give the flock a far better start for next year's lambing. In the event, however, we encountered difficulties. Lambing inside was all right, but putting out the ewes with their lambs in the spring was difficult even although they were going onto clean ground. With continuous use of the shed for long periods disease problems were accentuated. Two other unexpected aspects also appeared. The normal death rate of hill ewes from 'natural causes' can be expected to run between 2 and 4 per cent each year mainly in the winter months. Mathematically this poses the probability of some twelve to eighteen deaths during the period the ewes were in the shed. The shepherds didn't like this, nor having to bury carcases pretty regularly, which on the open hill would never have been counted, perhaps not even seen. Further, the reputation of our sheep suffered from public opinion (wrongly), thinking that all our sheep were in-wintered and therefore 'soft'. It took some years for this fear to die out.

After two years of full in-wintering of the Acharn hirsel we gradually evolved a system of only bringing in to the shed the weaker ewes towards the end of the winter period. The shed with its convenient pennage proved a godsend to Remony farming, allowing all the handlings of the sheep to be carried through conveniently and under cover, so avoiding many costly delays due to bad weather during the clippings. In the autumn and winter months wether lambs were brought into the shed for fattening to a good weight and so increasing their value. It continues in use for these purposes and is the centrepiece of our sheep activities.

Many are the stories of the dreadful clearances in the Highlands due to the introduction of sheep, sadly often true. But it has to be remembered that large movements of people from the glens had taken place before the introduction of sheep, primarily due to overpopulation. The economic circumstances made life in the Highlands so unbearably hard that many families voluntarily left to seek a better life in the New World. The sheep came: many are still there and without them today there would be still fewer people living in the Highlands. The subsidy for hill ewes introduced after World War II was as much to keep people in the glens as to provide food and, while recognising the ill-effects of encouraging over-stocking of hill ground, without today's continuing subsidies towards hill farming many glens would be uninhabited or covered with regimented arrays of spruce.

The crux of the sheep problem is the proper control of their numbers in relation to other animals grazing the hill. Heather is the mainstay of viable wildlife of all kinds on many Scottish hills, without which it cannot exist. Sheep, if overstocked, can graze out heather in very few years with that unfortunate result, but proper control of sheep numbers can coincide with good heather and all Nature's wild creatures that depend on it.

On Remony the numbers of sheep have shown small variation for almost a hundred years; it is good to observe that in some areas of open 'green' ground and in felled woodland, heather is slowly increasing, although there has been deterioration towards our western boundaries. While sheep numbers have been kept reasonably constant by man, the same cannot be said for deer numbers, of which more later.

It was just over two hundred years ago that the fourth Earl of Breadalbane found it worth employing gamekeepers to improve the sporting facilities and the rentals from his lands. All along the south side of Loch Tay heather predominates from almost the top of the range of hills with their summits about 1,000 metres above the sea down to the 'head dyke' which marked the division between the open hill and the enclosed farm lands, usually at about the 300 metre contour. Consequently, Remony estate lies in the middle of a considerable extent of territory ideal for grouse, nor has the heather been degraded by excessive grazing. Campbell care had helped in that, by its strict control of sheilings and of the grazing allowed on the hill. It was the attraction of good sport that had led my father first to come to Remony and he followed the practice of enjoying some of the sport himself and of letting part of it, very largely dependent on grouse numbers.

These numbers fluctuated greatly, rising to peaks and then falling drastically to almost zero. There had always been great interest in the causes of these fluctuations but in spite of all the inquiries and research carried out, grouse numbers still continue to fluctuate very much as before, some say in a cycle of perhaps seven to ten years. Remony was fortunate in being on a generally upward trend from 375 birds shot in 1959 to a peak of 1848 in 1974 before falling to zero in 1983. The grouse shooting was generally let in August and early September, bringing in good rents, while the family fitted in such additional days as numbers warranted, the important management factor being the ability to estimate correctly the numbers which could be offered to the tenant in his lease, and then deciding later in the season whether additional numbers should or could be shot. Even with the former decision, the weather could upset all intentions, since driving grouse in October is difficult enough and could be made more so if the grouse had congregated in large packs, making the taking of a worthwhile toll almost impossible.

Not only did the shooting rents greatly help the estate income, but shooting and stalking brought additional money into the neighbourhood by way of the tenants' accommodation and spending, while the beaters, who enjoyed their days on the hill and learned a lot about nature, were well paid for their work. All this encouraged proprietors to make every effort to have good numbers of grouse. In Victorian days keepers had a free hand and were often encouraged to kill every creature they thought might be harmful to grouse and so their livelihood. It was common for each keeper to display a 'rogues gallery' close to their house, hanging on it the carcases of foxes, cats, weasels, hawks of every kind and even eagles – any creature they thought might do harm to the grouse, to prove their keenness and efficiency. This changed only gradually, but however harmful to the environment this practice was, it undoubtedly helped to produce great numbers of grouse in their peak years, and the record bags made during the Victorian and Edwardian eras. Heather management was also important and on Remony we did our best to burn regularly in strips 20 to 30 metres wide to provide fresh young heather, good for both grouse and sheep, while leaving good cover against predation among the longer growth. Open draining of wet patches was also carried out, not only to encourage the heather but also to help provide grit in the upturned furrow. This practice was then heavily subsidised, now much less so because of the somewhat doubtful cost effectivness of the work.

Hill ponies were required to take the guns (and their ladies) up to the hill, but it was always a problem to find competent ponymen, later pony girls, and to have the ponies fit for their work and accustomed to it. Many were the worries as to whether an untried pony girl or pony would ever appear with the lunch!

During the 1939–45 war, Sir Malcolm Stewart, the wealthy ex-chairman of the London Brick Company and his wife, who lived in a charming Elizabethan house near Sandy, in Bedfordshire had shewn much kindness to me as a young Sapper officer helping to maintain Air Force landing grounds in the south. In 1944 while I was at home he briefly visited Remony with his wife and, being a keen sportsman, we had long talks about grouse and deer 'after the war'. It was not until August 1949 that he came again and this time, after careful reconnaissance to find a safe route, I drove him up to the Remony butts in our Land Rover. Then well over eighty years of age, he was delighted to get a right and left out of a covey of grouse during the drive we arranged for him. This was the first time a mechanical horse was used on our hill.

After that, our tractor, bought in 1948, was used with its trailer to take shooting parties up onto the hill, using the old peat road on the Acharn side. By the 1960s many of our tenants had their own Land Rovers and later, Range Rovers, which they naturally wished to use to get them to the butts. It was soon apparent that all powered vehicles left tracks through the heather which were slow to heal, so with good rents in the early seventies a start was made to make hill roads to convenient points by the use of a large bulldozer. Fortunately the roads proved cheap to make, since on scraping off the top layer of soil and vegetation the underlying ground did not usually require added bottoming and with a good driver plus good local knowledge rapid progress resulted in construction costs in the early days as low as 20p per metre of road for considerable stretches. There were snags, too, as when the bulldozer, while working on a known soft patch on the road leading to the Glen Quaich bothy, itself got bogged, requiring the hire of a still larger dozer to pull it out. Additions were made to the roads when shooting rents were good, but it was not until 1991 that the final link in the road going right round the Middle Hill was completed. Much was learned about the techniques of making these roads, drainage being the main problem not only in keeping surface water off the roads but in crossing the numerous small streams and rivulets running down the hillside. Wherever possible fords were used rather than culverts, themselves expensive and requiring haulage to their intended position and even then liable to be blocked by peat or gravel in a flood. Local knowledge was useful in avoiding hazards, in selecting crossing places of burns and of making the best use of gradients and contours, but however built these roads required regular maintainance, itself an additional burden on estate upkeep.

The hill roads proved a real boon to the estate, not only for sportsmen but also for the shepherds when they also were equipped with powered bicycles, or using Land Rovers to get them and their dogs out to the hill on gathering days. Although unsightly when newly constructed, with the help of grass seed the disturbed ground soon became covered by natural vegetation and when well sited the roads left little to ctch the eye. They were however sufficiently visible from the air for the satellite survey cameras to pick them up and to be shown clearly and accurately on modern Ordnance Survey sheets. This gave the impression to some people that, being marked on the map, they must also be public roads. Bad enough to meet walkers coming up the road in the middle of a grouse drive – disastrous in the middle of a stalk. The public have much to learn in their use of the countryside. Another important factor was the ease with which sportsmen could now reach and cover the ground on which they enjoyed their sport. This in turn could result in more game being shot as indeed happened in some places, giving the additional burden on landowners to ensure proper control of the annual cull of game from off their hills. Ultimately, it is this skill in conjunction with land management that produces a habitat where all wild life can flourish, including the predators in reasonable numbers; without it and with uncontrolled culling and the disturbance often associated with uncontrolled access a wilderness can soon grow, to be followed by depopulation of people as well as of wild creatures.

Historically, deer had always been reserved for the sport and enjoyment of kings. In Breadalbane days, deer hunts had been arranged, the deer driven by lines of men into or through narrow places where they could be killed by spears or arrows. Then, when rifles became available and increasingly accurate, they became the major means of culling deer. Stalking, in the modern sense, came into being, to be enjoyed principally by landowners and their sporting tenants.

Alongside the sport, deer had always been a source of food. No matter what legislation was passed there can be no doubt that hungry people living near the hills had always 'taken' a deer for consumption whenever it was easy to do so and that this was the principal reason why deer numbers remained relatively low. Being scarce and little seen except on the high ground it became fashionable and a display of wealth to have a herd of deer kept within a fenced area near the laird's principal dwelling, as was the case at Taymouth. The herd there included a white hind, almost certainly a direct descendent of the one Scandoner was sent to catch for King James in 1622. This herd was dispersed or, rather, escaped through holes on the ring fence no longer maintained, about 1920. The white strain is still evident, especially near the Coire Beith where deer with white faces or white on the lower leg area are occasionally seen and shot.

After that date stalking and the killing of deer in the central Scottish

Highlands was largely a source of income for the large landowners and their sporting tenants, who controlled numbers fairly strictly. After the 1939–45 war gamekeepers and stalkers became fewer and sporting tenancies tended to become short term rather than for a period of years. Deer numbers gradually increased, aided by the un-noticed factor of gradual climatic warming which with less severe winters caused fewer deaths and higher calving rates. The increase in deer numbers was noticed at Remony in 1974–5, and the annual culls were stepped up. It was not however because damage to grazing had been noticed, but rather because of a wish for a more accurate knowledge of actual numbers, that in 1982 Douglas Hutchison suggested that the five neighbouring estates of which Remony was central should come together to pool their knowledge of the number of deer each had culled, and to attempt regularly to census the total numbers. The first census took place in 1984 which showed the total number of deer on the five estates, Ardtalnaig, Auchnafree, Bolfracks, Garrows and Remony as 1,290.

While recovering in Stracathro hospital in 1944 from a gunshot wound in my left leg incurred soon after the Normandy landing, I was required to exercise the leg and did so by working a treadle fret-saw rather than on the more usual fixed bicycle. I used this opportunity to cut out in plywood contour lines enlarged off an ordnance survey sheet in order to construct a relief model of Remony estate, each contour being the thickness of the plywood, finally smoothed over with putty and painted. Many of my fellow-patients were completely puzzled as to what I was doing, and why, but in spite of criticism and the scarcity and difficulty of finding materials, I perservered and the model was duly completed. Now, forty years later, it proved its value when the deer counters, poring over it, could easily identify and agree where each lot of deer had been seen, so helping in the accuracy of the count.

A twice yearly census was continued, together with an annual 'get together' which took place on each of the five estates in turn and which became an important social occasion as well as a serious discussion. In fact, the greatest benefit from these regular meetings has been the increased friendship between all the proprietors and their families and, most important, between the stalkers/keepers, with the acceptance that more hinds required to be culled and great care taken in shooting the older stags with better heads.

To begin with, I acted as clerk to the group, arranging and then editing the census counts ready for each annual discussion and decisions on next season's policy. When my son James took over in 1987 other similar groups were being formed. By 1990 there was such widespread concern regarding excessive deer numbers in some parts of Scotland that the Red Deer Commission was actively advocating the formation of local deer management groups and the organisation of regional groups with representation on a centralised Scottish base.

So grows bureaucracy, but in this bit of Breadalbane the work had already been done by the landowners stepping up their deer cull so effectively that the five estates' count had been pulled back from its maximum of 2,850 in the autumn of 1992 to 1,809 in 1994, with consequent improvement in the quality and the numbers of older stags which helped with potential stalking rents. The culling of large numbers of hinds was an onerous and expensive job, not helped by very low venison prices, but some recognition of this and also of the big fluctuations in grouse numbers was made by the government by the abolition in 1995 of sporting rates, which had been levied by Local Authorities.

Traditionally the deer had been brought off the hill on ponies, usually with deer saddles. On Remony where there were patches of soft ground a light sledge or 'slype' had long been used, which had the advantage of being able to take more than one beast at a time, but always with the problems associated with ponies which have already been mentioned. In 1970 a three-wheeled machine called a Gnat was purchased on which a stalker and the rifle could get up the hill; it could go almost anywhere and could carry more than one beast at a time back off the hill. But it had the unfortunate habit of throwing the chain driving the rear pair of wheels, so now some knowledge of mechanics was required in place of ability with horses, plus an adequate supply of the proper fuel. The Gnat was superseded in 1976 by a Limpet, a small open four-wheeled truck with a fixed back axle driven by a shaft, which was rather more reliable. Limpets were the smallest and cheapest of a considerable range of cross-country vehicles developed at this time, the various types each having their peculiar advantages in certain terrains, but the Limpet proved very adequate on our ground and has continued in use well into the nineties.

So much for the management affecting the hill ground of the estate. Down below the head dyke farming went on after the gradual change from horses to tractors and from growing oats and potatoes to rape and turnips for the sheep and cattle. Perhaps the change to tractors was inevitable, but it was hastened by the difficulty in finding men able and willing to care for and to work the horses which in many ways were more suitable for the small fields and steep ground of hill farms. To go to buy a horse in the market was quite an event. One examined the horses in the stalls, talked to their owners, then watched as they were walked and then trotted up and down the 'ring' which wasn't circular but shaped like a cricket pitch to give the buyers a good chance to see how the horse they fancied moved. It was of course quite possible for a horse to pass all the obvious tests, age, height, conformation, sometimes past experience, but still to prove temperamentally quite unsuitable. At the end of the day and subject to passing the other tests, temperament was everything and here the skill of the purchaser came in and many were the tips given as to how temperament could be judged: by its eye, the way it carried its head, its speed of reaction to any sudden movement or sound and a host of others. Having got the new purchase home, it had to be fed and then tried out in the various tasks to which it might be put before any firm opinion of its worth might be given. With constant feeding, working and care, great friendships often developed between the horseman and his charge and only occasionally the reverse. How different with a tractor. In its choice horse power, tyre grip and the tricks it could perform with its equipment were important, perhaps most of all its reliability and the ease with which it might be repaired locally. And if it wouldn't start after a cold night one could at least vent one's exasperation by kicking it, which couldn't be done to a horse.

John Cameron was one of the last horsemen we had at Achianich in the late fifties and even he sometimes saw the use for a tractor. At that time we grew oats in the small steep fields below Lower Achianich, to be harvested with a binder which John reckoned could be pulled more easily by the tractor. So I was roped in and after a hair-raising descent down from the public road we started off, John on the binder seat operating its controls and me on the tractor. We got on famously for a time, until coming to an extra steep corner, where the binder capsized throwing John off, fortunately clear of it. He was none the worse; we went on and finished the field and when I look at it today I am not surprised when my grandchildren say they don't believe the tale.

Another habit which grew up in the sixties was the use of herbicides to control weeds in crops. In these days it was either MCPA which killed most of the weeds, or MCPB which in theory didn't kill the clover in a grass mixture and only seemed to kill a limited spectrum of the other weeds. The herbicide was sprayed by a wide boom fed from a tank carried on the back of the tractor, and this became one of my jobs because of the calculations required to have the mixture in the tank of the right strength and then to get it onto the ground at the right volume per acre. On the whole it worked fairly well but I have never liked general application of any principle or method when the need might vary. But I enjoyed going round the verges of certain fields using only one side arm of the boom to spray patches of nettles and such spot application was usually very effective provided one escaped the hazard of striking some fixed object hidden in the vegetation with the boom. Much later knapsack sprayers were used for spot application, in my view a much to be preferred system even with the weight of the tank on one's back.

During the 1970s we were frustrated in our efforts to grow foggage crops

for the lambs by the deer coming right down off the hill into these crops,
even in to the turnip pit at the Acharn steading, knocking down holes in
the fences and dykes in their passage. So in 1979 we decided to 'go electric'
and built an electric fence right along the head dyke from Callelochan to
the Bolfracks march. In the main this consisted of one or more live wires
strung onto the top of existing fences, with a 'stand off' wire carried on
short posts parallel to and about a metre away from the fence and about a
metre above ground. In theory any deer seeking to jump the fence would
find this stand off wire just where it would take off for the jump and any
contact with it would give the beast a nasty shock. I believe it is this single
wire which gives 90% of the effectiveness of the fence, but live wires strung
onto a fence do prevent stock rubbing on it and effectively prolong the life
of the fence for several years. An electric fence is cheap to erect and to run,
but being relatively flimsy it must be kept live, otherwise it quickly becomes
damaged, so regular inspection and maintenance is essential. Our fence proved
so effective that it is still being maintained, nor have we ever had other than
a very few odd deer below it and never again in numbers. It has proved
good for the estate and for the sheep, but the deer lost the occasional winter
use of the low ground, which did not prevent the steady increase in their
numbers.

Some buildings surplus to estate requirements were sold. The old meal
mill in Acharn, which I can recollect in its original use in the early 1920s
grinding oats, had been converted to a saw mill, first using the original water
wheel, then with a small diesel engine, since the water wheel lacked power.
In turn we had found it more convenient to use a mobile power saw, which
left the large building much underused, so in 1967 it was sold, with a small
area of ground which had largely been used as a rubbish dump, to Raymond
Morris. Raymond was an Englishman with a peculiar devotion to all things
Scottish. He had come to Remony in 1963 as our forester and had proved
a workaholic in certain things which interested him, for example in laying
out a nursery for young trees far beyond our requirements. The sale seemed
sensible and as intended Raymond set up a small shop, tourist orientated,
where he sold artifacts which he had made with great skill.

He also turned the nearby village rubbish dump into a most beautiful
garden beside the burn and arranged a display of old implements and items
of local interest which he had been given. However, the shop was not well
sited for passing trade and after a few years he sold it, with the ground except
for a few square metres, and the local objects, and moved to a shop in Cupar
but claiming the use after his name of 'of Eddergoll', Eddergoll being the
old place name of that area near Acharn of which he still owned a small
plot. Some years later, and I have no doubt after much hard work, he bought
the ancient castle of Balgonie in Fife and there his main life's work developed

in converting a ruin into an inhabited castle where he and his wife, now Baroness, live with their son, gaining considerable tourist recognition for the restoration carried out with their own hands, including a finely painted ceiling of coats of arms.

The charming cottage Burnbank with its croftland was sold in 1970, then Tighnaldon, originally Gavine Cottage and home for old people until converted to flats for retired estate staff, in 1975. Pine Cottage in Acharn followed in 1976 when it became vacant following the deaths of our retired gamekeeper, Charlie Ross, and his wife. The Gardener's Cottage came next in 1978 in the knowledge of the miniscule price paid for it by my father in the early days because even then it was thought not to have been of very good construction.

Next year the old school and schoolhouse at Acharn was sold, where all our children had had their primary education and which had reverted to the estate when the school moved to Kenmore. This was a big shake-up for the district, the Education Committee quite sensibly deciding that in place of old schools at Acharn and at Fearnan they should be replaced by a single modern school at Kenmore. With knowledge of this impending change, I as the local County Councillor, Rev. Kenneth Macvicar as District Councillor and my wife as Treasurer of the local Holder Hall combined to persuade the Authority to include a public hall facility within the new school. Eventually after many meetings and demonstration of at least one precedent elsewhere, this idea was accepted. A big local effort was made to raise funds, the old corrugated iron built Holder Hall was disposed of and with an agreed and very sizeable contribution towards the cost, the new school was provided with facilities for a badminton court and stage which could double as a hall, plus a purpose-made small kitchen solely for community use. This was of great benefit to the community, who could now hire the hall at a cost very little different to what they paid in the past but without the onus of raising funds each year for maintenance, particularly for the tons of coal required to keep the draughty old hall warm enough to sit in. Now with modern facilities and parking space provided by the Council, it became a benefit also to the scholars who gained a badminton court and a stage for school use. The arrangements for local administration between the community and the Education Authority were laid down but became a puzzle to newly appointed local authority staff when they found special differences applying only to Kenmore which they had not come across elsewhere. A bargain was also struck that children from the area previously served by Acharn school would have the benefit of transport to the school at Kenmore, particularly relevant in the changed conditions of heavy traffic instead of the occasional horse-drawn vehicle on the roads on which earlier generations were required to walk to school.

The house which Geoffrey Fairweather had helped me with in 1946 was sold too, the £19,000 it realised a far cry from its construction cost.

The biggest policy decision made in this period was the successive sale to the Local Authority of blocks of the old houses in Upper Acharn. The first sale was of the top or southernmost block, including the old smithy house, which was demolished and three new brick-built houses on a stone footing replaced them. There followed the block on the east side of the upper square and then much later ground to the east on which more houses were built. At the time we received much criticism from neighbouring landowners for allowing council houses to be built on our land because of the poor regard then held of council tenants. While such a sale did indeed mean lack of control of incoming tenants, it brought very considerable benefits to the estate. Chief of these was the provision of a water and a drainage system which served all the properties on the east side of the Acharn burn and of a local playing field for children. Not least was the fact of having council houses with reasonably low rents near at hand into which, if they took the appropriate steps, estate staff on retiral could expect to move, without the estate having to provide these houses. In 1994 two of the council houses were occupied by retired estate staff, beneficially to them and to the estate who gained from their willingness to carry out casual work which might be available and with their past experience of estate work. By increasing the population too, young people were there, with children at school, who did not find it difficult to get local employment increasingly orientated to the tourist industry, including the various sporting activities on the estate.

The estate was also busy on the other side of the balance sheet. Hendry Smith had two sons seeking work, one an ex-sergeant from the Scots Guards and his brother qualified as a blacksmith. A workshop and garage was purpose built for them in Acharn in 1964, not without an eye on the benefit to the estate from having these facilities on the door-step. It was also thought to be beneficial to have our own private petrol pump, but this proved illusory because of key and book-keeping problems in keeping it secure and later because the petrol companies charged heavily for supplying petrol in the relatively small quantities our tanks could handle and we found we could buy it cheaper in Aberfeldy. But Grant Smith went from strength to strength developing machines for timber extraction and after we had extended the premises for him he bought the workshop and some ground behind it in 1980, becoming a major employer of labour. Then disaster struck in 1991 when with overextended credit and recession in the timber trade his firm went bankrupt. The building and land are now back in the hands of the estate.

The estate houses on the west side of the Acharn burn which we had endeavoured to modernise in 1946–8 later required further attention, the old fashioned bathroom and kitchen facilities of twenty years ago being sadly outdated. Frustratingly, because the houses did have these old fashioned additions, they now did not rank for further modernisation grant, which greatly added to the cost. A new house for the gamekeeper, Lademill Cottage, was built in 1972 and a conversion made of the old keeper's cottage into a game larder and chill, a flat for temporary staff and a gun room in 1976.

Amid all these changes in and around the village of Acharn one continuing feature was the 'Comrade's Hut', the village hall and meeting place situated between Pine Cottage and the Old Mill on the east bank of the Acharn burn.

Unmentioned in any Valuation or Rent roll, this timber framed and corrugated iron clad building followed from a reunion held in Kenmore Hotel for those who had returned from World War I. The meeting was probably encouraged, if not arranged, by the then Marquis of Breadalbane, himself an ex-serving officer and holder of the MC together with the minister, then Rev. Gillies. The idea of a meeting place for those who had survived the war, and others, was well supported locally; the sum of £100 was subscribed by the Church of Scotland's Huts and Canteens Committee and support came from the British Legion. A Mr McLaren, who lived in Acharn, was elected as clerk to the committee to further the work which was carried out by himself and his father, joiner at Acharn, in 1921. The hall was eventually opened by my father, who presented a miniature billiard table and my mother a gramophone. The then Laird, Breadalbane, must have approved the site, but when the estate was sold to my father there was no sign of a lease, nor did my father ever execute a formal lease, although a draft was prepared, but goodwill continued to be extended by the proprietors.

Since then the hut has twice been extended, once to provide for a full length carpet bowls rink and once to give a scullery and washing facility and later a WC. Management continued in the hands of a local committee who raised funds from time to time by whist drives and other entertainments, so that the hall was much used and, because of its entirely local control, much appreciated by the local people.

In 1973 a 50th Anniversary Celebration Party was held, at which Mr McLaren, then aged eighty-nine and living in Blairgowrie, was guest of honour, with his daughter Mrs Mitchell from Stanley and grand-daughter Susan. Jim Moar, then secretary to the Hall Committee, was Master of Ceremonies. Mr McLaren told us that of the ten local men who went to France only five returned, and of these only three remained, a Mr McArthur who had been Road Surveyor and lived in Blair Atholl, Donald Walker in Acharn and himself. The list of those attending the event is in Appendix V.

This party marked the heyday of the Comrade's Hut and was a tremendous evening at which the playing, singing and dancing would have put to shame

many modern BBC entertainments. Robert Jamieson for many years ran a
local Dramatics group which each year put on a play at Kenmore and
elsewhere. The Bowling Club won honours all over Perthshire and other
functions were regularly held. But television and the indoor curling rinks at
Perth and Pitlochry were on the way, powerful disincentives to local entertainment. In spite of that, public-spirited figures, among whom Bessie Macdonald must rank high, continue to put time and effort into maintaining the
Comrade's Hut, which remains in good order and is the recognised Polling
Place for all local and general elections.

A major enterprise was the gutting of the row of old croft houses at right
angles to the public road in Lower Acharn, originally built by Breadalbane
crofters, and their rebuilding for use as six self-catering holiday lodges of
high standard, in 1982–3. This was expensive, but earned a good grant from
the Tourist Board, provisional on the lodges being maintained for holiday
letting for a period of at least ten years.

This was a considered step by the estate to diversify its interests by entry
into the tourist industry. The Acharn Point and adjacent ground offered
good opportunity for caravan development but this was rejected both on
amenity grounds and because of the number of casual strangers it would
bring into the neighbourhood. The maximum of thirty-two persons which
the six lodges provided, the majority resident for a week or more, was
thought to be an acceptable addition to the population of Acharn, having
in mind that many of them would be elsewhere in their cars for some of
the time. Although there is suitable space for further holiday accommodation
nearby, as yet this has not been thought desirable.

About the same period development also started at Croft-na-Caber, mid-
way between Acharn and Kenmore, with self catering and hotel accommodation offering in particular water recreation of all kinds which attracts many
young and active people interested in water sports. The excellent facilities
provided are also enjoyed by some of our Loch Tay Lodges visitors, while
the number of staff required to run the catering as well as the water resource
facilities is considerable.

So, these developments do much to give local employment and bring
many visitors into the area. The question pertinent to all holiday enterprises
is just how many visitors any environment can accept without adverse effects.
In this case, together with the water recreational facilities already available
at Kenmore and elsewhere, there is growing pressure on the use of the water
surface of the east end of Loch Tay and some obvious conflicts of interest,
for example between water skiing and angling or between speedboats and
sailing. There is no doubt that the residents of Lochtayside would prefer the
use of the loch restricted to angling and sailing and dislike the noise of high
powered engines, particularly the intermittent moaning of jet skis. This

striking of a balance of advantage between all the different interests is not easy, but quite apart from the environmental pollution of water and air caused by many powerful engines, the safety aspect arising from uncontrolled use and access gives cause for concern. The provision of bye-laws to control the use of the water surface seems highly desirable but unfortunately there are major difficulties in achieving this end.

After Hugh Fraser's death in 1979 his house at Lower Achianich which was in very poor condition was surplus to our needs and to obtain a good price it was offered for sale together with the farm lands below the public road which had originally formed Lower Achianich farm. This produced a tremendous response; Lois and I personally showed more than thirty applicants over the property which was eventually sold for a price far above our expectations. But we paid the penalty of making an outright sale, because the new owner, after producing ambitious plans for redevelopment, fell upon hard times, was unable to find the money for rebuilding and sadly has left his property unoccupied and unmaintained, to become a disgrace to the neighbourhood.

CHAPTER 21

The Next Generation Takes Over

Lois and I were fortunate in having four children, Caroline born in 1946, James in 1948, Ian in 1951 and Fiona in 1956. The girls before their marriage as well as the boys played their part in the family endeavour of running the farm and estate. No doubt it was because of their early experience of livestock, including our horses, and their mother's help with them, that Caroline is now a leader in her area in the Riding for the Disabled movement, while Fiona has a light-legged horse in her paddock alongside a Shetland cow and her calf.

Bringing up a family brings great joy but also poses many problems. Following on the provision of a good education for our children the thoughts of my wife and myself turned to looking ahead for the best means of making it possible that the estate of Remony should remain in the hands of the family.

Towards this end we took certain steps within the law, which included in 1966 passing one half of the estate to our son James, then eighteen years old, and taking our second son Ian into the partnership of A. and I. Duncan Millar in running the farms.

After leaving school James went through Sandhurst and became an officer in The Black Watch, very much a full time occupation, leaving his father to continue running the estate to the best of his ability. This however now required consultation with James on many matters and his signature on any deed concerning the land or buildings.

It gave us great pleasure when Ian decided to take a degree in Agriculture at Aberdeen University and further approval when he served an apprenticeship with the firm of Renton Finlayson, as it then was, in Aberfeldy and duly qualified as an Associate Member of the Institution of Chartered Surveyors. He also spent six months in New Zealand on a sheep farm and so very soon played an increasingly leading part in the running of the farms. Over the years I had persevered in clipping the sheep using the old fashioned shears or scissors, without great success. Ian arrived on the scene shortly after the introduction of electric power shears in the big sheep shed at Acharn and for a while was treated as a beginner in their use, but he put his mind to mastering them and in a short time was being consulted by the shepherds on the best setting for the blades or on any minor repair.

In 1979 Callum McCallum retired and was replaced by Jimmie Brown, who came from Lanarkshire. This coincided with the growing preference in many quarters for the barer-coated Blackface sheep, much favoured in Lanark and Galloway where rams sold there certainly fetched high prices. Encouraged by Ian the decision was made to change the Remony flock from the woollier Perthshire type to the barer-coated and hopefully better bodied Lanark type. That year Callum and I sold eight of the long-coated rams with which we had been working at the main Perth Ram Sales and averaged £366 each to a top of £1,600, the third best average of the sale. We also took four rams to the Lanark sale where they only averaged £79, which was not surprising as they were not well known there and being longer coated were not so well favoured, but we brought home three sires of the Lanark type for use on the flock. Next year the process was repeated when we spent £600 on a Plenderleith ram.

As every stockman knows, changing the type of beast in any flock or herd is a slow process and so it proved with us. Initially the most obvious effect of the introduction of the barer-coated sires was that many ewes and rams showed areas of barer fleece, a not uncommon thing and referred to in the sheep world as being 'double coated', a distinct blemish for breeding purposes. As a result, both the ewes and the rams we sold went through a disappointing period of slightly lower prices. Both Ian and Jimmie Brown stuck to their guns and continued to buy wisely from the barer flocks, paying particular attention to conformation, and ten years later Remony sheep were beginning to be recognised as being of good conformation among the barer type as well as being hardy.

In the meantime the argument as to which type was preferable continued, with the longer-coated sheep continuing to get some high prices at Perth and Stirling while the barer sheep were predominant at Lanark and Newton Stewart. At the end of the day, since the value of the carcase as the final end product is the governing economic factor, it is up to each breeder to do his best under the conditions of his land, the local climate and his own particular skills in breeding.

Ian, who married Hazel Hunter in 1976, continued to do great work on the Remony farms until 1990, when he took over full ownership and management of Tirinie farm where he had been living for some time and gradually relinquished his direct interest at Remony.

James meantime pursued a successful Army career. In 1974 he was Equerry to Her Majesty Queen Elizabeth the Queen Mother and was rewarded by becoming a Member of the Victorian Order. In 1976 he married Susan Marshall. Promoted to major, he successfully passed through the Staff College and then in 1985 came a nasty shock. Because of his very slight deafness, no doubt due to his proximity to rifles and guns, he was considered no longer fit to serve and had to leave the Army. This was not what anyone had expected, but fortunately there was a place for him at Remony and for almost a year he lived in the largest of our holiday cottages in Acharn while Lois and I designed and built the retirement home which we had not expected to require for some years. Reynock, situated just to the east of the old Remony farmhouse, became our home where we have lived since December 1986 in warmth and comfort, with every facility, yet still part of Remony estate. James, with his wife, son Andrew and daughter Fiona moved into 'the big house' the next year.

Running the estate, in which in theory I now only had a minor interest, was for him very different from Army life, but he gamely started at the bottom with periods of work as tractorman, stockman and assistant shepherd and in a few years was experienced in the work of the farms and of the estate. Meantime, I did my best to retire gracefully and not to criticise the new laird's decisions, which was not easy at first.

Management continued much as before. New plantations were established in Croftmartaig and on Balmacnaughton above the Queen's Drive to the east of the Remony burn. In 1993–4 the whole of the Queen's Drive wood was felled with the consequent mud and chaos associated with timber felling and only a poor return on the capital invested over sixty years before, reduced still further by the cost of fencing and replanting.

After an interregnum with Peter Lambie, Willie Nicol succeeded Jimmie Brown in charge of the sheepstock and although he had come from Dungarthill where he had helped Colonel Dewhurst to reach the top of the long-coated Perthshire type of sheepstocks, he joined with James in pursuing excellence of conformation when buying short-woolled sires and soon had our sheep winning the show championship at Aberfeldy once more. In 1993 we sold 43 rams at Perth, Stirling, Lanark, Dalmaily and Oban at an average price of £240 to a top of £850.

Relieved of most of my own duties, I had time to turn my mind and civil engineering instinct to making a pond at Remony, which I had long wished for. Many years previously I had employed Davie Harkness to dig a trench across the outlet hollow of the marshy area close to the site of the old Alekich farmstead. He dug the trench by hand to discover whether we could find and block the old drains which drained the hollow, but they proved to be so many and so deep that I considered it impossible to make a watertight blockage to hold water in the hollow above.

Now, in 1988, there were available the resources of powerful excavators and relatively cheap plastic watertight materials, so it was possible to dig a trench deep enough to hold an impervious membrane and so ensure there would be no underground escapement of water from the hollow above. The project required some thought, since these very drains were the head source

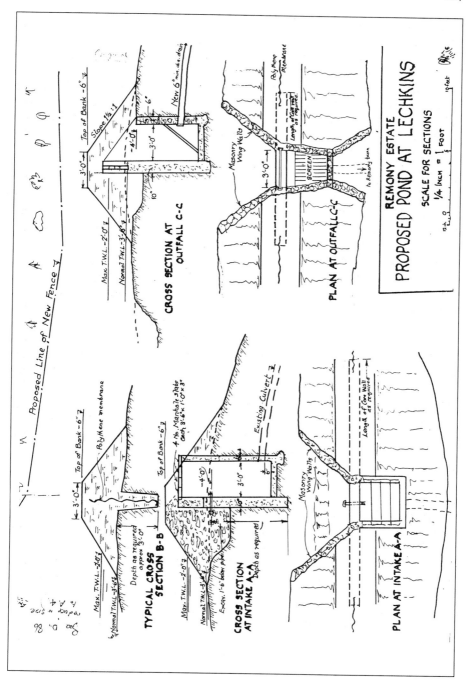

PROPOSED POND AT LECHKINS

REMONY ESTATE

SCALE FOR SECTIONS

¼ INCH = 1 FOOT

CROSS SECTION AT OUTFALL C-C

PLAN AT OUTFALL C-C

TYPICAL CROSS SECTION B-B

CROSS SECTION AT INTAKE A-A

PLAN AT INTAKE A-A

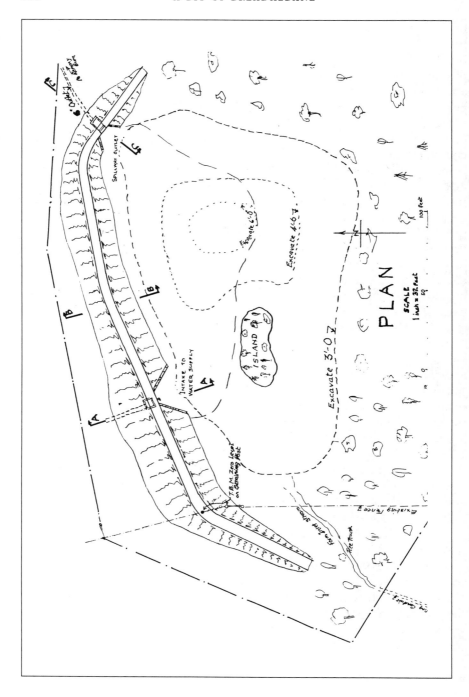

Proposed Pond of Lochkins

of the main water supply for Remony house and outbuildings, while there was very little running water to keep a pond topped up. The first of these problems was solved by building a section of deep concrete wall with a pipe through it fitted with a valve which allowed a controlled flow of water into a chamber at the top of the old drainage system. To supply water to the pond a small water course in the Queen's Drive wood was dammed with a 100 mm pipe through it, allowing water to flow down a channel and conduit to the pond but with a spillway so that all water in excess of that continued in the old channel leading to the Remony burn. A further complication was the fact that the old water supply conduits could not carry a big flow which might come from the pond in time of heavy rainfall or snow melt, so a separate overflow was constructed at the east end of the pond's bank with a concrete sill and side channels for screens or, if desired, splash boards to raise the water level above the sill, over which water could flow into another chamber with a 150 mm diameter pipe leading underground to the Remony burn. So the level of water in the pond can be controlled and also the flow from it into the house water supply system, now reinforced by the pond storage at its head. The old damp hollow was deepened by excavation and an island formed by tipping soil on top of the pile of large stones which we had come across during the excavation.

A plan of the works involved is shown on pages 167 and 168. The work was scheduled and put out to tender, then carried out by John McEwen and his son doing the concrete and manual work, Henry Murdoch and his JCB digging the trench and Robert Runciman with his Hy-Mac doing the main excavation, all between 6 June and the end of that month. After fencing the area around the pond we planted trees and shrubs and some yellow irises, while other water plants colonised the banks and verges of the pond of their own accord. Small brown trout from the Remony burn, caught by grandsons Andrew and Tom, were transferred into the pond; we now have a water resource attracting much wild life but have not as yet used it for curling although stones were carried up and circles scribed on the ice in the winter of 1993 just before a thaw set in.

The final cost was not high. Remony estate had recently been included in what was called an Environmentally Sensitive Area which meant that we were grant-aided in carrying out what was considered to be environmentally friendly work, such as the pond. These ESA schemes were a start of Government assistance to landowners or farmers on the sensible basis that if they carried out works thought to be in the taxpayer's interest, they would get some assistance from the taxpayer. The schemes were voluntary and had to have prior approval and were a change from subsidies paid on livestock, where the same 'green' thinking had led to quotas on eligible livestock to avoid environmental damage through overstocking.

In the course of the work two interesting discoveries were made. While digging for the cut-off trench a large stone slab was uncovered which at first we thought was part of the old drainage system, but which we soon found was in fact part of the cover of an ancient burial cist with stone-built side walls. We dug with trowels most carefully but found nothing except the leg bone of a sheep: our predecessors while carrying out drainage work, probably under progressive Breadalbane direction, had also came across the cist and they, like us, had left the stones as they found them, whatever they may have done with (judging from the size) the single corpse in it.

While excavating the deepest part of the pond to allow swimming and for safe overwintering of fish we came across a layer of dense black peat several feet deep lying below the ground surface. At the bottom of this peat were two baulks of blackened timber, well preserved by the peat. One of these, about 2.2 metres long, was roughly squared to a size of about 170 × 170 mm at its butt end with what appeared to be the marks of stone axes on its side. Its origin is questionable. Being below several feet of peat suggests it must have lain there for many hundreds of years, possibly dating as far back as two thousand years. Was it a beam used in some ancient dwelling house? If so, had the house been destroyed by some enemy and the beam thrown into the pool that was in all probability there, as a final act of destruction? Whatever the facts may have been these finds together with the stone circles and other stones not far away do suggest that there was a considerable population living on these upland slopes in ancient days, possibly when there had been a period of warmer climate; it is also certain that these ancient people of Breadalbane were a hardier lot than their present day successors.

The turbine and generator driven by water from the Acharn burn which my father had so wisely installed in 1925, after running non-stop for all these years, by the 1980s were showing signs of old age and were badly requiring renewal. James and I had many talks about what was best to be done but the cost of replacement was so high and the possible sale price of power to the Hydro Board so low that the only course of action was to keep the plant going just as long as we could, even in the face of the difficulties we were then experiencing in getting replacement parts and equipment to suit the Direct Current system installed at Remony.

Then in 1992 came a break in our favour. Under the Government's privatisation of the electricity industry they had inserted a clause in the acts requiring the generating authorities to accept power at premium rates from outside sources when produced by non fossil fuels. This was a direct result of 'green' pressure and aimed at reducing the emission of carbon dioxide and other gases without requiring further power from nuclear sources. But these acts applied only to the English boards, to the considerable indignation of a number of people in Scotland in the position to sell power to the electricity boards. After much argument and pressure on St. Andrew's House it was eventually accepted that this was contrary to the terms of the Act of Union and only a few weeks later an Order in Council was passed requiring the Scottish boards also to accept non fossil fuel generated power at the premium rate.

James and I rubbed our hands together in glee. After thought and a professional report on the resources we had available, by December 1992 we had up and running a new hydro electric system capable of producing 380 kilowatts, linked directly to the electricity grid, with all its output sold directly to Scottish Hydro Electric plc at the favourable premium rate. Without any ability to store water, power output is very much dependent on 'the run of the river', while the compensation flow required for the benefit of visitors viewing the Acharn falls reduces still further the output at low water flows. The capital cost and the borrowing required were high, but so is the total annual output, with every prospect of the sums borrowed being repaid within a very few years, and thereafter a continuing profit which would allow the estate to employ the extra labour we had always wished to have available to keep fences, drains, roads and buildings in the best state of repair. Having been associated with hydro work all my life I am particularly pleased now to have an estate scheme in working order. By making use of the original intake dam, heightened and with new intake chamber and screens, the whole pipe line being underground and so not visible and with a new turbine house tucked in beside the Acharn burn just upstream of Acharn village, the scheme is just as 'green' as it could be, so that few people are even aware of its existence. Our hope now is that this plant will run as successfully as the one my father installed all these years ago.

CHAPTER 22

Up to Date

Having progressed from Day One up to the present day (1994/5) there is every opportunity to take a broad look at the many changes affecting the land and the people, especially in recent times.

The land

The land, which a thousand years ago was covered by trees, rough scrub and thick vegetation, has been systematically cleared and cultivated in accessible places by the needs of the increasing population to feed themselves.

Since McArthur's survey in 1769 the appearance of the land in this bit of Breadalbane has changed relatively little. The main change has been the increase in the areas of man-planted trees and sometimes of scrub land as the population, which has remained remarkably stable within its limits of fluctuations, has gradually obtained more of its food from outwith its own bounds.

In the long term, the land can only produce a limited quantity of meat, milk or grain. There is little milk or grain produced today in Breadalbane but the supply of meat from sheep and cattle has changed remarkably little in the last two hundred years, the main difference being the more centralised control of large areas of land together with the stock on it. Increased efficiency together with the use of modern veterinary practice and fertilisers has undoubtedly increased unit output, but this has to be balanced against the loss of the exceedingly intimate care taken of all stock in the past, which was often the only source of wealth of the families working the land and to whom the loss of a single cow might mean disaster.

Man's efforts, his need for food, have pushed up the hillside the levels of cultivation or care of the land, leaving an ever smaller area of open hill above, but in this district the 'head dyke' separating the in-bye land from the hill has changed little since McArthur's day. On the open hill the biggest recent increase has been in the number of red deer which, together with the flocks of sheep, has produced pressure and consequent degradation of the natural heather where deer numbers have not been kept in check.

Man controls the environment and the pressures on it, so it is good to see the recent increased interest in the care of the environment and in the taking of only a sustainable output from its resources. This enlightened outlook itself can come under pressure from increased population, largely dwellers in cities or industrial areas, having little knowledge or experience of the complex processes involved in good land management but seeking to enjoy greater access to and use of the open countryside. This poses the major question of the intentions of those who will be in political control of our country, now and in the future.

The people

The evolutionary growth in population, reaching its peak in Beadalbane in the nineteenth century, was stemmed by the hardship of living off the land which forced excess numbers to emigrate either abroad or to the cities in search of a better life. In McArthur's time almost all the people on the farms he so carefully surveyed and listed lived solely off the land. Their tenure of it derived from past clan loyalty or allegiance, later from more formal legal contracts. Until the end of World War II it was taken for granted both by the lairds and their tenants that it was normal for sons to follow their fathers in occupation or control of the land.

The big changes which came after 1918 were closely associated with money, or the lack of it, and the power of money rather than past loyalties to acquire what was desired. As a result, landowners and occupiers changed more rapidly, each requiring time to learn and absorb the knowledge of sustainable systems of management, which teaches the undoubted lesson that frequent changes seldom lead to the best land management.

In the twentieth century the old established system of landlord and tenant came under pressure as more and more land was taken in hand by owners, provoked by legislation which meant that land once let on a regular tenancy could not easily be reoccupied by the owner, should he so desire. The optimum system for the land is one which combines intimate knowledge with sustainable use; for the people, the security of living without fear of sudden eviction and of benefiting directly from their efforts. Good relationships and a sound legal framework are the keys to these matters but there is still an important place for tenants living on and working the land, particularly when the owner may be a company or public body, or may have other primary interests elsewhere.

Remony Estate

Consideration must also be given to the 'Profit and Loss' account, the land and houses with their occupiers, of the estate in recent years.

As far as land surface area is concerned the sale of Callelochan farm land to the Forestry Commission in 1960 and later the sale of land at Lower Achianich totalled approximately 138 hectares of steep and unproductive land, while Remony Farm land which includes Balmacnaughton and the Target Wood extends to approximately 144 hectares of very much superior farming land. Allowing for the various small plots of land sold with houses and for building, there is a small credit balance in areas bought and sold, with a material betterment in land values apart from the convenience and amenity of including Remony Farm within Remony Estate.

Appendix III shows that in the period between 1930 and 1994 the estate sold into private hands fifteen houses of which five remain in whole time occupation, also eleven poorly built croft houses in Upper Acharn to the Local Authority who replaced them with nineteen new council houses as well as providing water and drainage systems for the eastern half of the village.

The estate built four completely new houses as well as reconditioning and modernising twenty-three houses, often after virtually complete gutting of the old shell. Five other new houses were built by other individuals, four after sale of plots of land to them.

By 1994 there were sixty-five habitations with all services of water, drainage, electricity (and television!) on the estate with a permanent resident population of 110 souls, rising to approximately 190 when all the holiday accommodation is occupied. This is probably a greater number of people than in the days of the last of the Breadalbanes, and certainly living in a very different standard of comfort and convenience.

Of the 110 residents, there are approximately twenty retired people, fifteen adults and children directly associated with the estate, twenty other children under the age of eighteen and the remainder in various other forms of local employment in which the tourist industry plays a big part. There is virtually no unemployment.

An interesting feature of recent times has been the increasingly rapid rate of change in the local population which has made me by far and away the person who has lived longest in the neighbourhood, with only a handful of others with more than forty years of life in, or associated with, the area.

All the changes above have come about relatively gradually, the greatest rate of change being in the value of money and its relationship to land, building and wages. The last leads the field in the rate of escalation, with a multiplication factor of almost × 20 between 1961 and 1994. There are variations in the rate of change in value in all categories, also differences between areas of Scotland, so that it is difficult to generalise. What is clear, however, is that the work of administration, with all the legal restrictions and orders now in force, together with the huge complexity of agricultural regulation, has increased out of all recognition. While values and sums of money to be handled have soared astronomically, the profit, if any, from the land has lagged far behind.

But by widening and diversifying the estate interests with direct control of them, I believe the land, the buildings, the farming and the people are all in as good if not better condition than when the Duncan Millar family first took over.

CHAPTER 23

Looking Ahead

It was Robert Burns who wrote 'an' forward tho' I canna see, I guess an' fear.' Like Burns, I cannot see far ahead and can only guess, but my fears are limited. In no way would I refer to a 'backward look' at this bit of Breadalbane, as 'prospects drear'.

It has taken a long time to reach the present situation, which in spite of some worrying features affecting society, finds much of the land in good heart, playing its part in sustaining people and welcoming visitors.

I have made clear my own interest in the land and my belief that continuity of its control is desirable. Control is not the same thing as occupation; even owner-occupiers cannot wholly control the land, but must also obey the law. And that is where my greatest fear for the future lies, since in our society laws are made by the politicians, democratically elected. *Demos*, the people, are unfortunately mainly town dwellers, with only a very small proportion living in or with any experience of the countryside. So their actions, even when taken with the best of intentions, ask the question 'for whose benefit?' – for the land, the people living on it or for the massive majority of town dwellers?

The last have in fact of recent years shown increasing awareness of the need for conserving the land of this country as the primary source of food, timber and certain minerals, of energy and for recreation, but they and those whom they elect are inevitably swayed by the most immediate considerations. For example, in the demand for increased agricultural production following the food shortages of World War II, the incentives then given have long been put in reverse, while in today's hopeful theme of beating swords into ploughshares questions of economics and of unemployment can put the cart before the horse in local situations.

The complexity of modern legislation as it affects the land and its users would have seemed unbearable to the Breadalbanes and a totally unacceptable imposition on their rights. Today, Town and Country Planning is taken for granted and I for one believe that in spite of its faults, the various Planning Acts have done more good than harm, although some of those who administer the law may be subject to criticism. Other Acts govern housing, employment and wages, while the minutiae of those concerned with farming occupy volumes. Through all this tangle those working the land today or seeking to improve it must struggle in order to achieve their objectives.

Now becomes apparent a major difficulty. Laws tend to apply to everyone, but our land surface has a multitude of different characteristics, geological, of altitude, soil types and mini-climates with large variations often in juxtaposition. The difficulty of framing laws to deal with all land is immense and can only become manageable by having a host of exceptions or of categories, the 'small print' so often of major importance at the bottom of any modern contract or bargain. Which leads me to the unshakeable belief that there are few laws or regulations affecting land use that can or should be applied universally, but to the acceptance of the principle that different conditions and places must receive different treatment.

An example of this thinking can be given by considering the important question of access to the countryside, with the difficulties even of defining what is the countryside in its progressive stages from front garden to mountain top. So far, this quesion has been handled, or sometimes not handled, remarkably well except by a few hot-heads, with the result that most people can go where they want to go with little or no hindrance. The law dealing with the control of land must deal with this question and I believe that in Scotland the answer cannot lie with any universal dictum but rather by making provision for the various viewpoints. It therefore seems that there is a good case for establishing several large areas of nationally owned land, National Parks, where everyone has the right to go where they wish, although even there *Demos* may find the need for some restrictions. Conversely, other areas of land linked with agriculture or sport and associated with the provision of employment particularly in remote areas, deserve recognition that at certain seasons and in some places it is necessary to prevent unauthorised access. There are already designated Areas of Great Landscape Value and Environmentally Sensitive Areas where special conditions and incentives are in force; there does not seem great difficulty in adding the two other categories described above.

There are already excellent provisions for walkers by the West Highland Way, the Southern Upland Way and in England the Pennine Way. These, together with recognised rights of way, through the Corrieyairack and the Lairig Ghru passes for example, along with many others, are widely known and used. No one can overcome the natural human desire to reach the top of any mountain summit, so provision must be made for this by recognisable footpaths to these and to other prominent features, but this need not mean access to them by any route climbers might happen to fancy, unless in the designated National Parks. Rock climbers of course like interesting and difficult climbs. Cannot climbing or mountaineering clubs get together to buy or rent mountain areas which particularly attract them for their own use, just as sporting syndicates buy or rent land for their sport? Similarly, why should not major cities or centres of population take powers to acquire by purchase or lease the undisputed rights to control a park or estate as the 'lungs' for their citizens?

Happily there are signs that we are moving in the right direction. Access agreements can be and are being made between local authorities and landowners, such as exists between Perth and Kinross District Council and Remony Estate, to the mutual benefit of both parties. In this case the public gain undisputed right to the beautiful and romantic Falls of Acharn with the added attraction of a purpose built viewing platform spanning the fantastic gorge above, constructed for the Local Authority by the officers and men of the 202 Field Squadron RE(V) as an interesting and useful summer camp exercise. The estate benefits from quietly signposted and maintained paths and the third party insurance cover of those using them. There is scope for a greater number of such agreements. Fundamentally, one cannot say: 'Thou shalt not' everywhere; rather: 'Here you can, but there only by complying with the land's requirements.'

Turning now to the individual control of smaller units or estates, it must be recognised that not everyone feels the desire or has the time or money to care for the land in the same way or as fully as it may deserve. Economic profitability must weigh heavily, which should be recognised and accepted by the public unless the Powers that Be can be persuaded to subsidise the area to achieve their particular desire.

It may be said that the procedures outlined above will result in a patchwork, but is not that exactly what exists at present and what nature presents to us? The deep cleft and savage hills of Glen Coe lie adjacent to the flat Moor of Rannoch, largely covered with water, the unmistakeable high rugged tops of the Cuillins in Skye are fortunately not far from the flat camping ground at Sligachan, while here in Breadalbane the steep and narrow entrance to Glen Lyon with the road clinging precariously to the rock face is close to the smiling and flat arable fields in the valley below. Such existing contrasts would not be greatly altered, if at all, by increased acceptance of areas set aside for particular end purposes. Whatever the sizes of the pieces of the patchwork, two factors are essential. Firstly, that consideration should be given to the well being of the people living in or near to the patch, and secondly that its controller, or his depute, should live on the patch and be directly answerable for his surroundings.

Unknown, too, in the future is how the argument between sport and conservation will develop. There is no doubt that blood sports involve some cruelty, but cruelty exists for all living creatures; nature's whole chain of life depends just on who eats whom. To see predators, be they lions or lizards, catching and eating their prey alive is prime viewing for many anti-blood sports television watchers, but it must at least be arguable whether it is preferable to end life in this way or by the sudden deaths involved in shooting. In nature, the predator gains food for himself and his family by his killing; in sport connected with grouse, pheasants, deer or fish the food element is only a minor one. But much betterment comes to an area where sport is enjoyed from all the expenses sportsmen are willing to meet in order to enjoy their sport, and this factor must be taken into account.

If one chooses to stop all blood sports it follows that death from natural causes is deemed the preferable alternative, whether it may be by being eaten alive or dying by accident or old age. To country people who see such deaths, they are not pretty and invariably slow. Townspeople just don't see them.

A far more powerful argument in favour of blood sports is the fact that those engaged in them are the principal preservers of their prey and of the environment in which their prey lives, if only for their own selfish ends. Without the huge sums made available in recent years by salmon fishermen, for example, for river improvement and control and for the buying off of netting rights, there can be no doubt that without this effort, and salmon being subject only to commercial forces and uncontrolled access, the Atlantic salmon would be on the verge of extinction.

In the case of deer, man having eliminated nature's only predators of them, their numbers are bound to increase, unless culled, with the consequent degradation of hill ground, of trees and ultimately of arable ground. Is it then better for the culling to be done by the state employing paid cullers, or by experienced stalkers knowing their ground and the deer on it, supported by those who enjoy the sport and who are willing to contribute towards it? Or can the anti-cruelty believers honestly prefer the more truly ecological idea that wolves should be reintroduced to control the deer numbers – by catching and eating the youngest and the oldest members of the herd as their easiest prey? Not to speak of all the other creatures wolves would prey on and the necessity to fence them in to the chosen habitat. Is there a similarity here to the ancient ploy of throwing Christians to the lions? To my mind the answer in favour of sport seems clear, because of the preponderance of its good as against its bad points.

There are many other complex questions unanswered as yet regarding the future, of which the unrestricted growth of the human population is probably the most important. It would seem that this question is at last being addressed, but an acceptable solution is not yet in sight. We in Scotland are fortunate to live on an island and still more fortunate if we happen to live in Breadalbane; it is up to us to maintain this situation as I believe we will. This does not mean that we should start building walls or other forms of protection around ourselves, but simply that while accepting the principle of being good neighbours, we should not pay too much attention when our neighbours start telling us how to run our own affairs.

Society itself is changing increasingly rapidly. Here the problems of vandalism, drug abuse and perverted sex must not blind our eyes to the enormous wellbeing of European society today and the encouraging trends to try to spread this wellbeing to the less fortunate. There was no vandalism or drugs-problem in my young days, but I remember children in Acharn running about barefoot, living in houses which today would be condemned. Are they better or worse off now? Clearly, far better physically, but yesterday's children did not have the constant drip of today's television, where the occasional brilliant programmes are surrounded by others in which bad language, sex and violence are the norm, quite apart from the easy availability and even pressure to acquire still more perverted viewing of indecency and bestiality. In 'The Good Book' it is written 'whatsoever things are true, honest, just, pure, lovely, whatsoever things are of good report; if there be any virtue and if there be any praise, think on these things.' When the opposite becomes commonplace daily viewing, should one be surprised at the consequences? There is no doubt that the increase in crime and in vandalism appears to have coincided with the diminishing influence of the Church in our lives and certainly in the number of people regularly attending church services. Churches of all denominations must cease to emphasise their differences and learn to gain support not only by singing hymns and listening to sermons. The Christian faith will not die, but it could be greatly revived by another Columba.

In the global sphere there have been fears of the effects of global warming – or cooling – and possible disastrous results. I have no doubt such changes will occur, as they have in the past, but so slowly that mankind will adjust to them gradually with minimum ill effect. There is of course always the possibility of a major catastrophe, but I doubt whether a nuclear holocaust, an unknown disease or even starvation would ever eliminate mankind, who are remarkably good survivors. There remains the possibility of a body from space colliding with planet Earth. This, too has happened many times in the past, but within the scope of our present knowledge the risk of a major collision seems considerably less than the possibility of man's spark of divinity enabling him to expand beyond planet Earth and to populate at least part of the universe.

I for one am well content with the land on which I live, but know well that while the land can exist without people, people cannot exist without the land, and so must ever strive to achieve the environment which they desire.

Those I Remember

Memory is a strange gift – some have it, some have not. It is also very personal, which excuses the use above of the first person singular. I can only describe my own memory as having many gaps but also of clear recollections, particularly in the more distant past. In the following pages I have set down some glimpses from my memories of people I have known. They may be biased or even incorrect, which is my fault; the omission of any name is no mark of disrespect.

The Marchioness of Breadalbane born Alma Imogen, youngest daughter of the 4th Duke of Montrose. Living through the summer months in the rather sparsely furnished Remony Lodge, for a ten-year-old boy to be called indoors and brushed up could only be called a bore. Lady Breadalbane was coming to call, no doubt in her capacity of Trustee soon after her husband's death, to have a look at the shooting tenant at Remony, where the estate was up for sale and perhaps some hint had escaped that my father could be a possible purchaser. She was an elderly lady, dressed in black and not very tall, but seemed kindly. Thankfully she soon became engaged in conversation with my mother and father, giving my sister and me the opportunity to escape. I little knew of her love and experience of the hills, or of her being the author of what later became a favourite book, *The High Tops of the Black Mount*, relating her many happy days at Blackmount on Loch Tulla. When next year we came again to Remony, she was gone.

There were sudden changes at Taymouth in the early 1920s. The seventh Earl died in 1922, leaving his widow whom I met so briefly to deal with his estate along with other Trustees. He was succeeded as eighth Earl by his nephew Iain Edward Herbert Campbell, who only lived to attend his uncle's funeral and then himself died, to be followed without dispute as ninth Earl by Charles William Campbell, descended from the earlier unsuccessful appellant for the Breadalbane title and estates in 1872 and a very distant relative.

Taymouth Castle was sold, and those living in it dispersed with little trace. The Breadalbanes had had their own private chaplain at Taymouth, an eccentric churchman in the habit of running barefoot round the district clad in little more than an ancient kilt – an early 'keep fit' enthusiast? I had met him thus more than once and been scared out of my wits, but I believe Mr Brandford was a kindly man.

After the break-up, **the ninth Earl** lived at Auchmore at the west end of Loch Tay. He took an active part in national and local affairs following a distinguished Army career, being both a Scottish Representative Peer and County Councillor for the parish of Kenmore. There must have been contact between the Duncan Millars at Remony and the Breadalbanes at Auchmore, possibly through mutual shooting friends, because I remember my sister, then sweet seventeen, being invited to dances at Auchmore somewhat to the concern of our parents. About that time also arrangements were made for me to have a day's fishing on Loch Breaclaich. I duly called at Auchmore and was escorted up to the loch by Hugo Nicholson, Lady Breadalbane's son by her first husband, a long uphill walk of which we made light work, but the loch only produced a single trout.

Many years later, on my return from the war, Dr Gillies persuaded me to stand as County Councillor in the December 1945 elections, saying that the sitting member, Lord Breadalbane, would not be standing. Whether or not that was correct, I was duly returned, unopposed. Quite possibly Lord Breadalbane had never been opposed either, but he evidently took a poor view of my candidature as a few days later, after stopping to have a look, he pointedly refused to give me a lift when he passed me in his car, walking up the glen road to Boreland where we both had been invited to shoot. I had left my car at the road end after the excuse of a business meeting with the factor, Mr Skelton, at Killin, not wishing as the very new councillor to be charged with any improper use of the scarce and tightly rationed petrol which left little manoeuvre for recreation. When we met a few minutes later as the guests gathered and were introduced by our host, Ronnie Stroyan, he was coldly polite.

About that time Lord Breadalbane's son, **John Romer Campbell, Lord Glenorchy**, was doing some work with the Forestry Commission not far away, so Lois and I asked him to Remony more than once, feeling that he was badly treated because of his slight impediment. We got on well with a polite, good looking young man, but he later moved away. He served some time in the Black Watch but never married and was reduced to many trivial jobs. In 1994, impoverished, he was living in London but still had a seat in the House of Lords.

Miss Brownlie: Catherine Mar Brownlie came to the Duncan Millar family while they lived in Edinburgh after World War I. My mother, as wife of an MP, had many social and travel obligations and employed a nurse to help in the care of the two children, me especially, being the younger.

Miss Brownlie had trained as a Norland Nurse and was interested in music as well as in children; she very soon became an indispensable member of the family, caring for all of us in our various indispositions. I particularly remember her taking me for trips across the Forth on the ferry boat from

Granton in theory to escape the pollen-laden air over the land when severe hay fever almost prostrated me during the summer. The sea trips were certainly fun and a welcome break from routine.

As soon as the family came to Remony, she it was who accompanied me up the burn to fish, until my link with Duncan McArthur made that no longer necessary. By the time my father died in 1932 Miss Brownlie had developed a deep feeling for my mother and remained as a companion to her, my sister and I being away from home for long periods during our youth. My mother suffered a severe stroke a few years later and it was with the help of Miss Brownlie's loving care that after being unable to walk or talk my mother made an almost complete recovery, waving goodbye to me from the platform of Stirling railway station when I was posted to the Middle East in 1941. Coming home to Remony after long periods at school, university, then work, she was always there to share in the welcome. When my mother died in 1943 the family Trustees asked her to stay on and keep Remony 'warm' for my hoped-for return. When that came in 1945 there she was to welcome and support me in my sadness.

My marriage came only a few weeks later, but Remony was a 'firm base' for my electioneering and my marriage and later was kept warm while my wife and I were away in London. As is recounted, one of the first decisions we made regarding the estate was to build two new houses. Miss Brownlie was the first to occupy one of them, Tighanlaggan, where she lived, still maintaining her strong interest in the family and the community, until her death in 1952. Remony owes a lot to her love and care of our home and deep interest in all our doings. The wall built across the north end of the Remony garden was the result of the legacy left to me on her death.

Helpers with Sport at Remony

As the son of the sporting tenant and now owner of Remony estate, I was natually keen on shooting. To begin with my father used to take me out with a .22 rifle with a silencer to shoot rabbits and taught me how to move quietly and to take careful aim so as not to wound the rabbit. They were exciting and wonderful outings for a schoolboy, a great improvement on only being allowed to walk with the guns when shooting grouse or partridges, even though armed with a catapult.

Donald Stewart was head keeper in the late twenties, a tall aquiline figure with sandy hair who lived with his striking looking white-haired wife, of whom I was rather afraid, in the then keeper's house, now the game larder with staff flat above. I was quite good with my catapult; on one occasion while walking with the guns near the summit of the Black Rock, where there were immense numbers of blue hares, I had succeeded in knocking over several hares with direct hits from the chuckie stones of my catapult, but they all ran off, none the worse. 'Hit them harrder, Mr Alastair, hit them harrder,' shouted Donald down the line to me. I couldn't, but next year with a stronger catapult and larger marble size stones I learned that if I could get really close to a hare lying in its form (as brown hares in particular often did) and hit them in the head, I could kill them, to my great triumph. How bloodthirsty!

Johnny Reid was underkeeper when I graduated to being able to shoot and stalk. It was he who accompanied me as stalker when I shot the big stag whose head is now mounted in Remony, as described in *A Countryman's Cog*. Supple and dark haired, Johnny was brother to Bessie Reid, later Bessie Macdonald, of whom more later. At that time the Reid family lived in a cottage below the public road just west of the Callelochan quarry. It was burned down while the Reids were there and is now a ruin.

Joe Elliot was the son of the headkeeper who succeeded Donald Stewart, and served with us for some years before moving to Drumour where he was head keeper for a long period. After retiring from that post he acted as head ghillie to the Fotheringhams at Murthly, where his good humour and kindly skills on the river enlightened many a dour day's fishing. Lois and I attended his funeral at Birnam where he had been living, along with a great number of mourners, a tribute to his high standing in the community. Joe was a good shot, a good companion and did fine work with Johnny Turner. One snowy winter we tried to teach him and Johnny how to ski, hoping it might help them to get across country in winter. The Greenlands made ideal nursery slopes, but not surprisingly they found it very difficult, not aided by the long and narrow skis then in use, inefficiently fixed onto old boots.

Johnny Turner to begin with had Joe Elliot to help him, and then a long spell of working single-handed. He took everything in his stride, quietly and efficiently, organising guns and beaters, keeping them all happy. Lady Auckland at Cromlix used to run trials of sporting dogs especially for the benefit of keepers, and Johnny, although little used to such things, usually came away with a prize – on one occasion for having the best excuse! Johnny lived with his wife in the same house as before and worked away at all the different tasks throughout the year with quiet efficiency. While he was being lowered in his coffin into his grave at Kenmore the wild geese flew honking their tribute overhead, joining with that of his many friends standing below.

Being warned of Johnny's retiral, we looked for a young man to replace him and struck gold when **Angus Hogg** came to join us. He is still with us and a whole generation of sportsmen have learned to respect and admire his ability, knowledge and invariable willingness to help on every occasion.

Johnny and some courses in his early days gave a sound foundation for the fund of knowledge and experience he has since acquired. His skill as a sheep clipper, learned from his early shepherding experience at Comrie, put him in the top class, further helped with the advent of power shears. There were few experts who came to help at the clippings who could take off a fleece cleaner or quicker than Angus, timed in seconds rather than minutes. I often noticed the sweat flowing from the faces of those competing, although they would never have admitted it, as to who was the fastest. Like Johnny, Angus is good with guns and beaters and is also a master at all work in connection with deer, being quite an exceptional shot with a rifle, turned to good effect in his war against foxes. As the deer numbers increased he played a full part in the expert but onerous work of culling sufficient hinds, and later in organising and taking part in the twice yearly census of deer, acknowledged by all his peers as the expert. He is also a talented musician, able to accompany any singer or player with his accordion purely by ear, or to play any air, making him much in demand at any social occasion. He is good at handling dogs and has won fame as a breeder of spaniels. We were delighted when he received his long service medal for twenty-seven years' service from the Duke of Atholl at the Scone Game Fair in 1993.

It was my love of fishing which first led me into contact which developed into a close relationship with **Duncan McArthur**, a short stockily built man with well bowed legs and very strong. My first trout at Remony was caught in the Remony burn just above what is now the ford between the Long Park and the Sixteen Acre, accompanied by my mother and aged about nine. I must have pestered everyone to 'go up the burn' and McArthur, Dochy to all his contemporaries and Carthy to me as a child, was a kindred spirit to whom his official task as gardener at The Lodge was perhaps not the most congenial after his varied career as mate on the *Sybilla*, crack shot in the volunteer force and several other more attractive jobs. Originally he must have been politely asked by my mother if he would help her by accompanying me up the burn to fish, but soon it was I who was clamouring to 'go with Carthy', which no doubt got me from under the family feet for considerable periods. First of all, worms had to be dug; McArthur as gardener knew just where the best could be found. He had plenty of small round tobacco tins with holes for air punched through the lids and when the tin was well filled we would set out with my little greenheart rod. It didn't take long for me to know all the best pools in the Remony burn, to know just what water conditions were best for fishing, after a spate when the water was still brown but running clear. Then we got on to exploring the Acharn burn, first in the easy places, then in the deep gorges and below the falls, with much climbing up and down and a few wettings. As I grew older we went on longer expeditions, to the upper reaches of the burns and on some red letter days for a whole day's expedition to fish up the Acharn burn, calling to take a few from the Bothy and the Civeac burns in passing, then a walk over the shoulder to the Coire Quaich burn, down it to the Quaich proper and then up the march and over the watershed to the head of the Remony burn and finally down it for home. Before being trusted with a sixteen bore shotgun we had done this more than once, with a record catch of just over a hundred trout. They were small, but made good eating and were beautifully coloured, real 'Highland Brownies'. Once, when quite unusually my sister was accompanying us up the Remony burn, she caught a trout bigger than any of mine and showed it to McArthur with pride. 'Yes,' he said, 'it is indeed just the largest, but,' taking a trout at random from my fishing basket, 'have you ever seen a bonnier one than that?'

McArthur lived in a ground floor house in the Manufactory block in Acharn, sleeping in a box bed let in to the side of the room and cared for by his sister. He also had a brother; they both suffered from being unable to take any form of alcohol without transformation from being quiet polite men into loudspoken ungainly customers. In his *Sybilla* days McArthur had a bicycle to travel from Acharn to Kenmore, until one day, having partaken too well at the Inn at Kenmore, the bicycle threw him off on the descent from the square. This was unacceptable; the bicycle was retrieved from the ditch, taken to the pier where the steamboats lay and cast into the loch, where it still lies, rusting. McArthur was a great smoker of black tobacco stuffed into an ancient pipe, a habit perhaps learned to repel the midges, when with the faithful garron Jess he had had long waits on the hill. On our good days up the burn when his job was to catch and unhook the trout I unceremoniously yanked out of the water, he would complain that I didn't even give him time to light his pipe. We remained the firmest of friends. When I motored home from Cambridge with my very first car in 1935, a Swift by name but not by nature, bought for ten pounds, its first outing after I got to Remony was a trip to Kenmore and back with McArthur. 'The finest car I ever travelled in,' he exclaimed. When he died a few years later, by then living alone in his den in Acharn with a small estate pension, there was no trace of any papers or cash, until a bundle of very soiled notes was found in the heel of one of his boots – his bank.

Workers of the Land

There had been few changes in the tenancies of the estate farms in my mother's day and when I came home to take full charge of the estate in 1951 I soon got to know my fellow sheep farmers. In these days, all the sheep clippings were done by hand, some clippers choosing to sit astride wooden stools, others bending over their sheep held on the ground, but it was a slow process and everyone possible was called in to help. The farmers each came to their neighbour's clipping, where the women folk were expected to, and did, provide refreshment: tea and buns for elevenses, then filled baps for lunch with more tea, beer or lemonade in between, and tea and biscuits in the afternoon. Our Mid Hill and Acharn sheep were both clipped in the old fank above Acharn, almost level with the Hermit's Cave, and the ladies toiled up the hill from Acharn with heavy baskets and kettles to keep the clippers going, usually a squad of twelve to fifteen. The home shepherds first gathered and brought down the sheep off the hill after an early start; they required their 'breakfast' and had earned it. The sheep were run through the shedder into their different categories and the clipping could then start. It was a great social occasion, with much wise-cracking, telling of tales and pulling of legs amid very hard work.

Tom Pringle was the tenant of Callelochan until 1960, a small dark man who had previously lived near Edzell but found life hard on this difficult farm. He joined cheerfully with his neighbours at the clippings until retiring.

Jimmie Sutherland farmed Lurglomand, a lugubrious man of middle height who often seemed to be in trouble of one sort or another. Like Tom Pringle, he didn't find life easy, but his small round wife fed us well at his clippings, with a smile. The clipping was done in the now abandoned fank above the beech wood at Lurglomand.

At Upper Achainich **the Macdonald family** had been longstanding tenants until retiring in the late twenties for McSwan to take over, who gave up in 1948 when I took over the farm and stock. The Macdonalds were a large family. John, the eldest of the brothers, moved to live in so-called retirement at Burnbank after working for some years as commonty shepherd on the Acharn hill. He invariably attended all the clippings with a good knowledge of all the sheep, always with words of wisdom. He chided me when I came to live at Remony with Lois, saying we ought to have enlarged the house at Tomgarrow, 'with the finest view in the county'. His brother Duncan lived for a while in the Smithy House in Upper Acharn and also helped with the sheep. He was a keen fisherman and used to take out the Remony boat alone in the cold spring weather to troll for salmon, often in difficult conditions. Christie married Bessie Reid and went to farm Portbane where they both toiled for many years until coming to live at Lonnaguy with their son Peter. Another brother ran a hotel at Pitlochry with considerable success. They were an outstanding family of fine country men, learned not only in country affairs but also in all that went on in broader spheres, full of wisdom.

Hugh Fraser had come from Ardradnaig to the west to take up the tenancy of Lower Achianich in the 1930s and lived with his kindly sister

Lizzie in the two up two down corrugated-iron roofed house which had
the last remaining 'cruck' roof of the district in its scullery. The cruck was
a piece of naturally shaped timber to support the roof, an important belonging
which in older times a crofter would have taken with him if obliged to
move to another house. When I took over the upper farm, Hugh gave up
his tenancy of Lower Achianich and became grieve for the combined farms.
Unmarried, well built, always with a twinkle in his eye, Hugh was a
tremendous character as well as being a splendid stockman and farmer of the
old school. More accustomed to horses rather than tractors, he was a stickler
for making good hay, not easy from the small steep fields he was used to,
and for having plenty of it. I have just come across a pencilled note from
my secretary scribbled many years ago: 'Hugh says he is out of hay, and
what are you going to do about it?' I must have done something, for we
remained good friends to the end. In 1969, at the party to mark the coming
of age of my son James, held high above Acharn on the Queen's Drive, it
was Hugh who presented a fine crook among the gifts from the staff to
James, making a most witty speech in which he said that as he had come
to Remony the same year as James, he had had a good chance to get to
know him! He was a good actor and took leading parts in local dramatics
in the 1950s, much encouraged by Robert Jamieson from Croftmartaig.

Lower Lurglomand had been occupied by an irascible old man called
John McNicholl, short of both stature and of temper. We were rather afraid
of him, but he died in the 1930s leaving his daughter **Maggie** with a fine
cow and not much else, to work the croft. She stuck it for a long time,
but in 1952 gave up and went to work at the Manse for Kenneth and Isobel
McVicar, to become their longstanding friend and mainstay for many a
long year.

Janet Campbell, invariably referred to as 'Janet West the road' lived at
Croftmartaig after the death of her father, old Robbie. She was large, rotund
and talkative, a never failing source of information on friends and neighbours,
consulted on many matters.

Nearer home in Acharn **John McArthur** ran the Post Office in what is
today called Drummond View. It was also the local grocery and the (to me)
rather elderly man presiding was always a friend, since he gave good measure
when I was allowed to buy 'mixed fancy' sweets from him. He had two
spinster sisters, the **Misses C. and J. C. McArthur** (I never got round to
using their Christian names, but knew they were Christina and Jessie) who
lived together in Rose Cottage opposite. They always went about together,
beaming at each other and to anyone with whom they spoke, but were shy
and retiring. It was indeed remarkable how many single people there were
in Acharn, but the school, which then catered for all of Kenmore as well
as the Acharn area, presided over by **Joseph Coull** had many pupils.

Jimmie McGregor, head shepherd at Remony, has already been mentioned but deserves more than a comment about his professional ability. A big, ranging man, strong and agile, he had the longest stride of anyone I have ever known. After we met about five o'clock on a gathering morning I was pushed to keep up with him in spite of the many years' age differential in my favour, as we walked together up the hill to Glen Quaich. There we separated, he going up and round the top of Coire Quaich while I remained below the ravine to prevent the ewes straggling back down the glen before they had been joined by those off the high ground. In his younger days Jimmie had worked at Achianich and on one hot summer day he had bathed in the loch from the Achianich point – then swam all the way across to the other side. History does not relate how he got back again. He had a wonderful fund of stories and was full of good humour. Every year, when the time came to mark the lambs which was done by taking a nip or a crop off one of the lamb's ears with a very sharp knife, he would come up behind whoever was holding the lamb for this operation, seize his ear and brandish the knife, saying, 'Now let me see, which ear is it to be this year?' New hands dropped everything and fled; the old stagers sat tight and grinned up at Jimmie, 'You ken fine, it's the left ear this hirsel!'

Sheep were his be-all and end-all. When I was out at the gatherings I was always interested to see how the grouse were doing a few weeks before the shooting started. One day, coming back with sheep below the Black Rock, I noticed Jimmie a short distance above me with a covey of grouse getting up all around him. When we met I said, 'How many grouse were in that big covey, Jimmie?' 'Grouse' he said, 'yes, I did see one a while back.' But when I came to buy rams keeping Jimmie beside me for advice, I didn't get the help I expected, since he saw every fault, with only a faultless or perfect ram suitable for use with his ewes. They were few and far between. We once went together by car to Newton Stewart in search of the perfect ram, passing Troloss Farm near the head of the Dalvine Pass on the way. It was pointed out to me as a place from where one of Jimmie's friends had once bought a good sheep. We did buy several rams which were loaded onto the railway and found waiting for us the next morning at Aberfeldy, but we never went there again.

Callum McCallum came as a head shepherd to Remony from the west, where he had herded sheep on the high and steep ground of Ben Cruachan, to succeed Jimmie McGregor. At the very first gathering which he attended before formally taking up his post, the shepherds were arguing in the fank one morning about the mother of an apparently motherless lamb left in one of the pens. Callum moved quietly over to the pen of ewes and studied them. Coming back, 'Could it be yon brokie faced ewe with the bare coat; she had a lamb with her as I brought her in, but doesn't seem to have one now?' It was, and what a wonderful example of observation and kenning after following a large bunch of strange sheep for only a few moments, a standard which he never lowered. Softly spoken and of middle height he was a good hill walker and came to know our hill and the sheep on it so well that he could go at once to any part of the hill to find a ewe that might have been missed during a gathering. I think we made a good team together, Callum with his knowledge and experience but always willing to listen to my own ideas and the problems of finance. We built up the reputation of the flock and in the hard work involved Callum could be counted on to be on time, cheerful and willing, on all the early morning starts when taking sheep to sometimes distant markets and meticulous in 'toshing up' the tups in their pens at crack of dawn to have them looking at their best before the buyers arrived at the market. Callum had friends everywhere and enjoyed taking up the invitations to judge sheep at shows, particularly in the west, where the complication of the same crofter's sheep appearing in several different classes could test the memory of any lesser man. Mrs McCallum's journeys from Acharn up the den road to the high fank with food and drink were innumerable; she was always attentive and helpful as well as preparing the best of fare. Callum is buried at Kenmore which he came to love and his widow and daughters continued at least until 1994 to attend many functions in Kenmore from their home in Crieff.

John Campbell followed the Macnaughtons as tenant of Remony Farm. My dealing with him tended to be on a business rather than on a farm or social basis. He came with polite requests from time to time requiring my attention until eventually he retired in 1963. Later still in the farmhouse, his wife became landlady to young **Geordie Reid**. He was working for me as a junior shepherd and was to become a great sheep man, but at that time was anathema to Mrs Campbell and a real source of trouble there.

Bessie Macdonald was born near Wester Kinloch on the north shore of Loch Freuchie near Amulree. Her father was the Breadalbane keeper there, but in course of the Breadalbane break up the family was shifted to Remony to live near Callelochan. Bessie, a bonny young girl, found her first job in the rebuilt Remony as laundry maid and as a schoolboy I well remember admiring her charm and vitality. No wonder she was courted: it was Christie Macdonald who won her hand when he got the tenancy of Portbane Farm, where they lived together for many years. It must have been the happiest period of Bessie's life, proud of her son Peter although concerned at his poor health, but a hard life with cattle, sheep and a horse to care for, all provisions carried up from Acharn or Kenmore except for a very occasional load of coal carted up the farm track. Whenever I called there, I was greeted like everyone else with a smile and the offer of tea and a scone, newly baked and delicious. As Christie grew older he was increasingly affected by his asthma and shortage of breath till he was eventually forced to give up, when they moved down to Lonnaguy, which was then available, leaving Portbane vacant, to become a ruin. Sadly, Peter, then a tall gangling youth, died soon after, to be followed by his father, leaving Bessie a widow and on her own. After her first desolation she put a brave face to the situation, fiercely determined to be independent and meticulous in meeting all her commit-ments, prompt in paying the rent. Slowly she became more and more involved in all that went on in Acharn and its neighbourhood, mainstay of the Comarade's Hut, first to offer help with teas or cakes and there in the scullery to help with the washing up. She could be counted on to aid every worthwhile cause. For a time she took in lodgers to add to her already wide circle of friends and correspondents; they little knew how fortunate they were to land in Lonnaguy. There was no social occasion in which she was not involved, and so busily involved that she almost ran rather than walked as she hastened from one task to another. Her death in 1992 left a huge gap in the life of the community. Bessie had had a sad life, seeing three of the houses she had lived in become ruins and losing those she had most loved. But there were glimpses of brightness and with an indomitable spirit she kept on smiling to the very end.

Ned McGibbon came to Remony as gardener where he and his wife lived in the staff flat there. He was a professional gardener of the highest order and after supporting my mother in her love of home and garden kept up the work following his wartime service in the Royal Air Force. Remony presents a difficult task for any gardener as there are so many areas and corners of rough ground that lack of attention could very soon result in a tangle of vegetation. Ned and my mother turned the dell to the west of the house with the small burn running through it into a charming natural garden, while in the formal garden above the house the herbaceous border flourished along with fruit and vegetables. Ned will be best remembered for his skill with the violin which he loved to play. There were few parties or social occasions where his fiddling did not keep all the feet tapping, often together with Angus Hogg and his accordion. After his death at Remony in 1963 Mrs McGibbon stayed on in the flat to help my wife, until she later obtained tenancy of one of the new council houses just below the Taymouth entrance gates at Kenmore, where, like Bessie Macdonald, she became the prime helper in every local affair, known and liked by everyone.

Hendry Smith was officially handyman at Remony from 1946 to 1966, but he was far more than that. A tall, dark, striking man with a slow and determined stride, he had hurt his back in previous employment but could turn his hand to anything and make a good job of it. In addition, he had a love of horses and while Lois and I kept hunters for much of the time he was also head groom. His aim was always for the best possible turn-out, gleaming coats as well as tack, and he gave us every encouragement and support in our mounted activities. After my first point-to-point ride, at the Eglinton Hunt races near Ayr when Golden Brooch and I finished somewhat exhausted and a poor last, he was there to meet me with encouragement for having completed the course and to cheer me up with my disappointment in so poor a result after all the hard work we had both put in. He and his wife lived at Laurel Bank in Acharn with four fine sons and one daughter, immaculately brought up under Mrs Smith's eagle eye. They are all living and doing well for themselves and their families, one in Australia and the remainder scattered over Britain. Hendry could be proud of them.

He was succeeded by **Bill Chalmers** another real expert with anything concerned with houses, their temperamental drains or wiring or in repairing anything mechanical. He retired to live in a small new council house in Acharn, where everyone still goes to him to make go any device requiring attention.

The Ministers

The Parish of Kenmore has in the past always been fortunate with its ministers. **Dr Gillies** has already been mentioned; how he found the time to research for and write *In Famed Breadalbane* as well as carrying out all his temporal and spiritual duties I find difficult to understand and he most fully deserved his Doctorate. Tall and latterly grey headed, he had a determined but kindly character, deeply interested in the history as well as the welfare of his parish, as the book shows. He christened both Caroline and James and did not fail to make his displeasure known when baby Caroline was late in reaching the church after an 'unfortunate event'. His wisdom included his cooperation with the **Rev. Atholl Gordon**, minister of the Free Church in Kenmore. During our early days at Remony I remember going to the Parish and to the Free Church on alternate Sundays, but in 1931 the two congregations were united and worshipped in the Kirk of Kenmore. Mr Gordon was a large man, living alone in the Free Church Manse, now Croft-na-caber. Calling for tea at Remony about 1926, my sister and I, unknown to our parents, placed a 'joke' wafer biscuit having a layer of pink flannel instead of sugar as its middle layer making it look very tasty, on the tea plate just as it was going in to the drawing room. Mr Gordon fell for it, chose the wafer and took a large bite, getting his false teeth hopelessly entangled in the flannel. He took the catastrophe very well, but our parents did not and we were both suitably chastised.

Following Dr Gillies's retiral, **Rev. Kenneth McVicar** took over in 1950 and after his forty years' service, in line with that of his predecessors, he lives in retirement in the house he built not far from the Manse, now occupied by Rev. John Mann. Kenneth and I had a long period of partnership in local affairs while I served as County and he as District Councillor from 1950 to 1978. I believe we did much to help the parish in many ways, not least in our succeeding in having council houses built at Kenmore, Acharn and Fearnan, sometimes after considerable difficulties. As Parish Minister, Kenneth could not be equalled. As a preacher he drew people from all walks of life to listen to his sermons; as a churchman he occupied high offices in the Church of Scotland where he had many friends and our only sadness was that the office of Moderator, in which he would have excelled, just failed to come his way. His outstanding ability was to find the right words and turn of phrase in any situation or office which he was carrying out – at weddings, funerals, as compère at the local sports, as auctioneer at church sales or on any special occasion he never failed to be outstanding with flowing phrases, invariably of the most suitable nature, rivalling in speech his brother Angus's fluency with the written word. A hard act for anyone to follow.

McArthur's Plans, 1769

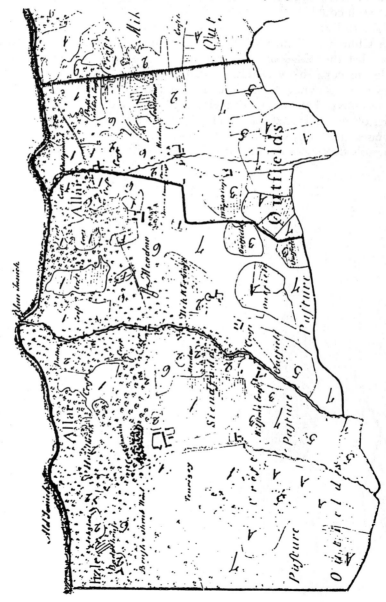

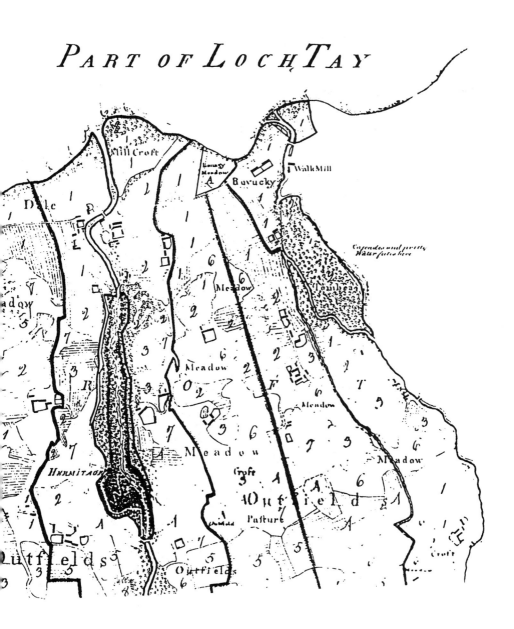

PART OF LOCH TAY

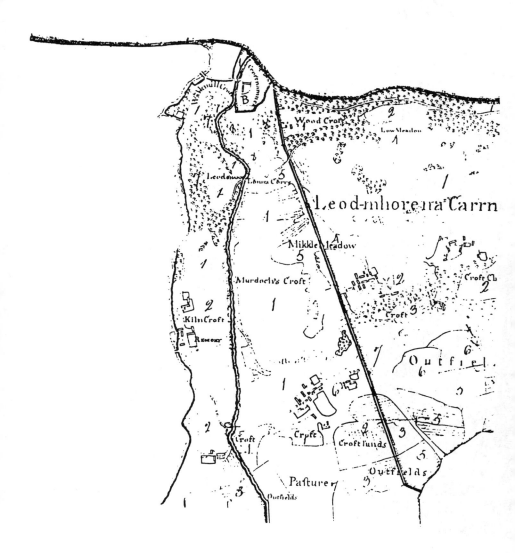

PART OF LOCH TAY

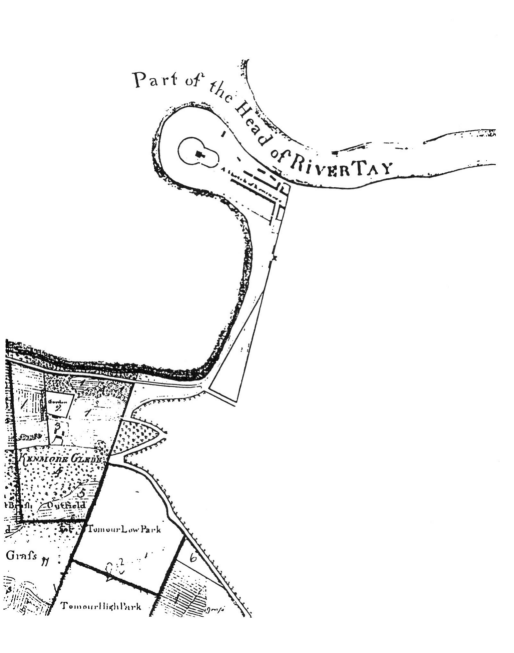

Part of the Head of River Tay

Officiary of Strymenich

	Croftlands	Infield	Meadow	Pasture	Wood	Moor	Total	
Tullochane								
Ashowich								
Wester Lerglomman								
Easter Do								
Wester Confpenmariage								
Easter Do								
Wester Achearn								
Easter Do								
Wester Ballimbreguard (Little Croft)								
Easter Do								
Meadow of Loregoy								
Tomgarrow								
Acchich								
Roure Ay								
Romeny								
Ballianacraistone								
Croftnamuck								
Portbane								
Croftnacabber								
Kinmore Glebe								
Brae of Ballomfeime								

Farm Statistics: McArthur.

APPENDIX III(A)

McArthur's figures for farms within Officiary of Taymouth, 1769

Extract summary of farms within the area of Remony Estate as it was in 1925

Farm unit	Rent	No. of souls	Cows	Horses	Harrowers	Sheep	Grass acres	Value £
Callelochan John Mackay, John McArthur, Patrick Crerar, Donald McNab, Patrick McKeown, Patrick McKeown Jnr, Katherine McKeown, Malcolm McCallum	29/10	8	15	16	8	160	1382	70/8/2
Achianich Patrick Carmichael, Duncan Robertson, John Anderson, Katherine McKay	16/–	4	28	8	4	116	415	28/5/6
Wester Lurgloman Gilbert Walker	8/–	1	16	4	4	50	241	16/8/9
Easter Lurgloman Patrik Haggart, Janet McVairn	7/10	2	14	4	4	60	231	14/19/2
Wester Croftmartage Donald Clark, Alex Anderson, Andrew Douglass	11/10	3	15	8	4	60	238	17/7/7
Easter Croftmartage Finley Hay, Donald Hay, Donal McTavish	11/–	3	15	8	4	60	240	17/8/11
Wester Acharn Donald Haggart Snr, Donald Haggart Jnr, John McNab	5/–	3	18	8	5	80	431	26/11/10
Easter Acharn Archie Cameron, Duncan Kippen Snr, Duncan Kippen Jnr	7/10	3	18	8	5	80	435	25/19/4
Wester Ballinlaggin and Mill Croft James Walker, Donald Walker	8/10	2	20	4	4	90	424	22/11/3
Easter Ballinlaggan Neal McArthur, John McArthur, John McAndrew, Janet McNaughton, possession of meadow of Lonagay	5/10	4	20	8	4	80	331	20/8/2
Aleckich John Anderson, Izabel McDougall, Donald McKerchar	10/–	3	15	6	3	60	324	18/19/7
Revucky John McKie, Wm. Rutherford, John McKinzie, Izabel Kippen, Margaret Haggart	3/4	5	4	4	–	24	110	6/11/2

Farm unit	Rent	No. of souls	Cows	Horses	Harrowers	Sheep	Grass acres	Value £
Tomgarrow	13/-	4	16	8	4	94	425	23/18/9
Daniel McNaughton, Patrick Kennedy, Neil McFell, Hugh Sincler								
Remony	13/10	4	25	8	4	60	448	27/16/8
Duncan Kippen, Duncan Anderson, Duncan Robertson, James Kippen								
Possessor of Waukmill, William Murray								
Bellamacnachtane	21/-	6	31	12	12	90	648	37/19/2
John Haggart, John McAndrew, Donald McKay, Dougall McDougall, Duncan McFell, Margaret McNaughton								
Croftnamuick	1/15	1	1				2	
James Campbell								
	172/19	56	271	114	59	1.164	6,326	377/1/2

List of Occupants at Acharn, 1850

September 1850

List of Occupants of Cottages at Acharn
north side of road, with the number of their families &c —

no. of Cottage	Inhabitants names & number of their family	Age	Occupation	Remarks —
1	James Brerar Wife & two Chil- -dren under 4 years	33	Labourer	employed at the Floating & Wood operations
1	James Brerar Wife & four of a family — oldest —	50 / 18	Labourer	employed at erecting & repairing fences — &c
2	John McNaughton Wife & five of a family — oldest —	70 / 44	Carpenter	Works at Taymouth sawmill
2	Widow McArthur eight of a family age of the oldest	45 / 22	mason	4 of the Children — under 12.
3	John Anderson Wife & three of a family. Eldest	53 / 23	Labourer	

No of Cottage	Inhabitants Names & number of their families	Age	Occupation	Remarks
3	Alext Frerar Wife & four in family – Eldest	41 / 17	Labourer	Works at Taymouth Garden –
4	James Shippen Wife & 1 daughter	66 / 25	dyke builder	Generally works by Contract
4	James McKag Wife	38 / 28	Painter	Works for P. Skeene not long Married –
5	Widow Sinclair Three in family Eldest	63 / 30	Shoemaker	1 Son in the Band –
6	James Taylor eight Children under 15 years of age	49	Surfaceman on the Public roads –	Wages 11/- per Week in Summer 10/- " – " in Winter
7	Duncan Anderson Wife & 6 Children Eldest	50 / 18	Mason	Generally works by Contract –
7	Colin McArthur Wife & 7 Children Eldest	46 / 11	Labourer	for some months past, unable to work, but now employed on the roads – 1 boy employed at Park roads &c 8/7d per day. –

No of Cottage	Inhabitants names & number of their families	age	Occupation	Remarks —
8	Widow Hazzard one son	79 48	Labourer	Employed at Wood Operation
8	Donald Dewar wife & 5 children Eldest	14	Labourer	Works at Taymouth Sawmill
9	Widow Campbell Three in family Eldest	53 24	Labourer	Employed at General work
	South side of road —			
1	James Walker wife 1 Son 1 Grandchild	72 75 41 14	Miller do	
2	Alexr Cameron wife & 3 young children	38	Carpenter on his own Account	
3	Widow Cameron 1 Daughter 1 Married Daughter & husband, John McCorkindale with 1 young child —	75 36 33	Labourer	Employed at Wood Operations

no of cottage	Inhabitants names with number of their families	age	Occupations	Remarks -
	South Side of road			
3	Widow Sinclair	80		Confined to bed
	1 Daughter	30		Weak in mind
	1 Son	39	Labourer	
	1 granddaughter	20		with 1 child, but not married _
4	Peter McKercher	40	Labourer	employed at the Floating
	Wife & 5 Children			_ & Fishing & Wood Operations
	Eldest	14		
5	Donald Cameron	38	Labourer	_ employed at Wood Operations
	Wife & five			
	Children - Eldest	12		
5	Widow Haggart			
	4 Children - Eldest	13		
6	Peter McDougel	53	Labourer	employed at Wood Operations, or
	Wife & three in			other general work —
	family - Eldest	24		
	also a Married			deserted by her husband
	daughter - with 3	30		
	young Children			_
6	Widow Crerar	84		
	1 Son	57	Mason	
	1 Daughter	40		
7	John McArthur	72	Labourer	
	Wife	39		
	1 Son			

No. 2 Age	Inhabitants names & number of their families	Age	Occupation	Remarks -
	South side of road			
8	Donald McNaughton Wife & 3 young children	38	Carpenter	Works at Taymouth Sawmill
	Peter Campbell Wife & 4 young children	38	Labourer	met with an accident on the railway, but now getting better not employed by us, for some time past, for selling Whiskey in defiance of all orders —
	Alex. Buchanan Wife & 5 in family Oldest	55 20	Smith	
	Widow Anderson 1 son 2 daughters (1 insane)	80 46	Guide to the Falls	
	Don.d McNaughton Wife & 6 in family Oldest	51 25	Grocer	
	Frances Suttie Wife & 1 young child	26	Labourer	

These sheets show a total of approximately 66 adults + 100 children (of all ages).

APPENDIX III(C)

Parish of Kenmore Valuation Roll, 1919/20

VALUATION ROLL of the COUNTY of PERTH for the Year 1919-1920.

No.	Description and Situation of Subject.	Proprietor.	Occupier
	BREADALBANE ESTATE.		
1	House (Fort Lodge), ...	The Most Hon. the Marquess of Breadalbane,	Proprietor. ... ...
2	do. (Tower Lodge), and Cow's Grass,	K.G., per Thomas Noble, factor, Kenmore.	John M'Pherson, joiner.
3	Lodge, Tombuie, ...	Aberfeldy.	Miss M. T. Murray. ...
4	a Corryvorrallan Grass Parks,	... ... do.	Proprietor. ...
5	House, Bigrow Cottages, ...	... ... do.	do. ...
6	do. do.	... ... do.	do.
7	do. do. ...	... ... do.	Loch Tay Steamboat Co. (Lim
8	do. Bigrow, ...	... ... do.	do. do.
9	Site of Garage, ...	... ... do.	Alexander M'Kerchar, ..
10	Water Privilege, Kenmore, ...	... ... do.	C.F.C. Manse, p.Rev. J. B.Ath
11	a Land at Croftnacabbar, ...	... ... do.	Rev. J. B. Ath ll Gordon.
12	House at Porthane, ...	... ... do.	James Morris, labourer.
13	do. do.	... ... do.	Vacant,
14	Porthane Cottage, ... ' ...	... ... do.	do.
15	House, Port Glas, ...	... ... do.	Proprietor. ...
16	Hotel, £102 5s 3d, a Farm, £53 19s, Ken-		
	more, ...	... ... do.	Duncan M'Intyre, innkeeper
17	House, Porthane.	... ... do.	... ...
18	a Land, do.	... ... do. ... —	Alex. M'Arthur, Acharn,
19	a Farm and House, Balmacnaughton, &c.,	... ... do. ... —	James and Peter M'Naughto
20	House, do.	... ... do. ... —	... ...
21	do. Pitmackie, ...	... ... do. ... —	... ...
22	do. Acharn (Tomgarrow), ...	... ... do. ... —	... ...
23	do. do. do. ...	... ... do. ... —	... ...
24	do. do. Tomgarrow, ...	... ... do. ... —	... ...
25	do. do. ...	... ... do. ... —	...
26	a Farm of Remony, ...	... ... do	James and Peter M'Naughton
27	Lodge, £40, Shootings of Acharn & Remony,	... ... do.	Proprietor for occupier,
28	House, do.	... ... do. ... —	... ...
29	Shootings, Tombuie, ...	... ... do. ... —	E. C. Kerr.
30	House, Pitmackie, ...	... ... do. ... —	do.
31	do. £3. & a Land £3, Revucky,	... ... do. ... —	Margaret M'Tavish, ...
32	a Land, Revucky, ...	... ... do. ... —	Peter M'Naughton, Remony,
33	a do.	... ... do. ... —	William Cameron, shepherd,
34	House, £2, a do £2, do.	... ... do. ... —	Miss Jane Walker. ...
35	a do. and Land, Revucky, ...	... ... do. ... —	John Mac pherson, senr., shoe
36	do. Revucky, ...	... ... do. ... —	J. & P. N'Naughton, Remon
37	do. do.	... ... do. ... —	Peter M' Naughton. ...
38	a Land, £6, & House, £4 9s 6d, Lower		
	Balinlaggan, ...	... ... do ... —	William Cameron, shepherd,
39	House & Meal Mill, £12, a Land £10, do.	... ... do. ... —	D. & J. M'Naughton, millers
40	House and Land, do.	... ... do. ... —	Donald M'Naughton, tailor,
41	do. £3 10s, a do. £4 10s 0d, do.	... ... do. ... —	D. M'Ewen, residenter,
42	do. £4 10s, a do. £3 19s 6d, do.	... ... do ... —	Alexander M'Kerchar, smith,
43	do. £15, a do. £3, do.	... ... do. ... —	Peter M' Laren, ...
44	House, Lower Balinlaggan, ...	... ... do ... —	Alexander M'Kerchar, ...
45	do. do.	... ... do ... —	Robert M'Owan, roadman,
46	do. do.	... ... do. ... —	Elizabeth M'Pherson,
47	do. do.	... ... do. ... —	Mrs. M'Naughton, ...
48	do. do.	... ... do. ... —	do.
49	do. do.	... ... do. ... —	... ...
50	do. do.	... ... do. ... —	... ...
51	do. do.	... ... do. ... —	Isabella M'Rae, ...
52	do. do. ...	... ... do. ... —	Peter M' Naughton, ...
53	do. do. ...	... ... do. ... —	Alexander Morison, ...
54	do. do.	... ... do. ... —	Mrs. Harris, ...
55	do. do.	... ... do. ... —	Dau M'Naughton, tailor,
			John M' Rae, gardener,

TRICT.—Parish of KENMORE.   351

Inhabitant Occupier, not rated (48 Vict. c. 3, sect. 8 and 9)	Annual Value of House (Lands Rept. Sect Act)	Yearly Rent or Value	No.	Amount of Feu-Duty Ground Annual, &c.	To whom Feu-Duty, &c., payable
					NOTE.—The letter a in italics indicates the classification of Agricultural Lands and Heritages for purposes of Occupiers' Rates, conform to 59 and 60 Vict., Chap. 37.
John M'Donald,	£4 0 0		1		
..	...	£3 0 0	2		
..	...	15 0 0	3		
..	...	2 2 6	4		
G. Walker,	2 10 0	2 10 0	5		
John Thomson,	2 10 0	2 10 0	6		
Vacant,	2 10 0	2 10 0	7		
do.	2 10 0	2 10 0	8		
...	...	1 0 0	9		
...	...	0 1 0	10		
...	...	7 17 9	11		
...	...	1 0 0	12		
...	...	1 10 0	13		
Vacant,	16 0 0	16 0 0	14		
..	5 0 0	5 0 0	15		
...	...	156 4 3	16		
Donald M'Lean,	2 0 0		17		
...	...	0 12 6	18		
...	...	220 0 0	19		
Alex. Robertson,	3 0 0		20		
John M'Lean,	2 0 0		21		
Vacant,	1 5 0		22		
do.	1 5 0		23		
James Gilmour,	1 10 0		24		
Vacant,	2 0 0		25		
...	...	47 11 1	26		
...	...	314 0 0	27		
Donald Stewart,	4 0 0		28		
Vacant,	4 0 0	162 0 0	29		
James Brydone,	3 0 0		30		
...	...	6 0 0	31		
...	...	2 10 0	32		
...	...	3 10 0	33		
...	...	1 0 0	34		
...	...	3 0 0	35		
Vacant,	1 5 0	3 5 0	36		
Hugh M'Laren,	2 10 0	2 10 0	37		
...	...	10 3 6	38		
...	...	22 0 0	39		
...	...	3 15 0	40		
...	...	2 0 0	41		
...	...	8 9 6	42		
...	...	18 0 0	43		
...	...	1 15 0	44		
...	...	2 0 0	45		
...	...	1 15 0	46		
...	...	1 15 0	47		
...	...	1 15 0	48		
...	...	1 15 0	49		
...	...	1 15 0	50		
Duncan M'Gregor,	4 0 0	4 0 0	51		
...	...	2 10 0	52		
...	...	2 10 0	53		
...	...	2 10 0	54		
...	...	2 10 0	55		

352   VALUATION ROLL of the COUNTY of PERTH for the YEAR 1919-1920.—HIGHLA⸺

No.	Description and Situation of Subject.	Proprietor.	Occupier.
	BREADALBANE ESTATE—continued.		
56	House, Lower Balinlaggan, ...	The Most Hon. The Marquess of Breadalbane, K.G.—continued,	Mrs. Elizabeth Cowan (widow),
57	do. do.		James Fraser, wood carter,
58	House, £4 10s, a Land £2 17s, Lower	do.	John Walker, joiner. ...
59	do. Balinlaggan,	do.	Miss Catherine M'Nab,
60	a Croft, do.	do.	Alexander M'Naughton,
61	a Land, £3 10s. do.	do.	Proprietor for Occupier, ...
62	a House and Land, do.	do.	Peter Cameron, ...
63	do. Manufactory,	do.	Mrs. Jane Cameron,
64	House, £4, and a Land, £4, do.	do.	Reps. of Alexander Campbell,
65	do. £3 10s, a do. £2 10s, do.	do.	Peter Stewart,
66	do. £3 10s, a do. £4, do.	do.	John M'Naughton, blacksmith,
67	a Land, Acharn Point, ...	do.	John M'Naughton, Manufac Acharn,
68	Steamboat Pier, Acharn, ...	do.	Loch Tay Steamboat Co. (Limit
69	House, £4 16s. a Land £3 12s, do.	do.	Heirs of Duncan M'Arthur.
70	do. £4 16s. a do. £3 12s, do.	do.	John Duff, labourer.
71	do. £4 2s, a do. £3 8s, do.	do.	Alexander M'Arthur, labourer,
72	do. Manufactory, ...	do.	John M'Pherson, shoemaker,
73	do. do.	do.	James Taylor's Heirs,
74	do. do.	do.	Alex. M'Kerchar, blacksmith,
75	do. Acharn, ...	do.	Miss Christina Sinclair, ...
76	a Land, do.	do.	John M'Pherson, shoemaker,
77	Cottage and Garden, Acharn, ...	do.	Miss Christina M'Arthur,
78	do. (£6 13s 9d) & a Land (£5) Acharn,	do.	William M'Rae,
79	do. and Garden, Acharn Post Office,	do.	John M'Arthur, merchant.
80	do. do. do. ...	do.	Mrs. Christian M'Callum or Smi
81	do. do. do. ...	do.	Robert A. Dick,
82	a Farm of Acharn & Grazing of Croftmartaig,	do.	James and Peter M'Naughton, I
83	House do. Acharn (Haugh cottage),	do.	... ...
84	a do. and Land at Croftmartaig,	do.	Thomas Dunn, labourer,
85	a do. do. do.	do.	James M'Kerchar, engineer,
86	do. £3 1s 10d a do. £6 5s 0d, do.	do.	Robert Campbell, ...
87	do. £6, a do. £2 4s 6d, Lurglomond,	do.	Mrs. A. M'Gregor, ...
88	a Farm and House. do.	do.	Mrs. Jane and Alex. M'Dougall.
89	House £3, and a Land £3 4s., do.	do.	Alexander M'Rae, ...
90	do. £3, & a land £4 14s 5d, do.	do.	do. ...
91	a do. do. do.	do.	Mrs. Donald Crawford, ...
92	a do. do. Achianich,	do.	John M'Nicoll, ...
93	a Farm and House, Achianich,	do.	Peter M'Donald, ...
94	a Farm. Easter Callelochan, ...	do.	do. ...
95	a do. and House, Wester Callelochan,	do.	Thomas Pringle, ...
96	Keeper's House, Callelochan, ...	do.	Proprietor, ...
97	a Farm and House, Ardradnaig, ...	do.	Peter Fraser, farmer, ...
98	a House & Land, Kepranich and Shenlarich,	do.	James Campbell Livingstone.
99	a do. do. Skiag, ...	do.	James M'Dougall and Reps. of D M'Dougall, ...
100	a Land at Leckbuie, £3, House, £1 1s,	do.	Donald Campbell, ...
101	Shootings, Ardtalnaig, ...	do.	Wm. H. Dixon, 81 Grace Chu⸺
102	Lodge, ...	do.	do. ... ...
103	House, do. ..	do.	... ...
104	a Farm and House. Milltown and Leckbuie,	do.	Archibald M'Dougall's heirs.
105	a Farm and House, Kindrochit,	do.	John M'Gregor,
106	a House and Land, do.	do.	Miss Annie M'Laren. ...
107	House, Smithy, £3, and a Land, £3, Ardtalnaig, ...	do.	Miss Margaret Campbell,

Parish of KENMORE—*Continued.*

Inhabitant Occupier, not rated (48 Vict. c. 3, sect. 3 and 9.)	Annual Value of House&Local Govt.Scot.Act. 1889.)	Yearly Rent or Value.	No.	Amount of feu-Duty, Ground Annual, &c.	To whom Feu-Duty, &c., payable.
...	..	£1 15 0	56		
...	...	2 0 0	57		
...	..	7 7 0	58		
...	...	3 10 0	59		
...	...	2 18 0	60		
...	...	3 10 0	61		
...		12 0 0	62		
...	...	4 0 0	63		
...		8 0 0	64		
...	...	6 0 0	65		
...	...	7 10 0	66		
...	...	1 15 0	67		
...	...	2 10 0	68		
...	...	8 8 0	69		
...	...	8 8 0	70		
...	...	7 10 0	71		
...	...	10 11 6	72		
James Taylor, sub. ten	2 0 0	2 10 0	73		
Thomas M'Rae,	2 0 0	2 0 0	74		
...	...	3 0 0	75		
...	...	3 0 0	76		
...	...	9 3 9	77		
...	...	11 13 9	78		
..	...	10 12 0	79		
...	...	9 13 9	80		
..	...	9 13 9	81		
...	...	102 0 0	82		
James M'Gregor,	8 0 0		83		
...	...	9 5 0	84		
...	...	13 5 0	85		
.	...	9 6 10	86		
.	...	8 4 6	87		
..	...	38 11 2	88		
.	...	6 4 0	89		
..	...	7 14 5	90		
...	...	12 6 1	91		
...	...	21 8 6	92		
...	...	45 17 4	93		
...	...	40 0 0	94		
...	...	40 9 8	95		
John Reid,	3 0 0		96		
...	...	33 11 6	97		
...	...	45 7 6	98		
...	...	43 15 6	99		
...	...	4 1 0	100		
...	...	140 0 0	101		
...	...	20 0 0	102		
Don. Campbell,	4 0 0		103		
...	...	77 11 4	104		
...	...	23 16 0	105		
...	...	6 2 0	106		
...	...	6 0 0	107		

Remony Estate Rent Roll, 1930–31

Subject		Tenant or Occupier	Rent (£)
SHOOTINGS			
Remony Shootings		R.H. Palmer	650
AGRICULTURAL POSSESSIONS			
Balmacnaughton, Tomgarrow, etc.		Proprietor	58
Acharn & Grazing of Croftmartaig		do.	92
1917–1926 Wester Callelochan		Thomas Pringle	40
Achianich & Easter Callelochan		Peter Macdonald	85
1917–1927 Achianich		John McNicoll	21
Lurglomond		Reps of Mr & Mrs Alex McDougall	38
SMALLER POSSESSIONS			
1922–1927 Croftmartaig	House & Land	Peter Cameron	9– 3– 9
1906–1927 do.	do.	Reps of James McKerchar	13– 9– 0
do.	do.	Robert Campbell	9– 3– 1
Lurglomond	House	Alex McDougall	8– 0– 0
do.	do.	Malcolm McNicoll	13– 9– 0
do.	do.	Mrs Donald Crawford	12– 0– 0
Holly Cottage		John Cameron	10–10– 9
Lower Ballinlaggan,	House & Shop	Reps of late G.L. Geddes	8–10– 0
do.	Land	James B. Coull	4– 0– 0
do.	House	Mrs McEwen	4– 0– 0
do.	Land	James B. Coull	4–10– 0
do.	House £6:10 & Land	Mrs Gillies	9– 0– 0
do.	House	Miss Cameron	5– 0– 0
do.	do.	Mrs Janet McOwen	2– 0– 0
do.	do.	Eliz. McPherson	1–15– 0
do.	do.	John McRae	10– 0– 0
do.	House £1:15 & Land	Alex Macnaughton	4–13– 0
do.	House	Isabella McRae	1–15– 0
do.	do.	Ruinous	–
do.	do.	Mrs Shorthouse	2–10– 0
do.	do.	Proprietor (£2)	2– 0– 0

Subject		Tenant or Occupier	Rent (£)
do.	do.	do. (£2:10)	2–10– 0
do.	do.	Hugh Cowan	1–15– 0
do.	do.	James Fraser	2– 0– 0
do.	do.	Mrs Elizabeth Walker	1– 3– 0
do.	do.Land	Proprietor (£2:17)	2–17– 0
do.	House	Miss Catherine McNab	3–10– 0
do.	House & Land	Proprietor	12–10– 0
do.	Land	Miss Jean Macnaughton	3–15– 0
do.	do.	Proprietor (£3:16)	3–16– 0
Manufactory	House	Mrs Jane Cameron	4– 0– 0
do.	House £2 & Land	Mrs Mills	6– 0– 0
do.	House	Miss Jane Walker	2– 0– 0
do.	do.	Donald McLean	3–10– 0
do.	Land	James B. Coull	2–10– 0
Lower Ballinlaggan	House	John Macnaughton	3–10– 0
do. do.	Land £4	Proprietor (£4)	–
Acharn Point Grazings		do. (£1)	–
do.		John Macnaughton	15– 0
Manufactory	House	John Duff	4–15– 0
do.	Land	Proprietor	–
do.	House	John McArthur	4– 2– 0
do.	do.	Mrs John Macpherson	10– 0– 0
do.	Land	Alex Macnaughton	3– 0– 0
do.	House	John McOwan	5– 0– 0
do.	do.	Donald McArthur	4– 0– 0
Acharn, House, Vacant			
do.	Sawmill	Alex Macdonald	6– 0– 0
do.	House	Miss Christina McArthur	9– 0– 0
do.	do. (£6:10) & Land £5	Walter McRae	11–10– 0
do.	House & Shop	John McArthur	10– 0– 0
do.	House	Philip Clacher	5– 0– –0
do.	do.	John Walker	9– 10– 0
Feu		Education Authority	14– 0
Grazing of Park at Acharn		Proprietor	5–10– 0
			£275–12– 5

ABSTRACT

SHOOTINGS	650– 0– 0
AGRICULTURAL POSSESSIONS	334– 0– 0
SMALLER POSSESSIONS	275–12– 5
	£1259– 12– 5

REMONY ESTATE ACCOUNT, YEAR 1931

EXPENDITURE	£
Public Burdens	462
Ins., supplies, various, misc.	432
Wages, incl 2 gamekeepers, Donald Stewart and John Reid	737
Estate upkeep and improvements	319
Factor, incl outlays	106
	1785
Gross Receipts	1356
Loss on year's working	£439

Remony Estate Rent Roll, 1961

SPORTINGS			
Estate Shootings	Proprietor	(Not Let)	115– 0– 0
Remony Farm Shootings	do.	do.	15– 0– 0
Forestry Comn. (Callelochan)	do.		1– 0– 0
Fishings, R. Lyon	do.		5– 0– 0
			136– 0– 0

ESTATE PROPERTIES		
Remony Farm & House	J. Campbell	63–12– 2
House, Balmacnaughton	do.	12– 0– 0
Remony (Acharn) Farm	Proprietor	229– 0– 0
Remony House	do.	122– 0– 0
do. Staff Flat	do. (Mrs Brown)	incl. above
Remony Stable Flat	do. (D. Wearing)	18– 0– 0
do. Keepers Cottage	do. (J. Turner)	27– 0– 0
do. Gardeners Cottage	do. (E. McGibbon)	42– 0– 0
Holly Cottage	Mrs. R. Backhouse	16– 0– 0
House, Lonnaguy	Proprietor (J. Paterson)	47– 0– 0
House, Tighanlaggan	do. (Mrs Macdonald)	47– 0– 0
Acharn Village		
House, Laurel Bank	Proprietor (H. Smith)	37– 0– 0
do. Tay View	D. Walker	35– 0– 0
do. Rose Cottage	Misses C. & J.C. McArthur	24– 0– 0
do. Fernbank	C. Walker	39– 0– 0
do. Haugh Cottage	Proprietor (M. McCallum)	48– 0– 0
Garage do.	M. McCallum (owner)	—
House & Shop	J. McArthur	44– 0– 0
Old Mill-store	Proprietor	17– 0– 0
House, Pine Cottage	C. Ross	35– 0– 0
Smithy House	D. Macdonald (rent free)	—
House, Uper Acharn	A. McDougall do.	—
do. do.	Miss E. McRae	2– 0– 0
House, No. 1 The Manufactory	Proprietor (G. Willocks)	34– 0– 0
do. 2 do.	Mrs & Mrs Liberkowski	43– 0– 0

do.	3	do.	T. Pringle	23– 0– 0
do.	4	do.	J. Saunders	22– 0– 0
do.	5	do.	J. Duff	18– 0– 0
do.	6	do.	Mrs J.R. Campbell	17– 0– 0
Garage,	No. 1		Proprietor (Estate Forestry)	8– 0– 0
do.	2		G. Willocks	8– 0– 0
do.	3		S Liberkowska	8– 0– 0
do.	4		H. Wesierski	8– 0– 0
do.	5		J. Paterson	8– 0– 0
do.	6		T. Pringle	8– 0– 0
House, Lower Acharn			J. McDougall	16– 0– 0
do.			J. Beaton	8– 0– 0
do.			A McOwan	15– 0– 0
do.			J. Fraser (rent free)	–
do.			J. Walker	16– 0– 0
do.			H. Wesierski	1– 0– 0
House, Tighnaldon (Upper)			D. Harkness (rent free)	–
do.			J. Macdonald	25– 0– 0
House, Burnbank			uninhabitable	–
Land,	do.		J. Macdonald	2– 0– 0
Croft & Land, Croftmartaig			A. Gair	15– 0– 0
Land, Croftmartaig			R.M. Jamieson	3–16– 0
Land, Croftmartaig			Proprietor	5–10– 0
Farm & House, Lurglomand			J.H. Sutherland	95– 0– 0
Croftland, Lurglomand			J.W. Moar	11– 8– 2
House, Lower Achianich			H. Fraser	9–10– 2
Farm & House, Achianich			Proprietor (R. Macnaughton)	90– 0– 0
Land for pier, Acharn Point			W.G. Innes	4– 0– 0
CC Water supply, Acharn			Perth County Council	7–10– 6
				£1434– 7– 0

WAYLEAVES, FEU DUTIES, ETC.

NSHEB Wayleaves			9–12– 4
PO Wayleaves			1–11– 3
School & Schoolhouse, Acharn	Perthshire Edn. Authority		8– 7
House & Land,	Viewfield	R. M. Jamieson	4–16–10
do.	Altchoaran	J. McGregor	2– 6– 3

do. Lurglomond	J. W. Moar	2– 9– 0
Land, Callelochan	Forestry Commission	15– 0– 2
House & Croftland, Callelochan	H.H. Fergusson	12– 5– 0
House & Lane, Croftmartaig	A. Gair	3– 1– 3
	Total	£51–10– 8

Remony Estate Account, 1961

INCOME		EXPENDITURE	
Remony (Acharn) Farm	9,000	Remony (Acharn) Farm	10,069
Achianich Farm	4,381	Achianich Farm	3,833
Estate Rentals excl. Farms in hand		Capital Expenditure	2,622
(no shootings let)	906	Estate maintenance	2,096
Miscellaneous	913	Shootings (incl. wages)	617
Paid in	9,206	Management, incl. burdens	1,467
		Personal	1,966
		Adjusted	–1,689
		Total	20,981
		Excess of Income	3,425
Total	24,406		24,406
		Total Estate & Farm Wages	
		(included above)	£7,481

Roll of Properties and their occupiers within the bounds at one time of Remony Estate, as at Nov. 1994

+ = pays rent to estate
★ = estate staff
- = outwith estate control
H = Holiday occupancy only

Subject	Occupier	Status	Number of souls	
House at Balmacnaughton	Mr & Mrs J. Shaw	—		2H
Reynock	Lois & Alastair Duncan Millar	+	2	
Remony Farm House	Mr & Mrs D. Reid	★	2	
Lademill Cottage	Mr & Mrs A. Hogg	★	3	
Remony House	James, Susan, Andrew & Fiona Duncan Millar	proprietors	4	
Flat at Remony House	Mr & Mrs M. Carry	+	3	
Marley Garages	Proprietor			
Gunroom Flat	Mr B. Edwards	★	1	
Stable Flat				
Shed at Remony Farm }	Kaimes Fish Farm	+		
Fish Farm				
Garage at Remony Farm	Mr A. Hogg	+		
Gardener's Cottage	Mr & Mrs Heirs	—	3	
Holly Cottage	Mr & Mrs I. Quin	—		2H
Lonnaguy	Mr & Mrs J. Kendall	—		4H
Tighanlaggan	Miss I. LeCorre	+	1	
ACHARN VILLAGE (see p. 217)			85	32H
Tighnaldon		—		4H
Burnbank	Mr & Mrs I. Anderson	—		2H
Croftmartaig	Miss G. Gair	—	1	
Viewfield	Mr & Mrs Black	—		2H
Altchoaran	Mr Oppenheim & M. Rutherford	—	2	
do., access to loch		+		

Lurglomand	(proprietor)		(2)
Lower Lurglomand	Mr & Mrs Hodge	—	2H
New House at			
Lurglomand	Mr F. Louden &		
	Mrs A. Salat	—	2
Achianich	Mr J. Hogg	★	1
Lower Achianich			
(ruinous)	Mr B. Walker	—	
Callelochan	Mr & Mrs Ferguson	—	2H

Total population	110	52H

Note. The holiday figure is a minimum.

Total rental paid to estate	£22,527
Annual Value of other land and buildings in use by estate or farm	£16,620
Gross Rental	£39,147

Remony Estate Account, Year to 31/5/94

	Income	Expenditure
Remony Farms (A. & I. Duncan Millar)	£185,733	£183,753 [3]
Remony Estate (A. & J. Duncan Millar)	£180,916 [1]	£148,523 [3]
Excess of Income £34,373 [2]		
	£366,649	£366,649

Notes

1. Includes Shootings, Loch Tay Lodges & Forestry
2. The excess income this year reflects that part of the timber sold during the year, amounting to £40,000, from the clear felling of the Queen's Drive Wood, planted in 1931
3. The total Farm and Estate wages amounting to £84,767 are included in the above figures.

APPENDIX III (G)

The Village of Acharn

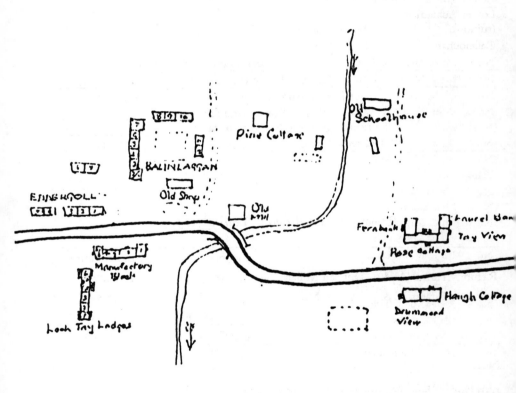

Village of Acharn
List of Inhabitants as at November 1944

Local Authority Houses

Occupier		Adults + children
Edergoll		
No 1	Mr & Mrs I. McDougall	2 + 3
No 2	Mr & Mrs M. Mitchell	2 + 2
No 3	Mr W. Stott	1 + 2
No 4	(Miss M. Ross)	1
No 5	Mr & Mrs A. Struthers	2
No 6	Mr & Mrs W. Chalmers	2
No 7	Mr & Mrs J. Moar	2
Balinlaggan		
No 1	Mr M. Gall	1
No 2	Miss A. Grieve	1
No 3	Mr & Mrs C. Smith	2 + 2
No 4	Mr & Mrs S. Wilson	2 + 1
No 5	Mr & Mrs P Lambie	2 + 1
No 6	Miss J. Jones	1 + 1
No 7	Mr & Mrs T. Bywater	2 + 2
No 8	Mr & Mrs J. Thomson	2 + 1
No 9	Mr M. Jones	1
No 10	(Mrs E. McInnes)	1
No 11	Mr A. Montgomery	1
No 12	Mr & Mrs P. Gregor	2 + 2
Local Authority Total		30 + 17

Privately Owned

Address	Occupier	Adults + children
Pine Cottage	Mr & Mrs Baird	2 (+B&B)
New House	Mr & Mrs S. Baird	2 + 2
Old Shop	Mr & Mrs A. May	2 + 2

Privately Owned (contd)

Address	Occupier	Adults + children
Old Mill	Mr & Mrs J. Troupe	2
Schoolhouse	Mrs Brodie (Registrar)	1 (+B&B)
New House	Mr & Mrs K. Mitchell	2 + 2
	Private Total	11 + 4

Estate Owned

The Manufactory

No 1	Mr & Mrs Green	2	+
No 2	Mr & Mrs H. Campbell	2	★
No 3	Miss M. Campbell	1	+
No 4	Miss M. Corstorphine	1	+
No 5	Mr J. Webb	1	+
No 6	Miss M. Brown	1	+

Loch Tay lodges. 6 Lodges, 32 beds.

Fern Bank	Mr & Mrs A. Grieve	2	★
Rose Cottage	Mr & Mrs D. Haigh	2 + 3	+
Tay View	Mr & Mrs M. Anderson	2 + 2	+
Laurel Bank	Miss D. Grieve	1	+
Haugh Cottage	Mr & Mrs W. Nicholl	2	★
Drummond View	Mr P. Saywell	1	+
Workshop	(Trewhell Bros.)		
	Estate Total	18 + 5	
Acharn Total		**59 + 26**	

The Coronation Photograph

About 1970 the author attempted to have names identified on the Coronation photograph (see p.111) with the help of James Walker, then aged ninety-two and living in Acharn village. He was the Estate's oldest tenant, but living in a house which had been condemned and from which he refused to move although offered a house in the renovated Manufactory block only a few yards away. 'The removal would be far too difficult and be a terrible upset.' He died shortly afterwards, still in his old house and aged ninety-three.

The photograph was left with him for some time to ponder over, with a notebook in which he entered his identifications with the aid of a numbered transparent overlay to the photo, which, however, was not very easy to decipher and place accurately, so that there are some errors in precise identification. The resulting record is a remarkable feat of memory, showing detailed knowledge of the relationships and lives especially of his nearest neighbours in Acharn. James Walker and his forebears set the standard of longevity for which the village has been well known.

2. Danny McArthur, with the pipes. A tailor to trade, who kept a shop in what was later to become Revard Holiday Lodge.

3. Hugh Cowan, batchelor. A tailor employed by Macnaughton's. Lived in Upper Acharn.

9. Alex Campbell, then living in Lower Acharn, but later moved to Dalmally as a Breadalbane gamekeeper.

14. James Duff, roadman. Worked on the Drummond Hill roads and later at Kenmore Hotel.

17a. Archibald Campbell, m., no family. Lived next to Walker in Lower Acharn.

16 & 17. Mr & Mrs Peter Cameron, m., family of 4. Lived at Tigh Claddich (?) after 1920.

26. James McLaren, farmer, Lurglomond.

27. Dan McNaughton. Had a tailor's shop.

28. Alexander McKerchar, son of Duncan McKerchar (no. 145, with bowler hat) who ran the blacksmith's shop in Upper Acharn.

29. Robert McEwen, son of D. McEwen, schoolmaster at Acharn. Robert started as a railway clerk and rose to become financial controller of the railways in the British sector of post war Western Germany before his retiral.

30. Alexander McNaughton, m., family of 3. Tailor's business in Upper Acharn.

34. Duncan Dewar, Head keeper at Remony. His wife is no. 52.

41. Thomas Dunn, m., with 12 of a family. Gardener to Rev. Atholl Gordon at the Free Church Manse, Portbane (?). All the family emigrated, 2 to South Africa and the remainder, including the parents, to Canada in 1920.

42. Duncan McKinnon, m., with 6 of a family. Lived at Lurglomand Croft with his parents.

44. John McGregor. Foreman on Breadalbane Home Farm before retiring to live at Revucky.

46. Robert Morris, son of David Morris the meal miller.

47. Robert Morrison, son of Sandy Morrison (no. 93).

47a. Peter McPherson, son of John McPherson, shoemaker. Mason to trade, he was burned to death in a house in Glenlyon where he was lodging in 1911.

48. Robert Campbell, Croftmartaig. (This house was much later occupied by Robert Jamieson.)

50. Lauchlan Duff. James Walker's grandfather, whose father lived to the age of ninety-nine. Duff was at one time dyer at the Remony mill.

51. Colin McArthur, blacksmith. Lived in Lower Acharn.

53. John Tailor, cattleman, m., with large family. Lived in Lower Acharn.

58. John Walker, joiner. Lived in the middle house of the top row in Upper Acharn.

61. D. McArthur (known as 'Donnachaidh Ruadh'—Red Duncan). Father of Duncan McArthur, later gardener at Remony.

65. Donal Dewar, shepherd, Tomgarrow.

69. – Rennie, shepherd with Peter McNaughton.

70. Miss Bella McRae, Fernbank.

71. Maggie McRae.

72. Bessie McRae. The McRae family lived in the end house of the top row in Upper Acharn.

73. Mrs William McRae, Fernbank. Her husband was a rabbit trapper.

74. Mrs Cowan, mother of Hugh Cowan (no. 3).

79. Bob McCowan, roadman. Father of John and Alex McCowan.

80. Donald Walker, labourer. Lived at Revucky. His sister is to the left.

82. Duncan Haggart, Had a business in Crieff. Lived in westmost house at Revucky.

83. Peter McNaughton. Father of Dan McNaughton, no. 27.

84. William Cameron, Holly Cottage. Shepherd. He accompanied sheep being away wintered, and went to the shooting in the summer (? father of 'Long John' Cameron).

85. Mrs Cameron, his wife.

86. John McPherson, shoemaker, Acharn, presently in Revucky. He had 10 of a family. Three of the boys were bankers, 2 in the West Indies, the others in Canada. His son Malcolm built the house later known as the Gardener's Cottage.

93. Sandy Morrison, general labourer and guide to the Falls, m., family of 7. Father of Mrs Shorthouse who lived in the upper village.

99 & 100 Mr & Mrs Cameron, Pine Cottage. Family of 3. He ran the joiner's business with water powered sawbench.

103. Miss Annie Duff. Lived in Lower Acharn next to Duncan McArthur.

110. Duncan McDonald, brother to John McDonald (no. 126).

111. Mrs Peter McNaughton. No family.

112. Alexander McArthur, Road surveyor, lived in Perth. Brother to no. 128.

115. Mrs McEwen, wife of the schoolmaster. She had been cut out of the picture; no doubt he would be sitting beside her when the photo was taken. They had a family of 5 sons and 3 daughters. The oldest, Jack, was a doctor in Doncaster. Polly was matron of a children's home in Glasgow. Walter and Maggie were in banks. Ina and Willie were school-teachers. They came to Acharn for summer holidays for a long number of years. They had the middle house of the west row in Upper Acharn.

116. Mrs Morrison, wife of Sandy Morrison, no. 93.

126. John McDonald, single. Achianich Farm.

127. Peter McNaughton (with bowler hat), Remony Farm.

128. Dochie McArthur ('Baldie') kept a shop in Drummond View. His brother John ran a tailor's business above.

128?. Jean McGregor, daughter of Archibald McGregor, under-keeper at Remony. She married Archibald McDougall, Lurglomand Farm.

130. Bessie Cameron, employed as a maid by Colin Campbell, the joiner.

134. Mrs Robert Campbell, Croftmartaig, wife of no. 48.

136. James Hendry. m., 1 of a family. Deck hand on Loch Tay steamers. Lived in Lower Acharn.

141. Mrs J.B. Mackenzie, wife of the Parish Minister, who took the photo.

143. Miss Kate McArthur. Lived in the second house from the west end in lower village with her two brothers (Duncan & ?) and a nephew.

144. Nettie McRae (sister to 71 and 72).

145. Mrs John McRae, mother of the above among family of 6 daughters and one son.

146. Mrs McKerchar, wife of Duncan McKerchar.

147. Mrs William Cameron, m., family of 6. Her husband was postman at this time. They lived in the middle house of the west row in Upper Acharn.

153. Duncan McArthur, gardener at Remony (later the author's fishing mentor).

It is noticeable that the different blocks of houses in the village of Acharn were not differentiated by name by James Walker, possibly because they were so easily known and, of course, there was no regular delivery of mail.

List of those attending the Comrade's Hut
50th Anniversary Party, 23 March 1973

Master of Ceremonies: Jim Moar, Schoolhouse, Acharn & Mrs Moar.
Guest of Honour: Mr McLaren, Blairgowrie, with Mrs Mitchell and her daughter Susan.
Others attending: Mrs McRae, widow of J. McRae, the Garage, Kenmore, the son of Bella McRae, Acharn.
Mrs Macdonald, Tighanlaggan, widow of Christie Macdonald.
Mrs McOwan, Acharn. Widow of Alex McOwan.
Hugh Fraser, Achianich.
(the above four were the only people of whom Mr McLaren had direct knowledge.)
Alec & Cathie Dott, Kenmore.
Miss McLaughlan, Kenmore.
Archie Irvine & his sister, Kenmore.
Mervyn & Mrs Browne & Deirdre, Milton of Ardtalnaig.
Mr & Mrs Charlie Ross, Pine Cottage.
Mr & Mrs Johnnie Turner.
Mr & Mrs Angus Hogg.
Mr & Mrs Jim Aitchison, Achianich.
Mrs & Elizabeth McDiarmid, Lawers.
Mr & Mrs McMillan (née Crichton), Garth.
Mr & Mrs & Stewart Morris, The Old Mill.
Mr & Mrs Hugh Livingston, Acharn.
Mrs Dickson, Acharn.
Mr & Mrs Jones, Acharn.
Mr & Mrs Kenny McInnes, roadman, Acharn.
Mr & Mrs Jim Wallace, gardener, Remony.
Mr & Mrs Alec Grieve, Elm Cottage.
Mr & Mrs Hector Campbell, shepherd, Acharn.
Mr & Mrs Jim Cumming, of G & R Smith, Acharn.
Miss Jean Paterson. Sister to Mrs Cumming.
Miss Christine McDiarmid.
Mrs Hourston.
Mr & Mrs Ferguson, Ardradnaig.
Mrs McGibbon, Remony (sometime secretary of C. Hut Com.).
Mrs Boynes.
Jock Finlay, Kenmore.
Rev. Kenneth McVicar.
Mrs McGregor (née Helen Wesieski, lately of Acharn).
Mr & Mrs Davidson, lately shepherd at Claggan.

Mrs Macdonald & son, Ardtalnaig.
Mr & Mrs T. Hay, Kenmore.
Mrs McLaren, Balnaskiag.
Miss McGregor, Balnaskiag.
Mrs Macdonald, (née Spence), Balnaskiag.
Mrs Mowbray, Balnaskiag.
Mr & Mrs H. McKinnon, Tullich.
Mrs Wright (née Fraser), Kenmore.
Mrs Bayne, Dalerb.
Mr & Mrs N. Menzies, G & R Smith, Acharn.
Mr & Mrs A. Duncan Millar & Ian, Remony.

In all about a hundred souls.

Entertainment by: Eddie Rose, Mrs Millie Morris (piano and singing) Douglas Macdonald (accordion), Hector Campbell, Weem.

APPENDIX 6 —The Macnaughton Family Tree

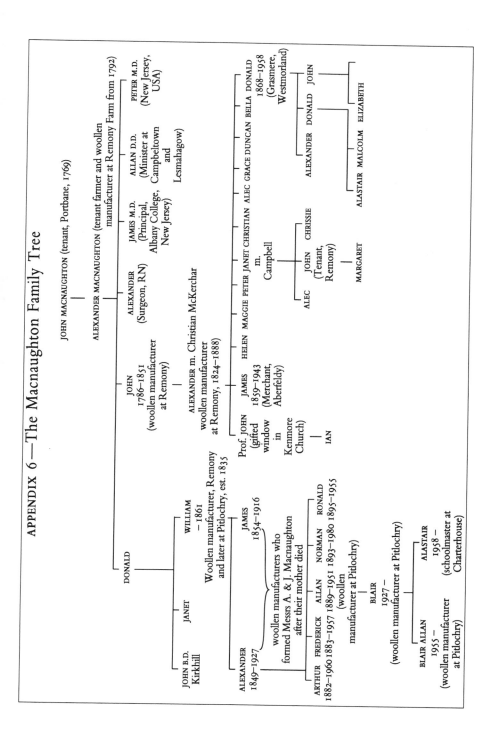

Bibliography

Michael Allaby & James Lovelock, *The Great Extinction* (Chatto & Windus, London, 1984)

William Bowie, *The Black Book of Taymouth* (privately printed by the Marquis of Breadalbane, 1855)

James Buist, *National record of the Visit of Queen Victoria to Scotland* (Perth Printing Company, Perth, 1844)

Nigel Calder, *Timescale* (Chatto & Windus, London, 1984)

H. Coutts, *Tayside Before History* (Dundee Museum, Dundee, 1971)

Frank Delaney, *The Celts* (Book Club Associates, 1986)

Gordon Donaldson, *Scotland—the Shaping of a Nation* (David & Charles, Newton Abbot, 1980)

Ian Finlay, *Columba* (Victor Gollancz, London, 1979)

Pat Geiber, *The Stone of Destiny* (Canongate Press, Edinburgh, 1992)

W.A. Gillies, *In Famed Breadalbane* (later edition, Clunie Press, Strathtay, Perthshire)

John Gowlett, *Ascent to Civilisation* (Book Club Associates, 1984)

Ian Grimble, *Scottish Islands* (BBC, London, 1985)

Evan Haddingham, *Early Man and the Cosmos* (William Heinemann, London, 1983)

Michael Howard, *Earth Mysteries* (Robert Hale, London, 1990)

Anthony Jackson, *The Symbol Stones of Scotland* (The Orkney Press, 1984)

Peter James, *Centuries of Darkness* (Jonathan Cape, London, 1991)

Donald C. Johanson & Maitland C. Edey, *Lucy* (Book Club Associates, 1987)

T.D. Kendrick, *The Druids* (Frank Constable, London, 1966)

Jonathon Kingdon, *Selfmade Man and his Undoing* (Simon & Schuster, London, 1993)

A.D. Lacaille, *The Stone Age in Scotland* (Oxford University Press, 1954)

Lloyd Laing, *Celtic Britain* (Book Club Associates, 1979)

T.C. Lethbridge, *The Painted Men* (Andrew Melrose, London, 1954)

D.A. Macnaughton, *A Highland Family: The Macnaughtons of Remony* (D.A. Macnaughton, Edinburgh, 1985)

Charles McKinnon, *The Scottish Highlanders* (Robert Hale, London, 1989)

Ann McSween & Mick Sharp, *Prehistoric Scotland* (B.T. Batsford, London, 1989)

Ralph Merrifield, *The Archaeology of Ritual and Magic* (Book Club Associates, 1987)

Ian Morrison, *Landscape with Lake Dwellings* (Edinburgh University Press, 1985)

W.H. Murray, *Rob Roy Macgregor* (Richard Drew, Glasgow, 1982)

Michael J. O'Kelly, *Newgrange* (Thames & Hudson, London, 1982)

John Peddie, *Invasion* (Book Club Associates, 1987)

Stuart Piggott, *The Druids* (Jarrold & Sons, Norwich, 1968)

Stuart Piggott, *Scotland Before History* (Edinburgh University Press, 1982)

John Prebble, *Mutiny* (Penguin Books Ltd., 1977)

Glanville Price, *The Language of Britain* (Edward Arnold, London, 1984)

A.A.W. Ramsay, *The Arrow of Glenlyon* (John Murray, London, 1930)

Anne Ross, *The Pagan Celts* (Batsford, London, 1986)

Tacitus (Penguin Books, London, 1948)

Geoffrey Wainwright, *The Henge Monuments* (Thames & Hudson, London, 1989)

Frederick Walker, *Tayside Geology* (Dundee Museum & Art Gallery, 1961)

Index